Women Viewing Violence

WOMEN VIEWING VIOLENCE

Philip Schlesinger
R. Emerson Dobash
Russell P. Dobash
C. Kay Weaver

BFI Publishing

Published in 1992 by the
British Film Institute
21 Stephen Street
London W1P 1PL

In association with
The Broadcasting Standards Council
5–8 The Sanctuary
London SW1P 3JS

British Library Cataloguing in Publication Data

  Women viewing violence.
    I. Schlesinger, Philip, *1948–*
    302.2345

ISBN 0 85170 327-5 pbk
     0 85170 330-5 hbk

Cover: Stella Crew, 2D Design

Typeset by Discript
London
and printed in Great Britain by Page Bros.
Norwich

To Ruth
for her courage

Contents

Notes on Contributors

Philip Schlesinger is Professor of Film and Media Studies and Director of the Film and Media Research Institute at the University of Stirling. He is the author of *Putting 'Reality' Together* (London: Methuen, 1987, 2nd ed.), *Media, State and Nation* (London, New York and Delhi: Sage, 1991) and co-author of *Televising 'Terrorism'* (London: Comedia, 1983). Currently he is completing a study of crime, criminal justice and the British media and writes regularly on questions of national and cultural identity in Europe. He is an editor of the journal *Media, Culture and Society* and a Fellow of the Royal Society of Arts.

Rebecca Emerson Dobash is Professor in the School of Social and Administrative Studies, University of Wales College of Cardiff and co-director of the Institute for the Study of Violence. She is co-author of *Violence Against Wives* (New York: Free Press and Basingstoke, England: Macmillan Distributing, 1979), now a classic in the field, and *Women, Violence and Social Change* (London: Routledge, 1992). Current research includes the legal and financial aspects of divorce, violent men and an evaluation of programmes for violent men.

Russell Dobash is Senior Lecturer in the School of Social and Administrative Studies, University of Wales College of Cardiff and co-director of the Institute for the Study of Violence. Along with Rebecca Dobash he has conducted numerous studies on violence against women. He is co-author of the award-winning book, *Violence Against Wives*, and of *Women, Violence and Social Change*. Other areas of work include the imprisonment of men and women, masculinity and male violence, and child sexual abusers.

Kay Weaver is a PhD candidate and part-time lecturer with the Department of Film and Media Studies at the University of Stirling. A graduate of the department and formerly research assistant with the Film and Media Research Institute at Stirling, she is co-author of *Cameras in the Commons* (London: Hansard Society, 1990) and is continuing to research women's interpretations of televised violence.

Acknowledgments

This research would not have been possible without the help of many people. First and foremost, we are especially grateful to the women who participated in the viewing sessions. We also wish to thank the following individuals and organisations who helped recruit women for the study:

In Scotland: Jacquie McPherson and Stirling Women's Aid; Shona Campbell and Falkirk and Grangemouth Women's Aid; Joyce Watkinson and Clackmannan Women's Aid; Central Region Rape Crisis and Stirling District Council; Clare Murray and all at Cross Roads in Glasgow; Gryffe Women's Aid; and Parmjit Purewal and Govanhill Neighbourhood Centre.

In England: Sandra Blendi-Mahota and The Croft Hostel in Birmingham; Debbie Fairley and Leamington Women's Aid; Preet Grewal and Panaghar Women's Refuge in Coventry; Anne Jackson, Michelle Batchelor and all at Northampton Women's Aid; Ann Nightingale and Coventry Haven Project; Barbara Zytkiewicz and The Haven Project in Wolverhampton; Alison Fielding, Sue Gorbing and Birmingham City Council Women's Unit; and National Women's Aid Federation England.

We are also grateful to Vicky McKeegan and her colleagues at Fusion Research in London for recruiting women with no experience of violence in both Scotland and England.

We are additionally indebted to Guy Cumberbatch at Aston University for providing facilities for the research in Birmingham, and to Jennifer Green, Elizabeth Lake, Cathryn O'Neill, Kathy Granger and Michelle Musgrove for assistance in managing and recording the group discussions.

Jean Park undertook the difficult task of transcribing the group discussions with great efficiency and Gordon Byron's computer wizardry was indispensable. We also acknowledge the great help provided by Ian Dey's software invention, 'Hypersoft', without which the process of completing this study would have been far slower and much more laborious. Sue Tickner provided invaluable assistance in completing the graphics.

The authors are grateful to the Broadcasting Standards Council – which, inter alia, undertakes research into the broadcast portrayal of violence and sexual conduct – for commissioning the study and to David Docherty, who, as the then Research Director of the Council, played a most helpful and constructive role in discussing the project's design. He took a personal interest in the study's evolution, without at any time infringing upon the research team's autonomy to do the work as we saw fit. We also appreciate the continuing support and constructive interest shown by Andrea Millwood Hargrave, the Council's current Research Director, and her response to an earlier draft. Although the BSC funded the study, the authors are solely responsible for its contents.

The authors have benefited enormously from the detailed, constructive and sympathetic comments offered by a group of much-valued colleagues. We are extremely grateful to John Corner, Peter Dahlgren, John Downing, Klaus Bruhn Jensen, Annette Kuhn and Sharon Vaughan for their generosity of spirit and their painstaking work. Sheila Hetherington cast a sharp eye over the typescript and saved us from many errors, while our publisher, Richard Paterson, has given imaginative support that has made the task of completion far easier.

Finally, we should say that, although undertaking a study of this scope in little more than a year was quite a daunting task, we have been fortunate in enjoying harmonious teamwork and have all been enriched by a process of discovery that has taken us into new territory.

1

MEDIA, AUDIENCES AND THE EXPERIENCE OF VIOLENCE

Many women live lives in which they are subjected to physical and sexual abuse by their male partners or face the risk of such abuse by strangers, and most women watch members of their sex being similarly abused, at times, on television. What do they think about this? And are those reactions different for women who have actually lived through the real experience of violence than for those who have not?

By asking these questions we have had to cross the traditional academic boundaries between sociology, criminology, and film and media studies. We have called upon women of diverse backgrounds to respond to a variety of programmes in which women are beaten, raped and/or murdered. The knowledge we have gained adds to the now rather large and established body of research on violence against women in sociology and criminology. It also forms part of research into the television audience in media studies and links into the burgeoning field of research into gender and the media that is now so central to women's cultural studies.

Apart from drawing upon feminist media studies, this book also needs to be understood in the context of another quite separate line of investigation which has focused upon violence in the intimate relations between men and women. The sociological study of domestic and sexual violence has so far simply not been connected with work on women as television viewers. Given the part that such violence – perpetrated by men against women – is increasingly recognised as playing in our society, there seemed to us to be an overwhelming rationale for exploring how it might relate to the viewing of television by women.

In this book, therefore, we bring together two separate issues for the first time: the feminist concern with representations and their consumption by women and the wholly separate study of domestic and sexual violence. To research such questions is, inevitably, to work from within – and, necessarily, to go beyond – some well-established lines of inquiry which we shall now indicate. There is no intention to offer a comprehensive review of the vast academic literatures that make up the fields of inquiry upon which we have drawn. On the contrary, this introductory overview is intended to be simple. It aims to set the stage for describing how the research was undertaken and for presenting our results.

Violence, fear and the media

How women view televised violence relates to a well-developed theme in media research. From the very outset of the rise of mass communication, researchers have tried to evaluate the effects of the media. Attention has been attracted successively by each major medium of communication. Although currently television is most central to this agenda of public concern, the press, radio, comic books and the cinema have each been a major focus of debate in the past, and still remain so on occasion.

To illustrate how press reporting of criminality, violence or disorderly behaviour might affect the wider population has been a long-standing matter of debate and research. So has official concern about the impact of crime and aggression in the cinema and how these might affect the conduct of the working class. There has also been a fear that watching unsuitable films might have a demoralising impact upon the sexual morality of young people.[1] Such concerns have been part of a well-established discourse upon social deviance, law and order, and threats to conventional morality which repeatedly comes onto the political agenda at times of social crisis.[2]

Contemporary concern about television, therefore, overlaps and is also continuous with a long-standing interest in various forms of mass communication and their wider social impact. Repeatedly, worry has been expressed about whether children spend too much time watching television, with negative consequences for their broader educational development, whether young people's exposure to adult problems and issues is harmful, and whether viewing crime and violence might result in delinquency. In similar vein, questions have been posed about whether violent fictional representations and crime reporting of disorder might bring about imitative behaviour or a deadening of public sensibilities. Such themes are part of a discourse upon the violent society in which the representations of such diverse phenomena as inner city riots, football hooliganism, political assassinations, terrorism and war have been the objects of often spirited debate and considerable research.[3]

Mass-mediated violence has been studied by using a wide range of models and theories, but there is no undisputed evidence of what the effects of such highly varied representations may be.[4] The predominant interest of the bulk of the work that has been done in this area has been in quantifying the presence of various forms of violence by means of content analysis, or, by a variety of social scientific methods, in trying to pin down how such concentration upon violent acts and contexts in both reporting and fiction might have effects upon the audience.[5] The effects of mass communication are of perennial interest because there is a seemingly unshakeable belief in the possibility of controlling them. At least this is so among many politicians and moral entrepreneurs, and also evidently in the public at large. This conviction persists despite the doubts periodically voiced by researchers who have had extreme difficulty in agreeing upon what a media 'effect' is and how one might actually measure it or evaluate its impact. While this line of inquiry has for long been a common starting-point, and remains on the agenda of much contemporary debate, it has not been the point of departure in the present study.

The unresolved state of research into the effects of mass-mediated violence does not appear to us to offer a potentially productive line of inquiry for the issues tackled here. Indeed, we have chosen to pose the question differently and instead to ask: What do women *make* of the violence that they see in the media? The underlying aim is to try to probe what representations of violence against women *mean* in their lives. By posing the question in this way one is able to find out a great deal about how such portrayals are actually received and how the impact of televised violence upon women's conceptions of themselves – their gender identities – might be variously described.

How women conceive of themselves is arguably closely related to the security or insecurity of their everyday lives. Most relevantly for present purposes, this matter has been one focus of analyses of the impact of television on the fear of crime. For instance, it has been held that portrayals of crime and crime-related themes on television have led to increased public anxiety and fear of going out on the streets. In fact, the evidence on the relationships between media coverage and fear of crime is far from clear-cut. The view taken here is that it would be mistaken to take an undifferentiated view either of the media or of the audience. It is important to recognise that crime and violence take different forms: for instance, given actions, the contexts in which they are performed and the reasons (or lack of reasons) provided may all vary. The genre or type of a particular film or programme, or the kind of newspaper consumed may also differ and affect how members of the public re-spond to what they see and hear.[6]

For instance, so far as the news media are concerned, it is important to distinguish between the press and broadcasting, for coverage of crime in general, and of violent crime in particular, differs significantly in each. It is also important to distinguish between different types of newspaper and different types of television programme. In each of these cases there are distinctive patterns of coverage. Popular, mid-market and quality newspapers tend to give varying emphases to violent crime, with most coverage found in the popular press, less in the middle-market papers, and least of all at the quality end of the market. How such stories are dealt with by different kinds of newspaper also varies substantially. Much the same could be said of television, with the grea-test concentration on violent crime occurring in local as opposed to national news, and with popular channels also covering many more of these stories than the minority ones.[7] If patterns of media content vary, then how they are variously consumed becomes rather important.

This raises questions about the distinctive ways in which different audiences make sense of the media. Most recent concern about the generation of fear of crime has focused on television and its relationship

3

to the viewing public. But it is too simplistic to take an undifferentiated view of audience responses to viewing either crime journalism or crime fiction, especially of the violent kind. Factors such as age, sex, class background, area of residence, and so forth, are all germane to the perceptions that audience members bring to bear upon their reading of television and the extent to which they might or might not personally be anxious about crime and violence.

Doubtless because of its cultural prominence and centrality, the overwhelming tendency in recent research has been to concentrate upon nationally networked television. However, this has tended to obscure the relative importance of other media. The local press, for instance, in common with the popular and mid-market national press, tends to exaggerate personal violence and robbery (when compared with the incidence of crimes as measured by official statistics) and this may well be significant in shaping how given social groups think about their localities and their perceptions of the sources of danger near to where they live. Such local news may be quite variously interpreted within a given community (for instance, on the basis of ethnic or class divisions) and further elaborated into rumours and scares by word of mouth.[8] Such considerations point towards seeing the relations between media and audiences as highly variable and complex.

In short, it is questionable whether any easily sustainable causal relationship can be drawn between exposure to television and public perceptions of crime. On the contrary, there is some evidence to suggest that the need to know about how given crimes might affect one's own life may at times provide the motivation to watch crime news and drama. If this is so, anxiety might foster heavy viewing, rather than the converse. Of course, this still remains an open question that is not easily resolved by empirical research.[9]

The view taken here is that if we cease to think in terms of causes and effects and look instead at the frameworks of interpretation that are brought to bear upon television watching, considerable insight is gained into the nature and sources of fear of crime and violence. In this study, the crucial starting-point is the experience of womanhood in our society and how being a woman interacts with what television has to offer. Such interaction, we shall argue, may vary significantly with differences based in social experience, ethnicity and class background.

A perspective on the audience

The approach developed here is situated in the current lively debate about how to research the television audience. Ever since television became the dominant medium in the latter half of this century, there has been considerable interest in its relationship to the viewing public. Historically, much of the research on this question has derived from the needs of the broadcasters themselves to collect information about their audiences.[10] The investigation of this question has gone through a number of distinct phases and has used different vocabularies for thinking

4

about the television-viewer relationship. These distinctive frameworks of analysis have been more than mere words: they have offered alternative ways of constructing the problem, although latterly it has been argued that a new synthesis of different approaches is beginning to emerge.

As we have already pointed out in relation to the question of violence, one long-standing preoccupation has been with media effects on audiences. Research into this has often begun with the underlying question 'What do the media do to people?' and, as alluded to already, there has been a tendency for this kind of approach to be fuelled by political and moral concern over how the media might influence vulnerable groups or those viewed in some official circles as potentially dangerous. Although such thinking first began by considering the individual recipient of media messages to be rather passive, this quite rapidly gave way to a growing recognition that members of the audience *actively* use the media on the basis of their needs, interests and values. In this respect, there has been a coming together with another line of research, the 'uses and gratifications' approach, where the leading question is 'What do people do with the media?'[11] Work in both the 'effects' and 'uses and gratifications' traditions have been firmly grounded in the fields of sociology and social psychology.

During the past fifteen years or so, yet another approach has been emerging and developing, concerned with analysis of the audience in terms derived from the field of cultural studies. Central to such work has been a strong focus on directly investigating television's 'reception' by studying a variety of audiences and by analysing how they make sense of different kinds of television programme.[12] Arguably this represents a change of approach and theoretical language from earlier work in the social sciences, although claims here may well have been overstated and there is a good case for pointing to the continuities rather than to the breaks.[13] The present new wave of research also marks a rejection of the idea once prevalent in film theory that the critic alone can determine what a particular audiovisual 'text' – a film or television programme – might mean. It has been supposed by some theorists that media texts act to determine the analytically definable 'subject positions' available to spectators, and therefore the actual 'readings' or interpretations available to the audience. From this point of view, in order to analyse what a given text might signify, real audiences were not needed (apart from the media analysts themselves, naturally, who were a special professional case, expert in cultural detective work).

In strong contrast to this rather formalistic approach, it has been precisely the guiding interest of recent research in the cultural studies tradition to analyse how actual audiences produce meaningful interpretations of television's output, and this in turn is premised upon the argument that viewers engage *actively* with what they see, whether as individuals or as members of various groups with distinctive characteristics. For some, this 'active' conception of the audience has been connected to a notion of 'empowerment'. For instance, it has been suggested that the viewer may enjoy potentially unlimited opportunities to make sense of what she or he sees, and in this sense be accorded considerable cultural power to define reality.[14] In line with this perspective, it has been argued that the televisual text is highly 'polysemic', that is, potentially open to a wide variety of interpretations and readings.

There is clearly something to be said for escaping from any simple deterministic conception – one where the viewer simply passively absorbs what is seen and heard, falling into line with whatever message television producers intend to convey or with what is supposedly 'inscribed in the text'. However, bending the stick too far in this direction does raise some problems. For one, there is a tendency to underrate the social, political, economic and cultural constraints that do operate to shape our readings of television. There is also a serious risk of conflating the capacity of each of us to interpret what we see and hear with the exercise of real social and political power.[15] Ultimately, it is what people actually do to try to change the world beyond the screen, rather than the mere act of interpretation of televisual texts, that brings us into the arena of how power is actually exercised. Currently, views differ about just how wide a range of meanings can be extracted in principle from any given text by the interpretative activities of audiences. Consequently, there is some dispute about the extent to which the relative power to construct versions of reality resides either in the media or in the audience – and, especially, what might be the broader implications of such readings for political action and social change.[16] The position adopted here is to side with those who see the audience as active but only within determinate limits. This general position is elaborated quite concretely throughout the book by reference to women's social experience of violence, and their class and ethnicity.

In brief, then, recent research has tended to react against deterministic lines of thinking about media audiences, insisting instead that we should pay attention to how real people actually make sense of viewing, listening or reading. So far as television is concerned, we can try to find out how these practices of interpretation work by analysing viewing activity in a variety of ways. Currently, there are two main approaches in reception studies. Some now argue that the best method for investigating viewing practices is to enter the home and see what viewers make of television in their domestic setting.[17] This may certainly offer valuable ethnographic insights into domestic consumption patterns and the dynamics of the family and not least, in the present context, into relations of power between men and women. Yet another approach – the one taken in the present study – focuses more centrally upon the variety of interpretations of the televisual text itself which, as we have said, may be more or less open to different constructions that depend upon the characteristics of specific audiences.

Apart from considering how given audiences make sense of television, the question of the genres into which a given television programme or film may be categorised and how its discourses are organised is also extremely important in determining the range of possible readings. The relevance of this point will become clear in the next chapter, where we discuss the programmes chosen for this study and the reasons that lay behind our selections. There, we shall also discuss the rationale for choosing particular groups of viewers, selected, for instance, in ways that allowed us to focus on key social differences, such as gender, ethnicity and class.[18]

Feminist media studies

This study quite consciously adds to contemporary feminist research on television by taking violence against women as its central theme. The neglect of violence in feminist television studies is particularly noteworthy because the analysis of women and their relationships to television viewing has become such a well-developed theme in the past two decades. This line of inquiry has been part of a much wider development in feminist studies of how culture is consumed by women, one that has extended to studying their interpretations and uses of, for instance, romantic fiction, of the arts in general, of women's and girls' magazines, of radio programmes and, especially, of televised soap operas.[19] Underlying such research has been an interest in seeing both how representations of gender are constructed by different media and how these are variously made sense of and integrated into the lives of women.

Implicitly, at least, the dominant tendency until recently has been to stress the study of 'women's media' or 'women's genres' as the best entry point into the question of gender identity. This has meant that much research has concentrated upon looking at those media products that women most favour. This stress upon television and radio programmes, films, books and magazines that women are known to like and consume does have a defensible logic. It has opened up a discourse on the cultural spaces that women try to make their own and the pleasures that they may derive from, say, enjoying melodrama or romance. But this kind of research strategy only gives us part of a much wider picture, as is increasingly being accepted.[20] The construction of the gender identities of women via the media needs to be understood in a context much broader than that of 'women's media' alone. This is not least because femininity is constructed in relation to masculinity in a comprehensive range of media and genres. The present study is a considered step in that direction. To overstate the case: there is much to be learned about women's consumption of television by looking beyond the soap opera. It is for that reason that, although we have touched base on this well-recognised focus of current research, we have studied other genres too. But we shall return to this point.

Although there are significant differences of approach among those who now practise the new style of reception analysis, there are also many shared reference points. Such work, on the whole, tends to be highly qualitative in nature, largely eschewing quantitative research.[21] There are good grounds for this emphasis, but not for making it into an article of faith that excludes any attempt at quantification. Among some feminist audience analysts, the use of qualitative methods is seen, in and of itself, as virtually 'empowering' women, as endowing them with the status of subjects. Conversely, quantitative analysis is seen as removing power from women and as turning them into objects.[22] Sometimes, even where quantitative methods are used in reception analysis (and these still remain quite rare), this is fudged, as though it were necessary for such work to be seen as purely qualitative to be respectable.[23] It will be evident, given our own commitment to the use of quantitative methods *in combination with* a qualitative approach, that we can see no theoretical rationale whatsoever for this position.

This is not our view alone, for there are signs that the combination of quantitative and qualititative methods is currently becoming more acceptable in the study of the television audience, although this tends to be among those who lay greater emphasis on social scientific rather than on cultural studies approaches.[24] This can only be welcomed as we regard the use of quantitative and qualitative techniques in combination as extending the kind of analysis possible. Our own thinking on this question – which is fundamentally informed by a sociological orientation – is elaborated in the next chapter.

Groups and genres

In the present study, we have been particularly concerned to consider how various discourses, rooted in particular contexts (such as class, gender and ethnic background) and given experiences (such as being at the receiving end of domestic or sexual violence), are brought to bear upon the interpretation of men's violence against women on television. The research strategy pursued has been to examine the variations that come about when we pay attention to differences among women. It should be said that there is a growing recognition of the need for such an analytical approach[25] and a number of feminist reception studies have begun to make more systematic use of different categories of women. Indeed, where these have been investigated they have been found to be illuminating.[26] It is a commitment to this overall approach that explains our methodology, which has involved screening a range of forms of televised violence at the same time as systematically varying the groups that have viewed it. The chapters that follow are an elaboration of the distinctive ways in which women viewers make sense of how violent gender relations are represented on television.

Apart from the systematic construction of viewing groups on the basis of socio-demographic characteristics, the approach adopted here has involved selecting a range of different types of programme or televisual genres for study, and there are several grounds for this.

First, as has already been noted, most work on women's viewing reception has occupied itself with 'women's media'. We are interested in looking beyond this rather self-limiting approach to take in a range of programming that extends the scope for potential responses and readings.

Second, in making our selection, we have quite consciously sought viewer responses both across different genres and across the televisual divide between factual and fictional programming. By considering how 'violence against women' is constructed in a range of output, we are following an earlier study of television's genres which investigated how 'terrorism' was handled. However, on that occasion, the focus of attention was the institution of television and its regulation rather than the television audience, although some attention was given to the relation between formats and audience size.[27] There is no reason why this broad cross-generic approach should not be taken up and adapted to the study of reception. Indeed, this has been done most productively in a recent study of the nuclear energy issue[28] in ways closely analogous to those developed here.

Third, given its subject matter, the present study does not investigate television reception by looking at the domestic setting. Again, we shall enlarge on the reasons for this in the next chapter. But, for the moment, let us simply note that the study of viewing activity in violent households would simply be impractical. This methodological limitation aside, we do in any case take the view that there is still much to be gained from treating as analytically distinct the text viewed and the process of reception itself. Moreover, if the purpose is the systematic thematic analysis of a particular field of representations – in this case, that of 'violence against women' – the method that we have adopted seems to us to be the only valid one.[29]

The lived experience of violence

For some members of the audience, reactions to televised violence involve an interaction with their experience of violence. For others, there is an awareness that they too could become the victims of violence, particularly rape. The lived experience of women's violence is also the material upon which producers build in creating the depictions for public consumption, and which, in turn, enter into the social world in which we all live.

Thus, it seems important to consider, even if briefly, a description of the violence that is actually experienced by women and which, in turn, becomes the subject of media productions for popular consumption. Physical assault, rape, sexual abuse and incest constitute most of the violence women experience at the hands of male relatives and acquaintances and, to a lesser extent, from strangers. In Britain, there have been few studies of the extent of violence against women, but one analysis of over 30,000 police records shows that 25% of all violent crime is wife assault. Another survey of over 1,000 women found that one in six had been raped, one in three sexually assaulted and one in five had been raped or sexually assaulted as a child. While in the United States, a study of 900 women found that 44% had experienced one attempted or completed rape and 20% had been assaulted during marriage.[30]

The following are descriptions of some of these events, and are best remembered as we consider women's responses to viewing violence against women on television. Del Martin opens her early book on violence against women in the United States with a letter, portions of which tell a now familiar story of abuse:

I am in my thirties and so is my husband. I have a high school diploma and am presently attending a local college, trying to obtain the additional education I need. My husband is a college graduate and a professional in his field. We are both attractive and, for the most part, respected and well-liked. We have four children and live in a middle-class home with all the comforts we could possibly want.

I have everything, except life without fear.

For most of my married life I have been periodically beaten by my husband. ...

I have had glasses thrown at me. I have been kicked in the abdomen when I was visibly pregnant. ... I have been whipped, kicked and thrown, picked up again and thrown down again. I have been punched and kicked in the head, chest, face, and abdomen more times than I can count. ...

Few people have ever seen my black and blue face or swollen lips because I have always stayed indoors afterwards, feeling ashamed. ...

Now, the first response to this story, which I myself think of, will be 'Why didn't you seek help?'

I did. Early in our marriage I went to a clergyman ... a friend ... professional family guidance agency ... two more doctors. ... I called the police one time. They not only did not respond to the call, they called several hours later to ask if things had 'settled down'. I could have been dead by then!

Everyone I have gone to for help has somehow wanted to blame me and vindicate my husband. I can see it lying there between their words and at the end of their sentences. ...

No one has to 'provoke' a wife-beater. He will strike out when he's ready and for whatever reason he has at the moment.

I may be his excuse, but I have never been the reason.

I know that I do not want to be hit. I know, too, that I will be beaten again unless I can find a way out for myself and my children. I am terrified for them also.

As a married woman I have no recourse but to remain in the situation which is causing me to be painfully abused. I have suffered physical and emotional battering and spiritual rape because the social structure of my world says I cannot do anything about a man who wants to beat me. ...

I know that I have to get out. But when you have nowhere to go, you know that you must go on your own and expect no support. I have to be ready for that. I have to be ready to support myself and the children completely, and still provide a decent environment for them. I pray that I can do that before I am murdered in my own home.

I have learned that no one believes me and that I cannot depend upon any outside help. All I have left is the hope that I can get away before it is too late. ...

My situation is so untenable I would guess that anyone who has not experienced one like it would find it incomprehensible. I find it difficult to believe myself. ...[31]

[American woman]

A broad range of women experience many different kinds of violence from male relatives, acquaintances and strangers. There are many forms of physical and sexual violation perpetrated by males against females. They range from non-violent, threatening encounters involving little or no direct body contact – albeit sometimes with the threat of attack and some uncertainty about the eventual outcome – to various forms of physical and sexual assault. Reactions and responses range from self-defence to a sense of discomfort, fear and anxiety. Domestic violence, rape, incest and sexual harassment have all been the subject of intensive study, and these accounts can only provide a brief glimpse into such experiences, but it is such experiences and a more general concern about them that form the core of the present study and should be understood, even if only in a cursory fashion. It is through the words of the women themselves that the nature and effects of such violence can best be described.

Flashing

Many, if not most, women and girls have been flashed at, and all are made aware of its likelihood. One study of flashing found that 63% of women had been flashed at.[32] Responses include fear, shock, disgust, giggling, anger, humiliation and no reaction. Freedom of movement may be curtailed for fear that such an event could occur virtually anywhere:[33]

> I was walking home from school. I was crossing the bridge. A bloke came towards me. Wanking. He had an erection. I have never been so scared in all my life. ... I felt hemmed in by him.[34]
> [English woman]

> The first two times I was flashed at I just hurried past. The last time I was with a friend [on the Underground] and he [an unknown man] came up and started exposing himself and saying obscenities. I got up and pushed him over and I felt much better because I'd actually done something and because he just shambled off.[35]
> [English woman]

When I saw his face, I think he was really pleased he was frightening

me. He was doing it to frighten women. Getting a sexual thrill from frightening women – doesn't it lead to other things? Maybe he would get a kick out of rape.[36]
[English woman]

Sexual harassment and molestation

I don't know if you'd call it incest or molestation or what ... it was the mental side. ... It would happen every night for a few weeks, and then it wouldn't happen for a few weeks, and then he'd be there, standing over the bed with no clothes on, and it'd start again. When he stood there ... I still get nightmares over it ... it's as if he sort of possessed me. Yes, that's it: I was sort of his, I was there for him. That's the way I feel. There was no way I could get out of it ... I'd just try and turn over, and ... when I turned back, he'd still be there![37]
[Australian girl]

I sang in a church choir [aged twelve]. One time a member of the church, a deacon, offered me a ride home. We were on the way home when he tried to pull me to him. He was feeling on my breasts and trying to rub them. I kept pushing his hand away and I told him I would tell if he didn't stop. ... He threatened to tell the church that I had tried to tempt him. He used to try to get me by myself, but I wouldn't cooperate after what happened.[38]
[American girl]

Domestic violence
The accounts by the following women reveal the nature of violence and the possible extent of injuries experienced by women at the hands of their male partners:

He punched me, he kicked me, he pulled me by the hair. ... I had a cracked cheek bone, two teeth knocked out, cracked ribs, broken nose, two beautiful black eyes – it wasn't even a black eye, it was my whole cheek was just purple from one eye to the other. And he had got me by the neck and he was trying, in fact practically succeeded in strangling me. I was choking, I was actually at the blacking out stage. ... I started to scream and I felt as if I'd been screaming for ages. When I came to he was pulling me up the stair by the hair. ... I can remember going up the stair on my hands and knees and the blood – I don't know where it was coming from – it was just dripping in front of my face and I was actually covered in blood.[39]
[Scottish woman]

He tried to strangle me last night. I was terrified. I did manage to get out of the house but I had to go back the next morning. You see it was Easter weekend and my two children were afraid the Easter

Bunny wouldn't come if mummy and daddy were fighting.[40]
[Canadian woman]

Although there have been some changes in public attitudes and responses to domestic violence during the last two decades,[41] the violence itself remains much the same.[42]

> *The first time?* We were talking and he slapped me. I didn't have any bruises or anything, but I was shocked. He apologized ... said he never meant to do it. I thought: 'People are human, they make mistakes.' We made love. I wasn't being honest with myself.
>
> *The worst* and *last time* was when he beat me until I was black and blue over my face and arms. He choked me and kicked me in the stomach. Sometimes it seems unreal. ... It's like I'd disown my body while talking about it. Sometimes I ask myself why didn't I crack up then, from battle fatigue. ... Maybe I'm going through it now.[43]
> [American woman]

Rape

Rape is another form of male violence that can be perpetrated upon women of any age and in a variety of settings. The fear of rape from a stranger seems to be almost universal. However, this is much less likely than physical assault from a male partner or sexual abuse or rape from a relative or acquaintance:

> I am seventy-three years old and I was raped when I was sixty-seven. A young fellow followed me into the elevator of my apartment building. He asked me if I knew the apartment number of a certain tenant but I told him that name was unfamiliar to me. I said, 'Oh, are you the man from United Parcels? I'm expecting a package.' ... A few minutes later my doorbell rang. I look through the peephole and there was the young man with a package. Of course I opened the door right away. He had a wrench in one hand. He shoved me against the wall and started hitting my head. Later I had to have five stitches. He told me not to make a sound and he started walking through my apartment. I think he wanted to see if I was really alone, or he might have been looking for things to steal. ... He told me to get on the bed. He pulled off my underthings and then he tore into me. ... Finally he left, after warning me to keep quiet.[44]
> [American woman]

> I was nineteen and I was coming home from a Harvard weekend. I missed my bus connection so I decided to hitch. I had to get back to school for an eight o'clock Monday class. I accepted a ride with a young man who seemed okay. We went for some coffee and doughnuts so that I could get an idea of who he was. There was nothing to get me alarmed. When we got back into the car he told me he had to

stop and pick up some friends. I still didn't think anything was wrong. His friends got into the car and then they drove me to a deserted garage.

They told me I'd better co-operate or I'd be buried there and nobody would ever know. There were three of them and one of me. It was about one a.m. and no people were around. I decided to co-operate.[45]
[American woman]

Child sex abuse and incest
Child sex abuse and incest are now known to be far more prevalent than once thought, as increasingly more women have become willing to disclose what was once a secret and unshareable problem:

He totally ignored me until eleven. When I started my periods, he started to sort of take notice. In fact, he took me out for a meal, started to buy me presents. I was quite pleased 'cos he was actually taking an interest in me. Then after that it started.[46]
[English girl]

I'd be in bed and hear the sound of his trousers and he'd sit down and I'd pretend to be asleep. You think 'If I pretend to be asleep nothing's going to happen' – but it does.[47]
[English girl]

I could feel myself splitting, becoming two quite different little girls: one was the sharer of The Secret ... the other heard screaming voices, couldn't eat, couldn't concentrate, felt scared and on edge all the time, and dreamed non-stop of a nice future, of running away, of having a loving family, of being left alone.[48]
[Canadian woman]

Kids are terrible at keeping secrets but, by God, you keep this one.[49]
[English girl]

Coping, fear and avoidance
The fear of male violence is a reasonable, predictable and sensible response to having been victimised, and anxiety is often heightened. Anger is also a reasonable response, although women are often censured for expressions of anger, no matter how legitimate. Such anger may lead to more active forms of defence and public rejection of the male sense of privilege that underpins so much of their violent behaviour:

I think my attitudes have changed permanently – I will never feel safe walking down the street by myself ever again. I will never feel safe in a situation where I'm alone with a man I don't know very well, I will

14

never trust men totally again. Also I will never be able to cope with harassment as well as I could before. But then that's another thing, maybe my getting angry is coping with it in a different way. I'm just learning a lot about myself at the moment and how to adapt that experience into my life.[50]
[English woman]

The accumulation of all these incidents made me frightened *all the time* – and angry. I couldn't walk down the street normally. I walked down the street scared and angry.[51]
[English woman]

My being raped moved something in me so deeply that I could no longer not look at it: I'd had a fear of men all of my life.[52]
[American woman]

Re-experiencing violence through the media
In one study, some of the women who had experienced violence indicated that it affected their response to films, books, television programmes and pornography. They objected to the portrayal of violence against women as 'entertainment' and resented how such representations elicited painful memories.[53] Such views were sometimes expressed in very strong terms:

There are things that bring it back. ... I can't watch extremely violent things, I just want to turn off because the thoughts will start and I just don't want to know. That's the way I cope – by suppressing it.[54]

At the extreme, the reaction could be one of complete rejection of television:

It's just sensitized me more and more to violence, to almost a ridiculous point where I can't – as soon as violence comes up in a book it makes me feel *physically sick*. I can make myself read it, but I really do have to *make myself*. If it comes up on the television – and it's there all the time – I find it very difficult to watch.[55]

This book analyses how women view violence against women on television – a topic oddly neglected until now, failing thus far to attract any sustained research of the kind reported here. It is our contention that the representation and interpretation of violence between men and women are central to conceptions of masculinity and femininity. So the failure to take this matter on as a major theme in the study of television – which after all occupies such a central place in our culture and our daily lives – is all the more puzzling. In *Women Viewing Violence* we attempt to open up new perspectives both in media studies and in the study of violence against women.

15

INVESTIGATING EXPERIENCE
AND RESPONSE

Women Viewing Violence is grounded in a one-year study of women's interpretations of and responses to the portrayal of violence against women on television. The study is based on the assumption that the reception and interpretation of television programmes mobilise the cultural, social and material experiences of viewers. Gender is significant in shaping viewing patterns and interpretations, and we were particularly interested in assessing the different reactions of women who had been the victims of violence and of those who had not. We sought to explore whether and how these experiences shape interpretations and responses to televised violence. Experience of violence may not necessarily be the only, or possibly the most significant, factor affecting readings. We also considered it important to examine whether ethnicity, nationality (Scottish/English) and class background structured viewings of violence.

In order to achieve these aims a comparative research design was employed which involved the screening of selected programmes to two broad categories of women formed into fourteen viewing groups. The two categories included women who had experienced violent attacks against them by men and those who had not. The study employed a distinctive approach to audience research by combining both qualitative and quantitative methods. Two main data-gathering techniques were employed: quantitative data was obtained through individual questionnaires concerning personal backgrounds and individual responses to the screenings; and qualitative information was gathered from group discussions of the programmes. This fieldwork resulted in over 100 hours of group discussions and 546 completed questionnaires.

Locating the study
As discussed in the previous chapter, the approach taken here lays stress upon the 'active audience' which must be understood and located through interpretative methods. These locate reception within a complex of cultural, social and material experiences. Going beyond the text means that researchers have had to attend to the significance of viewers' actual reactions and this has required new, more anthropological and sociological approaches. Within this growing tradition, scholars are currently employing in-depth interviews with individuals and families

and particularly group discussions as a means of assessing audience reactions. Generally rejecting positivistic methods, these researchers have stressed the need for sensitive, intensive research as a means of teasing out cultural readings. Feminist scholars have claimed that these methods are particularly important in the investigation of women's accounts since they 'empower' women through a process of knowing.[1]

The research conducted for *Women Viewing Violence* follows in an interpretative tradition with a commitment to the representation of the actor's point of view, as reflected in the use of women's discussions about watching television. By using focused group discussions, we sought to allow women participating in the study an opportunity to express their views in a generally supportive environment. We ruled out the interviewing of families because this would be unlikely to enable women to express their views, especially in cases where violent domestic relations prevailed. Research has revealed the ways in which the social order inside families is rooted in gender-based conflicts and the exercise of male power which often suppress the views and sentiments of women. Only by allowing women a space of their own will we be able to learn about their views. Past research had also convinced us that the groups should be composed entirely of women and that discussions should be conducted by a woman. It was considered that the presence of males would inhibit and distort women's responses and interpretations. We also decided that an environment most conducive to uninhibited discussion and debate would be achieved by creating groups of women with broadly similar backgrounds.

We judged generally homogeneous groups to be most likely to facilitate meaningful participatory discussion. It is not that group discussions necessarily result in some sort of consensual or singular reading. If that were so it would be possible to conclude that 'groups' hold certain views.[2] Approaches based on consensus or singularity reify groups and place a gloss on group discussions which is often unwarranted. Our view is that typifications and conclusions about readings emerging from group discussions must be based on tendencies or patterns. The outcomes of group discussions are indicative and symptomatic of certain views and lines of argument, rather than definitive.

According significance to the interpretations of viewers does not mean that further analysis ceases. Perceptions and reactions must in turn be located through a wider contextual approach.[3] Contextual, interpretative analysis must situate women in the specifics of their everyday lives and relationships. Understanding the commonalities and variations in women's readings of television requires knowledge of their biographies and, for this study, particularly their relationships with men and their experiences of violence. Violence at the hands of men is not the only experience which differentiates women from one another. We also considered it important to explore the ways in which nationality, ethnicity and class shaped reactions. Once women are located in these terms through their own biographies, it is further necessary to place these cultural and social experiences in the much wider context of women's existence within the family and wider social structures.

Women Viewing Violence departs somewhat from many other media studies committed to an interpretative approach. By adopting a standardised approach to group discussions together with systematic qualitative analysis, we seek to extend the range of existing work. While we think 'unstructured interviews' and other impressionistic approaches are important, it is nonetheless the case that genuine comparative work aimed at assessing the impact of different backgrounds and experiences on how television is interpreted requires a degree of standardisation. The use of focused groups in which participants were systematically faced with similar points of reference for discussion ensured that all participants were presented with the same frameworks, allowing for specific and direct comparisons to be made.

The use of standardised questionnaires to gather information on participants' backgrounds and individual reactions to programmes constituted further departures from many interpretative approaches. Background information and individual responses to questionnaires meant that we could more accurately depict and understand how cultural and social experiences shaped reactions to televised violence.

Using quantitative and qualitative information from these three sources meant that we could portray women's interpretations and how these related to some key dimensions of their lives more fully than would have been possible if only *one* empirical strategy had been employed. Triangulation of methods and sources of information – that is, using several approaches, is a method increasingly used in the social sciences.[4] Quantitative results aid the assessment of major trends and patterns and qualitative accounts allow for more meaningful representations of what people think and of the complexities of their everyday lives. The use of quantitative results, which show overall patterns, may assist researchers in avoiding the temptation to present qualitative results which concentrate on only one or a few discourses and interpretative positions to the neglect of others.

An approach such as this means that quantitative and qualitative results can be synthesised into an overall 'interpretative analytic' aimed at providing more comprehensive, contextual knowledge than would be possible without the use of such diverse methods.[5] Interpretative approaches also suggest the need for more self-consciousness in the presentation of research results. Thus researchers ought to provide developed accounts of the conduct of their investigations and how they have conducted their analysis. Such reconstructions of research are always difficult and partial, but they are necessary if others are to judge the basis of the claims made in any particular study and they act as useful pointers for further work. Unfortunately, much media research in the cultural studies tradition seems to provide only the briefest of details about its rationale for and the nature of the research process itself.[6] In the following sections we provide a partial account of what we consider to be the most salient features of this study.

Designing the study

Pilot study and programme selection
A pilot study was carried out in order to establish which programmes and programme forms would be best suited to achieving the stated aims of the proposed investigation. It also enabled us to gain an initial insight into the reactions of women to such programmes in a group setting. More pragmatically, it provided indications of the time required for discussion and how such discussion was likely to evolve. Participants in the pilot study were students of the University of Stirling.

Four separate viewing groups were constituted for the pilot study. Group one was shown an episode of *EastEnders,* which contained a scene of domestic conflict and violence, and the television drama *Closing Ranks,* which contained scenes of domestic violence and other forms of violence. Group two watched *Crimewatch UK* and *Crimewatch UK Update,* containing a report of a rape and murder of a young woman, and *Distant Voices, Still Lives* (Terence Davies, 1988), a film containing scenes of domestic violence. Group three viewed *A Nightmare on Elm Street 4: The Dream Master* (Remy Harlin, 1988), a film in the horror/slasher movie genre. Group four was shown *Blue Velvet* (David Lynch, 1987), a film containing scenes of sexual violence.

After each group-viewing, the reactions to the programmes were evaluated and the structure to be used in the group discussions was refined. The pilot phase was also used by the researchers to view, evaluate and select potential programmes. We further considered a range of programmes containing instances of violence against women not included in the pilot viewings. For example, *Friday the 13th* (Sean S. Cunningham, 1980), although not in fact viewed by any of the pilot groups, was discussed extensively with women taking part in the pilot studies, most of whom had seen it. It was considered to be a portrayal of deliberately unrealistic violence, where violence was intended to entertain by producing fear. The film was not taken seriously by pilot group members. When the research team viewed *Friday the 13th,* it was eliminated as a candidate for the project mainly because the film portrayed a female protagonist who committed multiple murders, an extremely unrealistic portrayal of the known patterns of violence. It was decided that it would be of greater value to use material likely to have a relationship with the real incidence of violent crime (mainly committed by men) and with public perceptions of violence.

Although *A Nightmare on Elm Street 4, Blue Velvet* and *Distant Voices* were seriously considered for inclusion in the research project, these were ultimately rejected. *A Nightmare on Elm Street 4,* like *Friday the 13th,* was not taken seriously by women viewing it in the pilot study, who considered the violence exhibited in the film to be totally unrealistic and far-fetched. It was judged to be a purely escapist film, intended for teenagers, and quite unlikely to be taken seriously by mature women or to provide a meaningful focus for the questions addressed in this project.

The pilot group which had viewed *Distant Voices, Still Lives* regarded it as an 'art movie'. While the film includes some very realistic scenes of domestic violence, these are set within the context of working-class Northern England in the 1930s: this historical setting, combined with an unconventional artistic narrative, made comprehension difficult for those in the pilot group. The research team decided that more pertinent films were available for consideration.

The content and format of *Blue Velvet*, with its perceived denigration of women, its portrayal and apparent condoning of serious violence, its use of extreme language and its potential impact on both female and male viewers, suggested that this film was ideally suited to the research project. That the film is widely available in video shops and had been broadcast on satellite television, and that its director, David Lynch, has become established as a highly acclaimed figure – a contemporary cultural hero for some – underlined the case for its inclusion. The outcome of the pilot study led to a different decision. Group discussions of *Blue Velvet* revealed that this film could be extremely disturbing to women. The violence portrayed was regarded by some members of the pilot viewing group as grossly offensive and upsetting. After carefully considering the possible consequences of showing *Blue Velvet* to women who had been victims of male violence – such as rape, domestic assault and marital rape – it was decided that the film was far too disturbing. The research team concluded that it would be unethical to expose women, particularly those who had experience of violence, to such material and agreed that it could also raise practical problems of group management.

In making its final choices, the research team took account of reactions to the pilot studies, made its own assessments of possible programmes and considered the contemporary debates surrounding violence against women. We sought to present a range of programming and genres that might evoke a variety of responses, considering actuality and fiction programming to be the two most pertinent broad categories with which to start. It was decided that programmes to be used should be selected according to the following criteria. They should:

(i) contain portrayals bearing a significant relation to actual acts of violence committed against women;
(ii) portray violence within a variety of narrative forms and genres. Variation was considered necessary since, in contained narratives such as films and plays, the very form itself brings the story to an end. This compares to continuous narrative forms, such as soap operas, where various lines of development are deliberately left open to retain the audience's further interest. It was also thought necess-

ary to compare women's perceptions of 'real world' violence as presented in factual programmes with its fictional presentation, to explore how, if at all, women might relate differently to these. The pilot study of *Crimewatch UK* had already indicated that, among one group of women, perceptions of the representation of factual violence were by no means identical;

(iii) range from those concerned solely with violence against women to those that represented such violence as subsidiary to wider themes and issues;

(iv) encompass a variety of types of violence against women;

(v) include portrayals of different female character types as victims of violence, offering the possibility of a range of interpretations about why women are subjected to violence;

(vi) contribute to wider debates on violence against women.

Programmes used in the study

These deliberations resulted in the selection of four programmes, *Crimewatch UK*, *EastEnders*, *Closing Ranks* and the film, *The Accused* (all described in greater detail in subsequent chapters). Given the substantial discussion and controversy that has surrounded *Crimewatch UK,* it was decided to make use of an example of this programme.[7] *Crimewatch*, like similar programmes such as *America's Most Wanted*, attracts very large audiences and also raises provocative questions about the use of drama-documentary techniques in its 'reconstructions'. The research team was particularly interested in the use of *Crimewatch* because of debates concerning the role of this kind of televised programme in heightening fear of crime. In showing the entire programme – which dealt with a whole menu of crimes in a variety of formats – we hoped to gain some understanding of women's general perceptions of crime as presented on television, as well as to assess in particular how they reacted to the presentation of the murder of a young woman. The *Crimewatch UK Update* – a follow-up to the main programme that reports on public reaction to police appeals for help – was also included. The screening and discussion of the *Update* was conducted after group reactions to the main programme.

Turning to fiction, we considered what would best represent the kind of material available to the television audience. The main concern was to offer a range of programmes touching on violence against women where that violence was embedded in a variety of narrative forms (or ways of telling the story). We considered the key typical forms or genres and decided to include an episode from a soap opera in which violence was incidental to a wider continuing saga (*EastEnders*), as well as one television drama in which marital violence was a key theme, interlaced with that of police corruption (*Closing Ranks*). Both cases, then, placed violent acts and the relations between men and women in broader, quite complex, contexts.

Soap operas such as *EastEnders* have elicited a great deal of interest in academic circles, with a particular focus on women viewers' relationships to this genre.[8] It was therefore thought to be particularly important to assess women's interpretations of an episode within this genre portraying violence inflicted upon a woman. We were specifically interested in assessing to what extent the viewing groups found the episode to be realistic, particularly those scenes involving domestic violence. We anticipated that some women in the viewing groups were likely to be more familiar with *EastEnders* than others. Some would have extensive prior knowledge of the characters which others lacked. It was felt that such differing levels of familiarity with the programme could have a bearing upon the interpretations of the violence portrayed.

The television drama, *Closing Ranks,* was considered to be a particularly realistic portrayal of violence in a domestic relationship. It accurately portrays the intimidating and coercive behaviour associated with violence against women, as well as marital rape. Additionally, the level of violence portrayed exceeds that demonstrated in the *EastEnders* episode, thereby potentially broadening the scope for discussion.

The drama presented an extensive range of issues: for instance, women's place in the home and in society, the influence of a violent husband upon his son's attitudes, police reactions to reports of domestic violence, and corruption and violence within the police force. The programme portrayed not only violence in the domestic setting but also a case of police assault against an innocent male member of the public, allowing comparison of the interpretations of these two essentially different violent acts.

Discussions with the study's funding agency focused upon the desire to consider major film releases, given that these are often presented on television. Considerable discussion ensued about what might be most appropriate. The funding agency suggested that a 'slasher' film be included because such films are popular and have specific ways of representing violence. Although doubtful, we included such films in the pilot study. For reasons already discussed, a different choice was eventually made, namely *The Accused.* This major Hollywood production (dealing with gang rape) was the subject of considerable critical commentary. Widely available in video shops, it was acquired by British Satellite Broadcasting for transmission on its Movie Channel and was broadcast on B Sky B in April 1991. It was also transmitted on BBC1 in January 1992.

The research team considered it vital to include a film which portrayed graphic scenes of violence committed against a woman while remaining within the bounds of that which women could ethically be expected to view in a group situation. *Blue Velvet* had breached the bounds of acceptability so far as this research was concerned, and although *The Accused* contains a rape scene of more than five minutes in length, we judged that it would probably be acceptable to the various viewing groups. However, on ethical grounds, it was considered necessary to inform members of the viewing groups that they would be seeing the film, that it did contain an explicit rape scene, and that should they feel unable to view that part of the film they would be free to leave the room during the scene. Three women actually acted upon this warning and withdrew.

The programmes selected for this study provide a meaningful representation of a range of violence presented within diverse genres. The following genres are represented: 1) a factual programme rooted in realist conventions of crime reporting (*Crimewatch*); 2) a prime-time soap opera rooted in realism and with a strong social-issues orientation (*EastEnders*); 3) a single play made for television by a recognised documentary 'auteur' (*Closing Ranks*); 4) a feature film made for cinematic release but also available to satellite television and video audiences (*The Accused*).

Sample and viewing groups

In order to explore reactions to televised violence, a total of ninety-one women were selected and formed into groups. Each group spent one day viewing the selected programmes. Just over half (fifty-two) of the women were identified as having previously been subjected to some form of violence, usually at the hands of a male partner, while the other half had no such experience. A total of fourteen viewing groups were constituted, varying not only in terms of experience of violence, but also in terms of national background (Scottish/English), ethnicity, and class.

The distribution of ethnicity in the overall sample is presented in Figure I. Fifteen Afro-Caribbean women (16% of the sample) and twenty-eight Asian women (31% of the sample) participated in the study. The majority of the Asian women (79%) were born in Pakistan or India, migrating to Great Britain later in life. They were about equally divided in terms of religious background: 41% identified themselves as Muslims and 37% as Sikhs; the remainder were Hindus. The number of Afro-Caribbean and Asian women included in the sample constitutes an over-representation in relation to their numbers in the wider population. Overall, however, the two categories of women, those 'with experience of violence' and those 'with no experience of violence', contained approximately the same proportion of white women (52% with experience of violence and 54% with none), Asian women (31% in each case) and Afro-Caribbean women (17% and 15% respectively).

In order to create settings in which detailed discussion could develop, it was decided that the optimum size of a group should be six women, although the achieved groups ranged in size from five to nine. The formation of appropriate groups took considerable time and included considerations of experience of violence, class membership, and ethnic and cultural background. These various criteria of selection were combined to produce the following groups:

Scotland: Groups with no experience of violence
1. White working-class women.
2. White middle-class women.
3. Asian women.

Scotland: Groups with experience of violence[9]
4. White women.
5. White women.
6. Asian women.

England: Groups with no experience of violence[10]
7. White working-class women.
8. White middle-class women.
9. Asian women.
10. Afro-Caribbean women.

England: Groups with experience of violence[11]
12. White women.
13. Asian women.
14. Afro-Caribbean women.

Figure 1: Ethnicity of respondents

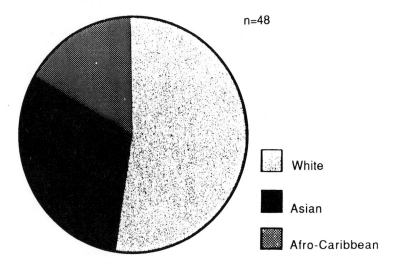

n=48

☐ White

■ Asian

▨ Afro-Caribbean

Recruiting group members

Women with experience of violence
Efforts to form the fourteen viewing groups proved to be one of the most time-consuming and difficult aspects of the research. Recruiting women for groups with experience of violence was always conducted through third parties, usually women's organisations. Organisations contacted for recruitment purposes were rightly concerned about the nature of the research, and a great deal of consultation and discussion was therefore necessary. In discussing the project with organisations and prospective participants we were scrupulously honest about the levels of televised violence to which women would be exposed, and were as concerned as the women's groups through which we were recruiting about the possible effects on women.

In Scotland, most of the women who had experience of violence were recruited through Women's Aid groups, who each year provide support and refuge for thousands of physically abused women and their children.[11] In England, Women's Aid as well as other organisations assisted in recruiting women with experience of violence. After assurances of confidentiality and anonymity, co-ordinators of local Women's Aid groups and the other organisations recruited women for the project and explained the nature and aims of the study to prospective participants. Once women agreed to participate they were approached by the researcher. These groups were also prepared to provide the necessary follow-up support for those who took part in the research, should this prove necessary. Contact with Women's Aid organisations proved especially fruitful, not only as a means of recruiting women but also as a key to contact with other victim support groups for women. Through Women's Aid we were directed to community organisations and action groups who provided additional women willing to take part in the project.

Because of long-standing relationships between two of the researchers and Women's Aid groups in Scotland, the recruitment of women living in Scotland proved relatively straightforward. Recruitment of women who had been victims of violence in England proved much more difficult. At an early stage in the research project, the team decided that English viewing groups should be based in Birmingham and the Midlands, principally because the English Midlands is a populous and culturally diverse region. As a major city, Birmingham was thought to have a sufficient number of Women's Aid groups available to assist in recruiting women with experience of violence, but it proved difficult to recruit an adequate number of women through these contacts. Women were eventually recruited from Coventry, Leamington and Northampton, as well as Birmingham. These women were recruited through a diverse range of organisations, from Women's Aid, refuges unaffiliated to Women's Aid, Victim Support Schemes, women's hostels and ethnic community groups.

It was particularly difficult to recruit groups of middle-class women with experience of violence, who are often reluctant to make public the violence and their predicament. Nevertheless, some middle-class victims of violence did participate, in groups that included women from working-class backgrounds.

Women with no experience of violence
Women without experience of sexual or domestic violence were recruited by a market research organisation. Using a quota sampling technique, street recruiters chose women at random on the basis of criteria considered important for the study. Recruiters were informed of the essential need to exclude any victims of violence from these groups, and during the street interview they asked interviewees whether they had ever experienced any violence; those who indicated that they had were excluded. A wide variety of women were approached and selected on the basis of variations in class, ethnic background and age.

Women recruited through the market research organisation and those recruited via Women's Aid and other organisations were informed that they would be taking part in a television survey, and that the survey was concerned with issues of violence on television, but also with representations of women, men, family life, and crime. It was important not to make prospective participants too sensitive to the aims of the project. However, women were informed that taking part in the group sessions would involve viewing examples of portrayals of violence.

All participants were given £20.00 (about $35.00) for their attendance at the one-day session. Crèche facilities were provided, or the cost of child-minders was covered by the project. All expenses incurred by interviewees in the groups were covered, including travel costs to and from the session, lunch and child care.

Conducting the screenings and focused group discussions

Screenings
The screenings were conducted in a seven-hour period of a single day, interrupted only for lunch and tea-breaks. In an attempt to standardise viewing venues, all but three group sessions were held in University surroundings. The sessions with a group of Scottish Asian women and two groups of English women with experience of violence were held in community locations. This change of venue did not seem to affect the nature of responses or discussion.

Before each day's viewing women were again told that they would be viewing scenes of violence and that if they felt the need to leave during any particular scene they should do so. Participants were shown entire programmes and then asked to fill in a short questionnaire aimed at assessing their immediate reactions. This was followed by a discussion of the programme and then a second opportunity to fill in the same questionnaire in order to capture any changes in interpretations arising from the discussions. Discussions of each programme ranged in length from thirty minutes to one-and-a-half hours, with an average duration of one hour. In the mornings, all groups were shown *Crimewatch UK* and the *Update* as well as one episode of the soap opera, *EastEnders.* In the afternoon, groups were shown either the television drama *Closing Ranks* (four groups), or the feature film *The Accused* (ten groups).

As group sessions lasted for at least seven hours, it was essential to make participants feel as relaxed as possible throughout the day. Comfortable chairs were used, plenty of food and refreshments were freely available throughout the day and a buffet lunch was provided. Where necessary, dietary and Asian meals were provided. Seven hours of viewing and discussion, whatever the setting, constitutes an arduous task and although women commented that they felt 'knackered' at the end of the day, in those groups where time allowed for discussion of the session itself, most women expressed positive views about the experience.

Group members were asked to view the programmes as though they were in their own homes. Although we sought to create a comfortable atmosphere we did not seek to minimise the undoubted artificiality of these conditions when compared with the normal viewing experience. All research, whatever the method, creates a unique reality and alters the 'natural' setting. We judge the established viewing groups to fall somewhere between the tightly controlled artificiality of the psychological experiment and the naturalness of the domestic setting.

The established groups appear to have facilitated and concentrated thinking and discussion. Participants, particularly those with experience of violence, noted the way the supportive group setting encouraged discussion. As two women put it, 'Other people spark you off thinking', and, 'It's interesting to get other people's point of view and to actually discuss what you've seen. I mean, I don't get a chance to discuss things, you know, with being on my own with my little boy.'

One of the important intentionally 'contrived' aspects of the study was that women were able to watch entire programmes without being interrupted and otherwise influenced by male partners and children. Women commented on this 'unnatural', albeit positive, aspect of the study, contrasting the viewing groups with the demands of the domestic setting which make it difficult to concentrate attention on television viewing:[12]

You've usually got your mind on other things as well as just sitting down and watching television in your own home.

[At home] you can't relax because you've got the kids all the time and, you know, you're concerned about the kids in bed. Even if they're okay [you worry] if they're going up and down the stairs.

At all group sessions, the female researcher and a female assistant were on hand to provide support for the women. The assistant was free throughout the day for this purpose. Although three women did leave during the rape scene in *The Accused* (subsequently returning for the discussion) and the programmes did appear to be viewed with considerable emotion by many women, the effect did not curtail discussion.

Focused group discussion
The format for programme discussions was broadly standardised, although where necessary, due allowance was made for specific issues raised within a given group. After filling in the short questionnaire on immediate reactions, the discussion of each programme opened with a request for initial reactions and responses. Group members were invited to offer judgments on specific aspects of the programme: for example, whether they liked or disliked the programme, regarded it as 'good' or 'bad', or found it entertaining. By permitting the initial reaction to remain open, we sought to elicit the themes and issues which were most salient for group members. Initial reactions were followed by more focused discussions guided by a series of questions posed by the researcher, who acted as a moderator (see Appendix III, Guiding Questions for Discussion).[13] Although group members were free to raise any topic they wished, the researcher raised a standardised set of issues in each session, thus ensuring a degree of comparability across groups.

The focused discussions concentrated on a number of themes such as the main characters in the programmes or – in the case of *Crimewatch* – the presenters, the victims and the perpetrators of the three reconstructed crimes. Of particular interest were the points of identification with the screen characters, especially for those who had been victims of violence. The focus then moved to a consideration of specific scenes and situations depicted in each programme. In *Crimewatch* the principal focus was the reconstruction of the activities of the murder victim prior to her death. The *EastEnders* discussion focused specifically on scenes portraying the couple involved in domestic violence, as well as those situations involving other families. Scenes selected from *Closing Ranks* concentrated on the violent policeman and his wife, though again including situations outside this relationship. The discussion of *The Accused* predominantly considered the main character, scenes leading up to the rape, and its portrayal (see Appendix III).

During the discussions of specific scenes, women were asked about their reactions and evaluations while viewing and why such scenes might have been included within the programmes. They were also invited to consider the motivational contexts associated with scenes, particularly those including violence, and to consider the intentions of characters. Finally, group members were asked to consider the programmes' value for women.

The discussions involved a funnelling process which was designed to allow groups initially to determine their own agendas as much as possible, before urging them to focus on specific issues. The research team was anxious not to predetermine responses. This problem occurred in one pilot study, where group members discussed issues with which they perceived the research to be concerned. Such 'demand characteristics' cannot be eliminated entirely, but they can be minimised.[14]

Data collection instruments and analysis
Group discussions were tape-recorded and transcribed for computer analysis (producing over 1,400 pages). The verbatim transcripts were categorised and analysed using the computer programme 'Hypersoft'.[15] The systematic analysis of these discussions provides one basis for our accounts of women's interpretations of and reactions to the programmes. In addition, quantitative data were gathered on each participant using seven separate instruments: the 'Background Questionnaire', administered before the day's viewing, and six 'Programme Questionnaires', administered before and after the discussion of each of the three programmes viewed during the one-day session. These quantitative results were analysed using the software packages 'StatView II SE+ Graphics'.[16]

While group discussions provide an important basis for developing and assessing interpretations, there must be considerable concern about the validity of generalising about individuals or the 'group' solely on the basis of these discussions or from the transcripts of such discussions. Small-group processes and conversational conventions play a significant role in the production of specific readings within groups. Homogeneous groups and skilled moderators can play an important role in facilitating the fullest participation and the moderator can at least partially direct the course of discussion. But there will always be reticent, domineering and influential group members, and dissenting opinions may often be 'restrained' or silenced.[17] Therefore, it is important to pay particular attention to group processes and to reach informed judgments about how these might affect interpretations emerging from discussions. It may also be important to use more than one method of gathering data or information on individual interpretations and reactions. This was one of the main reasons for employing Programme Questionnaires to determine immediate reactions unaffected by group discussions. In this way we have an additional method for assessing the reactions and relating them to lived experiences. We do not suggest that statistically aggregated data generated from these questionnaires can replace, or are superior to, qualitative forms of information (e.g., transcriptions of discussions) but seek to demonstrate that each serves to complement the other.

The standardised Programme Questionnaires were used to determine individual reactions immediately after each viewing and immediately following each discussion.[18] This method provided evidence about participants' responses to the programmes that could be compared to the qualitative findings. The quantitative statistical results based on these questionnaires are useful in illustrating overall patterns and tendencies and in allowing for more systematic comparisons between groups and categories of respondents.

The Programme Questionnaires were brief and contained both closed and open-ended items (see Appendix II for examples). They provided systematic information about evaluative and aesthetic judgments on each programme and the participants' assessments of characters and situations. Questionnaires were designed specifically for each programme, but there was considerable commonality in the issues explored. Group members were asked whether they had seen the specific programme and, for *Crimewatch* and *EastEnders*, how often they watched them. They were also asked to rate each programme on a Likert-type scale, scoring from one to five on a series of items including whether the programme was: Realistic, Entertaining, Violent, Offensive, Serious, Disturbing, Exciting, and Believable.[19] Concentrating on the format of the programme, we asked members of viewing groups to identify what they saw as the main issue being presented and if they could personally relate to any of the characters or situations. Finally, for *Closing Ranks*, *EastEnders* and *The Accused*, the women were asked whether they thought such programmes or films should be made. In the case of *The Accused*, which at the time had not yet been screened on British television, they were also asked whether it should be broadcast.

We were also interested in identifying the backgrounds, cultural locations and explicit experiences of the women who participated in the group discussions. Audience research sometimes treats groups as 'representatives' of social and demographic categories with little effort to validate this assumption or to assess intra-group variations in the supposedly significant variables. The results of the Background Questionnaire completed by every participant enabled us to locate specific variations in backgrounds (such as experience of violence) and to make a more informed and direct assessment of the relationship between these factors and the women's interpretations as evident in the Programme Questionnaires. While interpretations may not be direct 'expressions' of socio-demographic categories, the interpretations made by the participants in this study were affected significantly by ethnicity, class, and the experience of violence . It is not that belonging to a given social category or having had a particular experience crudely determines responses; rather they tend to provide a discourse, or variety of discourses, for the interpretation of the wider culture, of which television is a significant part. Such discourses contain quite distinctive assumptions, values, interpretations and vocabularies, and these can be seen in the detailed analysis of the reactions to the various programmes screened.

Where possible, the Background Questionnaires were completed prior to arrival. Most often, however, women filled them out just before the screenings. The Background Questionnaire explored the usual social and demographic issues, such as age, location of residence, educational achievement, employment, living arrangements and leisure-time activities (see Appendix I). Data were also collected on patterns of television viewing and media consumption, including favourite stations and programmes, average weekly viewing, radio-listening habits, newspaper consumption, and major media sources of information and entertainment.

Given the central research question, much of the Background Questionnaire was devoted to an exploration of women's experiences of crime and violence. Respondents were asked about their experiences of physical attacks in public and in the home, and provided rudimentary information about the nature of such attacks. Information was also obtained about a wide range of specific forms of sexual aggression and violence, including obscene phone calls, sexual harassment at work, groping, flashing, incest and rape. Women were asked about their fears and apprehensions of becoming victims of property crimes and about their use of the criminal justice system as a consequence of being a victim of a property or violent crime. They also gave us their views on the impact of various media on their own fear of crime. The questionnaire finished with a series of questions about the respondents' identification with 'women's issues'.

Analysis of results proceeded on two parallel and overlapping paths. Qualitative results arising from interpretative methods, such as participant observation, in-depth interviews and group discussions, present researchers with a series of dilemmas regarding analysis and presentation. Various strategies, such as case studies and the presentation of verbatim accounts, are often employed. These have the benefit of 'fleshing out' and illustrating the significant themes and patterns identified by the researcher(s). Often, however, it is difficult for readers to understand *how* certain materials are chosen over others and *why* certain quotes take precedence over those which never appear. In this study we have attempted a systematic approach to the development of significant themes and illustrative quotes arising from group interviews.

Screening specific programmes and employing a focused group interview meant that we, like all researchers, had already directed participants to certain themes and issues, while not of course determining what they thought. Once the fieldwork was completed, members of the research team discussed preliminary interpretations of results and developed a set of general categories for grouping and analysing the recorded transcripts (see Appendix IV). Using the Macintosh-based 'Hypersoft' qualitative data analysis package, quotes were grouped into these categories. For example, two of the main categories were 'Victims' and 'Perpetrators'. Under these headings we grouped all comments about these two categories and, using a further refinement, the interpretations of causes, motives and justifications were also classified.

Although qualitative data analysis packages such as 'Hypersoft' facilitate the categorising and manipulation of results, they do not eliminate the time-consuming and laborious task of reading and classifying what people tell us. The initial articulation of analytical and operational categories does, however, avoid the *ad hoc* approaches associated with the unfounded assumption that the results 'speak for themselves' since all data-collection techniques shape results. Initial categories were used in an interactive way to assess initial assumptions and to classify segments of transcripts. Preliminary readings of transcripts and the process of classification also informed and altered initially identified categories and significant themes.

Proceeding in a self-conscious manner also means researchers should be open to the discovery of themes not recognised in early deliberations. The reading, grouping and analysing of transcripts yielded a number of new insights, most notably the significance of women's relationships with children and the importance of ethnicity in shaping interpretations. Using this method means that overall analytical categories and forms of presentation are embedded in, although never completely determined by, the discourses of those participating in the study. The development of categories was also shaped by the systematic comparison and synthesis of quantitative and qualitative results and through the construction of a narrative of presentation. Writing up the results, discussing and sometimes debating the form and style of presentation also meant formulating and reformulating categories and overall results. The quotes used in *Women Viewing Violence* to illustrate major analytical categories have emerged from a complex process. Those chosen for inclusion best represent the dominant themes emerging from group discussions.

The Programme Questionnaire and the Background Questionnaire yielded results which were most amenable to quantitative statistical analysis. Using 'StatView' we explored the commonalities and differences in backgrounds and responses of women who participated, with a specific focus on the way experience of violence, ethnicity, and class shape response patterns. Preliminary data analysis revealed the extraordinary importance of the experience of violence and ethnic background in shaping interpretations. In the remainder of this chapter, and subsequently, we demonstrate, through summary statistics and measures of statistical association, how these two factors affect reactions to viewing violence.

Background characteristics of the respondents

Results of the Background Questionnaire show that the women participating in this study come from diverse backgrounds. The youngest woman was nineteen, the oldest fifty-five, the average age was thirty-three and the majority (50%) were between the ages of twenty-six and thirty-five (see Figure II). Well over three-quarters of the women had children, usually two.

Educationally, the sample ranged from those with little formal education (principally those who had migrated from the Indian subcontinent) to women with higher and further education. Thirty-six per cent of the group with no experience of violence and 29% of the women who had experienced violence obtained 'O' level results, while 8% and 10% respectively achieved Scottish Highers or 'A' levels (roughly equivalent to completing an American high school education). Approximately the same proportion of each group, one quarter, finished a technical or vocational course or part of a university course. Six per cent of the women who experienced violence had completed a university degree and 3% of women with no experience finished technical college. One woman in the group with no experience of violence had completed a postgraduate course.

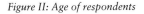

Figure II: Age of respondents

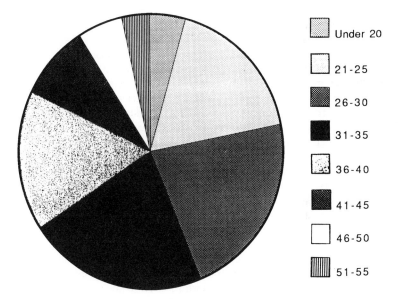

Under 20

21-25

26-30

31-35

36-40

41-45

46-50

51-55

Overall, women who had experienced violence and those who had not were not strikingly different in terms of their educational backgrounds, but they were different in their patterns of employment and current marital and living arrangements. The majority (56%) of women with no experience of violence were married and living with their husbands and children, while only 13% of the women who had previously experienced violence lived in such a household. Most of the women with experience of violence were either separated (31%) or divorced

(33%) and the vast majority were living alone with their children. Many of the women were fully occupied in the home (42% of those with experience of violence and 26% of those with none). Women from the groups who had no experience of violence were likely to be in full-time (41%) or part-time (20%) employment, whereas only 17% of women who had experienced violence described themselves as fully employed. Women employed in wage labour in both groups were primarily in unskilled or clerical occupations.

The type of accommodation also varied between the two categories of women. Most of the women participating in the study lived in cities and towns, but, because of the nature of the sample, about one-third of the physically abused women were living in a refuge or hostel. Of those women not in a refuge or hostel, most were renting, either from the local authority or private landlords. Only 15% were owner-occupiers. By contrast, most of the women with no experience of violence were owner-occupiers (62%) while others were living in either council (23%) or private rented accommodation (13%). The reason for the difference is not difficult to discern: basically the one category is primarily composed of single-parent families, whereas the other generally includes women from intact families with a male wage-earner.

Women participating in this study were not particularly active in politics. However, 58% of women with experience of violence and 47% of those with none did express an interest in politics. Although only eighteen women (26% of those with experience and 16% of those without) identified themselves as feminists, the vast majority of participants (86%) said that they were interested in women's issues and 93% said that they were interested in women's rights. It is important to remember that these women were not chosen for their expressed interest in women's issues, so these results may be rather surprising.

Media consumption

Our findings show that media consumption was broadly similar for women who had experienced violence and those who had no experience. As illustrated in Figure III, the women watched from one to ten hours of television on weekdays, with the vast majority (62%) watching less than four hours of television a day.

Independent Television (ITV) was watched in the households of most of the women (63% with experience, 51% with no experience) although there was nearly an even split between ITV and BBC1 in the households of women who had no experience of violence. This may reflect the preponderance of middle-class respondents in that category. BBC1 was most often mentioned as the favourite channel among women who had not experienced violence (47%), while ITV was favoured by more of the women who had been the victims of violence (40%).

When asked to choose their favourite television programme, most women mentioned soap operas (56% with experience, and 44% with no experience of violence). *Neighbours* was by far the most frequently mentioned soap (about 16% in each category). Other favourite genres included documentaries and the news, although they were never chosen by more than 12% of either category. Other popular forms included films, game/quiz shows, comedy series and current affairs. Interestingly, when asked what sorts of programmes they disliked, the participants often named specific soap operas. Women who had experienced violence also singled out specific genres, such as violent films (19%) and horror films (8%). Only one woman from the group without experience of violence singled out such programmes. Many respondents also told us that they disliked sports programmes (29% of women with experience and 11% without). With the exception of violent films and sports, no other specific type of programme was singled out as disliked by a sizeable proportion of either category.

Figure III: Hours of weekday viewing

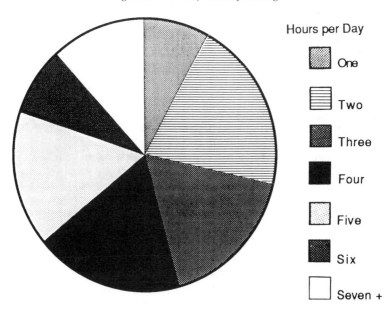

Hours per Day

One

Two

Three

Four

Five

Six

Seven +

Other media, radio and newspapers, are also used. The women told us that they listened to music on Radio One (29% with experience, and 56% with no experience of violence) or independent local radio (51% with experience and 26% with no experience). Patterns of newspaper consumption were predictable, with nearly 60% of both categories of women reading popular or mid-market newspapers. Almost the same percentage of women in the two categories (40%) indicated that they usually read popular newspapers such as the *Sun, Daily Mirror, Daily Star* or *Daily Record*. Mid-market papers such as the *Daily Mail, Daily Express* and *Scottish Daily Express* were read by 40% of women with no experience of violence and 28% of those with experience. Women who had not experienced violence were much more likely to read newspapers on a daily basis than those who had (59% and 35% respectively). When asked which medium they found most entertaining, the vast majority in both categories (67% with experience and 80% with none) opted for television. Exactly the same percentage of women from both categories (69%) indicated that they also found television the most informative medium.

The findings on radio and television consumption patterns are consistent with the broad picture emerging from quantitative research by the broadcasters. The women who participated in the study were average consumers of television, their tastes for radio output were in line with other data, and the strong preference for soap operas also accorded with well-documented findings.[20]

The nature of violence against women
In seeking to locate the experiences of women in this research, we have drawn upon a wealth of research literature about violence against women. Physical abuse of women in the home, rape, sexual assault and child sexual abuse have all been documented. This research shows that women and girls are the most likely victims of physical and sexual assault within the domestic setting. Official crime reports and surveys of experiences of crime in Great Britain, Canada and the United States confirm that women are the victims in 90–97% of assaults in the home and that this violence is usually perpetrated by their male partners, sometimes after separation or divorce.[21]

Intensive research on the nature of violent events against women in the home reveals that the violence is persistent and severe and often results in serious physical and emotional damage. The physical force used by men against their female partners includes slapping, punching, kicking, the use of weapons, rape, and sometimes murder. A particular violent event is often associated with threatening, intimidating or terrorising forms of behaviour which, for some women, becomes a continual aspect of their daily existence. Violence of this nature is usually associated with men's attempts to punish, control, dominate and/or humiliate women.

As abuse continues, it usually becomes more frequent and severe. Physical abuse is often associated with attempts to isolate the woman from family, relations, friends and social agencies who might provide support and assistance for her and/or attempt to control the man and his violent behaviour. Women may be isolated to such an extent that they feel entrapped and imprisoned in their own home. Traditionally, and still today, women find it difficult to share this problem because of the behaviour of men and the shame associated with exposing family problems to public scrutiny. As women struggle to create a violence-free relationship or to escape from violence and seek help, they have traditionally encountered unhelpful responses from social and legal agencies, thus further increasing their sense of isolation and the man's feelings of control. Women living with a violent man often find it difficult to attain the economic means and the social support necessary to escape and live a life free from violence and intimidation – a point reflected in the demographic characteristics outlined earlier. Research shows that men sometimes pursue women for years after separation, continuing their violent and threatening behaviour. Investigations of homicide reveal that women are most at risk when they separate from, or try to leave, a violent man.[22]

Experience of violence

Evidence from the Background Questionnaires provided information on women's experience of crimes and of violence. Most of the women identified initially as having been the victims of violence reported physical assaults, some having been raped, while the experiences of a few were identified as primarily serious emotional abuse and intimidation. Most of the women (89%) were the victims of violence in their homes, but half of this category had also been victimised in a public setting. Fourteen women (28% of the identified group) told us that they had been raped and eight (16%) reported being the victims of incest.

Violent attacks on the women who participated in this study were similar to those reported in other studies.[23] Women described being slapped, punched, kicked, beaten up and having had weapons used against them. Whether this violence occurred within the home or in a public place, most women (80%) reported that they had been attacked and/or raped by husbands or boyfriends, whereas only a few reported attacks by strangers.

Nearly half of the participants were initially selected on the basis of screening questions indicating that they had had no experience of physical or sexual violence. However, a few later indicated on the Background Questionnaire that they had been the victims of less serious forms of abusive behaviour, such as obscene phone calls or men exposing themselves in public. Three women, identified initially as having had no experience of violence, subsequently reported being the victims of violence in the home, which in one case had been incest.

Women from both categories reported quite similar experiences of some of the less serious forms of abusive behaviour from men. For example, 42% of both categories had been subjected to obscene phone calls, while 34% of the women who had experienced violence, and 24% of women who had not, indicated that they had been subjected to men exposing themselves in public.[24] These results confirm past research in revealing that a sizeable proportion of women have been subjected to a wide range of abusive forms of behaviour at the hands of men.[25] They also show that some women experience persistent and severe forms of violence, usually occurring in intimate relationships with men. Although most women participating in this study could be located on a single, wide continuum of abusive and violent behaviour, for the purposes of this research we can assume that the two categories of initially identified women approach the opposite ends of that continuum.

Fear of crime

Violence and fear of crime
The two categories of women also differed in the levels of their fear of crime. Not surprisingly, most of the women in the study who had been the victims of crimes of violence felt more vulnerable than women with no such experiences.[26] This was most pronounced in fears of physical violence within the home. Well over half (61%) of the women who had experienced violence said they worried about physical attacks in their home, whereas only a quarter (23%) of women without experience reported the same concern. Differences between the two categories were less pronounced with reference to fear of crime in a public setting, with nearly the same proportions in each category (67% with experience and 56% without) indicating that they were worried about physical violence in public.

The two categories of women differed in their concern about going out at night. Sixty-five per cent of women who had experienced violence said they *were worried* about going out at night in their local area, whereas nearly the same proportion (63%) of women who had not experienced violence said that they *were not worried* about going out at night in their local area. When asked if there was 'anything about the area in which you live that you feel is threatening', over 43% of those with experience of violence and 21% of those with none said 'yes'. Similar differences were apparent in general concerns about crime. While around three-quarters of the women with no experience of violence indicated they worried about crime, 90% of the women with experience of violence were similarly concerned. Overall, these data show that the women in this study who had been the victims of violence generally expressed a greater sense of vulnerability and fear regarding crime than those women who had not experienced violence.

These findings are generally in line with the results of other research on women's fear of crime. They differ, however, in that they show a strong and direct relationship between fear of crime and victimisation. Women who have been the victims of violent attacks within the home are more likely, it seems, to express a sense of vulnerability extending beyond the home.[27] We also know, as Elizabeth Stanko has pointed out, that despite the under-representation of women as victims in official crime statistics and victim surveys, their sense of personal safety is conditioned by a wide range of harassment, intimidation and violence by men in public and private places.[28] As Stanko indicates, many women exist in a 'hostile and intimidating atmosphere', and the results of this study illustrate the impact of this atmosphere and of direct experiences of violence on women's perception of personal safety.

The media and fear of crime

Fear and apprehension about crime and violence are generated through a number of social and cultural experiences, perhaps the most important being the personal experience of violence. Some commentators have, however, sought to assess what contribution, if any, the media may make to these fears and anxieties.[29] When asked whether certain types of media *increased* or *decreased* their fear of crime, there were few discernible differences between the two categories. Over half of the women in both categories (56% with experience of violence and 61% without experience) indicated that certain types of media tended to *increase* their anxieties about crime.

When asked to choose from a list of those formats most likely to *increase* fear of crime, women were most likely to choose television news, television dramas and documentaries, television films, and the tabloid press. Very few women felt that radio news, the cinema, magazines, local free-sheets, and the quality newspapers were likely to increase their fear of crime. When asked if there was any '... one particular type of newspaper or TV programme which increases your fear of crime' fourteen women (15% of the entire sample) spontaneously mentioned *Crimewatch*. A small number of women also mentioned pornographic magazines, 'page three' nude photographs published in popular newspapers, and sensationalist forms of reporting as likely to increase their fear of crime and violence.

When queried about the role media play in reducing their fears of crime, a small proportion of women in both categories said that these could play such a role. Twenty-eight per cent of the women who had experienced violence and 19% of those who had no experience agreed that the media might function to reduce their fear of crime, usually mentioning television documentaries and current affairs programmes. When asked if there was any specific type of television programming or newspaper reporting that *reduced* their fear of crime, seven women spontaneously mentioned *Crimewatch*. These results indicate that over half of those involved in the *Women Viewing Violence* project considered that the media play an important role in *increasing* their anxieties and fear of crime, and that, for most women, the media play no role in *decreasing* those fears.

Mass-mediated violence and real violence

When asked specifically about what they thought of media reporting of crimes committed against women, our sample gave us some surprising and complex answers. Many indicated that they were not sure of the impact of this reporting, although in a number of instances they gave very clear and strong indications of their views. For example, an over-whelming majority from both categories (87% with experience, 90% with no experience of violence) thought that crime reporting might help make women become more aware and more safety-conscious. How-ever, over three-quarters of women in both categories also thought that crime reporting might actually increase women's fear of being attacked. Group participants were more equivocal about what impact such pres-entations might have on men. Large numbers across both categories (forty-six women, 50% of the entire sample), indicated that they did not know whether crime reporting would 'encourage men to commit violent acts against women'. Slightly over half of the thirty-nine women who had not experienced violence and slightly less than one-third of the fifty-two women who had experience of violence indicated that they did not know if crime reporting would encourage male violence. Of those women who did offer an opinion, there was a strong and significant difference between the two categories, with nearly three-quarters of women with experience of violence believing that crime reporting would encourage male violence, and almost the same proportion of women without experience believing the contrary.

Women who had been victims of violence felt strongly about the possible negative impact of crime reporting, yet they also felt that such reporting might have positive effects in making some men aware of 'other men's [violent] actions against women'. Almost all of the women with experience of violence who expressed an opinion on this subject felt that reporting crimes of violence against women could make other men more aware. Women with no experience of violence also endorsed this idea, with only 22% saying that they did not think it would make men more aware of the violent acts of other men.

When women were asked whether they thought that there should be more explicit control of the depictions of women in the media, the vast majority indicated that there should be more control. Ninety per cent of women with experience of violence and 70% of those with no experi-ence indicated that they would like to see more control. These senti-ments were most likely to be expressed by Afro-Caribbean and Asian women. All but one of the fourteen Afro-Caribbean women participat-ing in the study indicated that they would like to see more control and all but three of the twenty-three Asian women concurred. When women in this study were asked about specific media portrayals of women in 'page three' pin-ups often presented in popular daily British newspapers and in 'adult' magazines, and the presentation of violence against women on television, in the cinema and in videos, there was a strong and consistent pattern. Of the women indicating that they thought more control was appropriate, most were not concerned about the cinema; whereas the majority in both categories (with and without experience of violence) indicated that there should be more control of page three pin-ups, adult magazines and the portrayal of violence against women in videos and on television.

These results indicate that the women in this study generally thought that media presentations increased their fear of crime. Those who have experienced violence are concerned that the reporting of such crimes might make women generally more fearful of attack and encourage male violence, although a fair proportion of our respondents were unsure about the latter effect. Many felt that media coverage of crimes against women could have an educational impact upon some men. Most women in the study also thought that there should be greater control on media portrayals of women, particularly on television and video.

Conclusion

The research for *Women Viewing Violence* was preceded by a pilot study which enabled the researchers to evaluate and choose the most appropriate programmes for screening and to assess the potential problems associated with conducting group discussions. Four programmes were chosen as providing important features essential to the main aims of the research: *Crimewatch UK*, an episode of *EastEnders*, *Closing Ranks* and the film, *The Accused*. Group discussions and individual questionnaires were used for gathering information about participants' reactions to the programmes. A Background Questionnaire was also employed to gather data from participants on a number of issues, including their social, ethnic and educational backgrounds, experience of violence, fear of crime, patterns of television viewing, other media consumption and orientations to control of the media.

The results of this Background Questionnaire have revealed a number of important differences and similarities between women who have experienced violence and those who have had no such experience. The two groups did not differ in terms of age-distribution and educational achievement. However, they did differ in patterns of accommodation and employment. Women who had no experience of violence were often employed and the majority were married and living in their own homes. The majority of women in this study who had experienced violence were primarily unemployed single parents living in rented accommodation.

Analysis of data derived from the Background Questionnaires has revealed the importance of the experience of violence and of ethnicity in shaping interpretations and reactions. For example, women with experience of violence were more likely to express fear of crime and to voice concern about the reporting of violence against women in the media. They were also more likely to say that they would like to see more control over the portrayal of women in the media. Two other potentially significant background variables, class and nationality, were not of major importance in shaping reactions and interpretations. Analysis of the relationship between socio-economic variables and viewing patterns, fear of crime and interpretations of the programmes revealed no important patterns. Questionnaire results (and group discussions) also revealed very little relationship between nationality (Scottish/ English) and interpretations of the selected programmes.

Therefore in subsequent chapters we concentrate on the experience of violence and on ethnicity as the major determinants of varying interpretations of media representations of violence against women. We present the results of group discussions and the responses to the Programme Questionnaires, illustrating the significance of experience, ethnicity and, where relevant, class in shaping reactions. The presentation of the results of group discussions and programme questionnaires is preceded by a description of each programme.

All four of the programmes used in the research are detailed at some length, providing readers with a simple narrative account of what respondents viewed. The descriptions are not textual analyses, nor do they provide shot-by-shot visual detail, but stand as accounts of the main story-lines of the programmes. Rarely do expositions of audience research provide lengthy descriptions of the programmes used in analysis, a deficiency which prevents readers from having a fuller awareness of what viewers are responding to. Here, the intention is to provide a 'feel' for what was viewed, and a backdrop for an appreciation and evaluation of the responses given by our group members. As the responses of the women participating in this study indicate, there is no fixed interpretation of any one programme. Viewers create their own meanings and understandings and draw their own conclusions in structured ways. Therefore, the programme descriptions detailed are not intended to be conclusive or to privilege any specific reading.

3

CRIMEWATCH UK

About the programme

Crimewatch UK is a very popular programme, broadcast by the BBC, which aims to mobilise the television audience in order to assist the police in catching criminals. It was the initiator of a new genre that also includes *Crimestoppers* (broadcast in many of the Independent Television regions) and *Crime Monthly* (broadcast by London Weekend Television). Similar programmes are now broadcast in several other countries. *America's Most Wanted* is perhaps the best known such example.[1] Although considered to be factual television, *Crimewatch* might be seen as using some of the devices of crime fiction to entertain and hold its audience. Running for forty minutes each month (apart from a summer break), it is also able to attract an average audience on the BBC's main channel, BBC1, of 11.5 million. This is higher than some of the less popular soap operas, and much greater than that of the national main nightly news, whether on BBC or ITV. *Crimewatch* attains high audience appreciation ratings and is distinguished from comparable ITV programmes by its appeal to a national audience rather than to regional ones.

It is no accident that *Crimewatch* has achieved popularity in a period of law and order politics and fear of crime. It is also part of the new wave of 'participative' television. The BBC's research suggests that members of the television audience tend to group it with programmes that have a consumer/public watchdog function, distinguishing it from documentary programmes and police fiction.[2]

Although intended to mobilise audiences to help the police solve crimes, *Crimewatch* entertains to hold its audiences. In doing so, apart from the use of reconstructions (which raise interesting questions about the relation of the documentary dramatisation of a crime to actuality) the programme team select their crime stories from the popular end of the market, with murder, armed robbery with violence, and sexual crime as the staple items of coverage. Corporate crime, which is seen as difficult to visualise, and political crime, which is seen as too sensitive (especially in the case of Northern Ireland), do not figure in *Crimewatch's* menu. The style is fast-moving and visually varied.[3]

As the interpretation of sexual crime has proved to be of special importance in this chapter, it is worth noting that two types of crime later discussed by women viewers – sexual assaults on young children and rapes of adult women – figure routinely in both national and local

43

newspapers. These are part of a developing pattern over the past two decades in which sexual violence has been increasingly pervasive in everyday press coverage, with occasional stories meriting extensive and long-running treatment. In a comprehensive study of sexual crime coverage in the British press, Keith Soothill and Sylvia Walby underline the way in which rape cases, in particular, have moved out of the formerly restricted domain of smutty Sunday coverage to become a staple of popular (and even much quality) journalism.[4] The changed norms of the press in general have evidently had an increasing impact upon both general television news coverage of sexual crimes, and more specialised coverage such as *Crimewatch*.

It is also pertinent to note that the press coverage of rape cases uses a distinctive framework, in which there are three elements: the search for the offender, courtroom reporting, and post-conviction coverage.[5] Whereas courtroom reporting is a central issue in our later analysis of *The Accused*, it is the search phase that most directly relates to this chapter. This involves a style of coverage where 'the newspapers typically focus upon the criminal and deviant nature' of the offender, who is usually unknown to the victim and therefore to the police. Cases of serial rape (and sometimes murder) may become major newspaper narratives. However, there is a relevant distinction between the national newspapers, which often construct titillating 'sex fiend' stories in cases seen as of general interest, and the local press which more typically offers sustained and often detailed coverage in local cases.[6] *Crimewatch* has elements of these approaches. At times, for instance, it has concerned itself with major serial rapist cases that preoccupy the popular press. But its reconstructive approach and concentration on detail bear a similarity to aspects of local coverage. Significantly, when the BBC investigated audience views on the programme, one evident demand was precisely for local variants of *Crimewatch* – a role that in certain rather limited respects is fulfilled by ITV's *Crimestoppers*, and also in the London region by *Crime Monthly* .[7]

The *Crimewatch* production team necessarily has a close relationship to the various police forces that provide access to the details of the crimes covered. The programme is premised upon an identification with the fight against crime. Although the programme team insist upon their editorial independence, the police have a right of veto (never used to date) over the broadcasting of material put together in the programme's characteristic 'reconstructions'. For the broadcasters, it is essential that their programme be seen as independent of police control, an objective also shared by the police themselves. Particular importance is attached by the programme team to the need to have a good 'clear-up rate' for the crimes presented. This functions as a measure of *Crimewatch*'s value to the public and is seen as a defence against those critics who accuse it of a sensationalism and gratuitous violence that provoke public fear of crime.

Recently, in the Home Office's *Report of the Working Group on the*

Fear of Crime, chaired by the Chief Executive of Channel Four Television, Michael Grade, considerable concern was expressed about 'crime scarer' styles of media coverage.[8] *Crimestoppers* was singled out as an instance of this. The *Fear of Crime* report observed that *Crimewatch* did issue a 'health warning' to its viewers by informing them that the crimes featured are uncommon.[9] Research by the BBC into *Crimewatch* and by the Independent Broadcasting Authority (IBA) into *Crimestoppers* suggests (in drawing overall conclusions) that there is little hard evidence that television crime coverage of this kind induces fear in the audience.[10] However, looking at the detail of the BBC's report, we note the following observations in its discussion of the five groups (three of them made up solely of women, two solely of men) constituted by the audience researchers:

> ... some of the women, but none of the men, said they had been frightened by the programme. A few informants also mentioned the possibility of elderly viewers being frightened.

> The women who felt more inclined to say they felt frightened were the ones living or viewing alone – their imagination starts to run away with them.

> But most of those who had ever felt afraid said they understood why the programme has to be that way ...[11]

It would be fair to say that fear of crime is not accorded much weight in the BBC's research (which preceded the *Report of the Working Group on the Fear of Crime*); it is much more concerned with audience views on the reconstructions of crimes against property and the extent of violence shown in these.

By contrast, the IBA's research was commissioned as a direct outcome of the Home Office report. In the summary of the findings, the researchers observe:

> Among respondents who reported viewing *Crimestoppers,* over half agreed that although they themselves had not been made afraid by the programme, viewers should be warned beforehand when it is due to show a reconstruction of a violent crime. Just one in three respondents indicated that they thought that *Crimestoppers* had made them feel more cautious about going out alone in the dark or that other people had probably become more afraid of crime as a result of watching the programme. At the same time, a similar proportion said they were reassured by *Crimestoppers* that the police solve a great many crimes.[12]

The evidence, therefore, is complex and ambivalent: a crime reconstruction may cause anxiety at one level and reassure at another. The

IBA survey results do not distinguish between male and female respondents' views. Nevertheless, for fully one third to link their viewing with fear of crime does suggest that the issue cannot readily be dismissed. Given our own findings, reported below, we are inclined to think that the broadcasters' research may not have tapped adequately into some of the complex anxieties about personal safety that we have uncovered among women.

What the respondents saw

The *Crimewatch* programme used in this research project was broadcast on BBC1 at 9.30 p.m. on 10 November 1987 and the *Crimewatch Update* was broadcast on the same evening at 11.50 p.m. Since this particular programme was originally broadcast, the title sequence has been changed, but in all major respects the programme concept remains the same.

Crimewatch runs for forty minutes and is broadcast live. It contains elaborate reconstructions of selected crimes, usually two or three, interspersed with shorter descriptions of several others. The public are asked to watch, recall events, and ring the police in the studio if they have information that might help solve the crime. *Crimewatch UK Update* is ten minutes long and is broadcast later the same evening to inform the public about any progress with the cases shown. *Crimewatch* opens to a punchy drumbeat which runs throughout the opening titles. A series of crimes, watched by a series of pairs of eyes is followed by a sequence in which we see telephone calls being made to the police. Images of police response are then shown in the shape of a police car and motorcyclists. The *Crimewatch* logo of ultramarine blue block letters takes shape. As the music fades along with the logo, a dimly lit studio appears before us, with two presenters seated in the foreground and a large number of people working at desks behind them.

The programme begins with the presenter Sue Cook:

> Good evening, and welcome to the programme where once a month instead of just hearing about crimes you can perhaps actually do something about them. As always we're live, and the detectives here from all round the country are waiting for your call.

The telephone number that can be called by members of the public is given. Presenter Nick Ross then continues:

> This month, some advice about how *not* to have your car stolen, and three reconstructions: the cool car thieves who pose as friendly mechanics and persuade drivers to simply hand over their car keys; the fraudsters who conned a bank out of almost a quarter of a million pounds – maybe you'll recognise a voice; and the murder of a girl who was hitchhiking home in Oxfordshire.

As the reconstructions that are to follow in the programme are detailed, extracts from each appear inset in a blue box carrying the *Crimewatch* logo with a headline underneath it. The car thefts extract shows a man in an orange boiler suit talking to a man on a street and walking towards a car with the headline reading 'Mercedes Thefts'. In the case of the fraud, the administration section of a large bank is shown followed by a close-up of two large turning tape spools with the headline 'Hitchin Bank Fraud'. The final reconstruction extract reveals a young woman dressed in jeans and a brown suede jacket hitchhiking against a background of grass verge and trees with the headline 'Rachael Partridge Murder'. Details of some previous cases carried on *Crimewatch* are then given with the results of the programme's appeals for public help.

The first reconstruction, the bank fraud, runs for seven minutes and, like most *Crimewatch* reconstructions, uses actors to illustrate how the crime was committed. The reconstruction opens in West London. It is a complex tale of a man who, just before business hours, poses first as an employee of a firm and then as a cleaning contractor, to get past the night cleaner and then the secretary, in order to obtain company stationery and copies of signatures of the company directors. With these, the intruder and an accomplice managed to remove £236,000 by fraud from the company bank account and exchange this into Deutschmarks through a small city bank, using the company's name to gain authority for the exchange. The bank had recorded the telephone call arranging this exchange, and it was played in case viewers might recognise the voice. Photo-fit images of the crime's perpetrators are shown. The two fraudsters are described as white and middle-aged, and black and younger. A 'substantial reward' is also mentioned. While appealing for the public's help, the presenter states: 'We are all victims of this sort of fraud, because we pay for it in either bank charges or through our insurance.' Telephone numbers are then provided for the public to call in with information.

Moving away from the reconstruction, 'Incident Desk', presented by a woman police constable and a male police superintendent, briefly outlines several other cases in England: the disappearance of a couple from Jersey, an assault on two young girls by a man armed with a putty knife in Merseyside, an armed gang's unsuccessful hold-up and ramming of a security van in Hertfordshire, and the theft of £90,000 worth of toys in the south-east of England.

The second reconstruction concerns the theft of Mercedes cars. It opens in an expensive residential area of London with a wealthy-looking woman beside a red Mercedes. An oil leak has been temporarily repaired, and she is cleaning spilt oil from the wheel. The owner of an old broken-down brown car is in the same road and suggests that his mechanic friend, who is on his way, check her car too. The mechanic explains that the car has not been properly repaired and needs an oil seal. He says the owner of the brown car will take the Mercedes owner to buy one, now that his car is working. The woman accepts the offer and leaves her car keys with the mechanic so that he can start work while she is away. She is taken to several garages in an attempt to purchase the oil seal, and at one of these is abandoned by the man in the brown car. Meanwhile the 'mechanic' has driven off the Mercedes which, we are told, has never been seen since. A second theft by the same perpetrators is shown in the reconstruction, this time involving a Middle Eastern couple in western dress near Waterloo Bridge. A further six thefts of Mercedes have occurred under similar circumstances.

After the reconstruction, a police constable in the studio provides further information on these crimes and their perpetrators, telling of a man who had his Mercedes stolen in the same way but who was too embarrassed to report the theft at the time of the incident. This is followed by a presentation of details of car-theft prevention devices with which the public can protect their cars, and an item from the New Scotland Yard car pound on how to inspect serial and chassis numbers to discover whether a car you are considering purchasing is stolen.

'Photo Call' follows next, described by the presenter as 'television's version of the Wanted Poster', in which closed-circuit camera recordings of crimes are screened. The programme's resident police presenters briefly show more crimes in London and elsewhere in England, including some black youths committing an armed robbery at a jeweller's, white men suspected of robbing a bureau de change, a burglary in which a woman was violently attacked and, finally, a black man who has committed a number of raids on building societies.

The final reconstruction depicts what the presenter describes as 'yet another that highlights the dangers of hitchhiking'. He continues by stating:

Now, young people, especially young women, of course know the risks of hitchhiking. But the truth is, if you don't have a bike or a car, and there are no buses where you want to go when you want to go, the temptation to hitch is overwhelming. Rachael Partridge took that risk. She was seventeen years old.

The five-minute-long reconstruction, with the male presenter's voice-over and an actress playing the part of Rachael Partridge, tells the story of a young apprentice dental assistant. A photograph is inserted of Rachael, the youngest of three sisters, who lived with her parents in the English countryside. An actress is then shown playing Rachael at her boyfriend's house in a village several miles away, where she went most evenings after work. She and her boyfriend are sitting together on a sofa, laughing at one another's passport photographs. We are told that the couple, who met at school, were planning to go to Italy on their first holiday together. Rachael's mother comes to pick her up from the boyfriend's house and the young woman leaves, promising to telephone him later. When in the car, Rachael says that she does not want to go home but had planned to go to her girlfriend's house to use a sun-bed. The mother says this is not possible, as her father needs the car to go to a meeting and therefore it would be impossible to collect her later. She nevertheless insists on going to her friend's, and is dropped back in the boyfriend's village where she gets a lift from a work colleague to the friend's house in another village nearby. Here we see Rachael using the sun-bed in a mid-shot wearing her bra, and we are told that after this she has the problem of how to get home.

The boyfriend had heard that she was at her girlfriend's and knew there were no buses back to her home. He is shown looking for her on his motorcycle. Apparently the only means of getting home is to hitch a lift. We see her leaving her friend's house and then thumbing a lift in the direction of her home on a busy secondary road. The reconstruction then shows a white van at a spot where she had been seen talking to the driver. She was again seen hitching some minutes later on the outskirts of the village, where the street lighting stopped. The presenter explains that 'Rachael was frightened of the dark, and there were six miles of black country lanes between Rachael and her home. ...' The boyfriend was worried and again searched, but eventually gave up.

The final scene of the reconstruction shows an isolated barn and the voice-over states:

> Next morning: seven miles from [the girlfriend's village] and two-and-a-half miles from Rachael's home lies Bledlow Ridge ... at 11.40 two farm workers saw someone lying in the corner of the barn. They'd discovered the naked body of a young woman. There was blood around her head and neck.

Over a photograph of her the voice continues: 'Rachael was struck heavily on the face, sexually assaulted, and asphyxiated.' The reconstruction ends and, in the studio, the presenter introduces 'the man who is seeking Rachael's killer', a detective inspector who goes into further detail concerning the time and place of the murder, and gives information about a white van the police are interested in locating. A plaster cast of what is believed to be a male's footprint taken from the barn where the young woman died is also shown. The appropriate telephone numbers are once again given for viewers to call.

In the customary 'pay-off' presented at the end of each programme, the presenter stresses that such crimes are unusual and urges the viewers, 'Don't have nightmares, do please sleep well.' The programme ends, and the credits roll to the sound of the theme music.

The *Crimewatch Update* opens to the same titles and theme music as the main programme. Sue Cook states that the response has been very good to this evening's programme. The fraud is dealt with first, where the photo-fits are shown again and an appeal is made to a particular caller to telephone again, as he had some particularly relevant information which the police wished to pursue further. The Mercedes car thefts are then covered, accompanied by a small extract from the reconstruction: we are shown the wealthy-looking woman handing over her car keys to the supposed car mechanic. Again, details of public responses to the crime are given, suggesting that the police may now have a lead on the thieves and their whereabouts.

The Rachael Partridge murder follows with extracts from the reconstruction, this time short clips of the girl and her boyfriend on the sofa in his house, of her lying on the sun-bed in her bra, and finally of her hitchhiking along the main road where she was last sighted. We are told that there has been a large number of telephone calls to the programme regarding this murder. One call came from a woman who had been approached by a man in a white van very similar to the one featured. We are told that this woman had to struggle to get away from the driver, and is very frightened. An appeal is made to her to call back, as she 'rang off before we could obtain full details'. The detective inspector assures this caller that anything she says will be dealt with in the strictest confidence. This is repeated by Nick Ross. Viewers are then reminded of the clothes that Rachael was wearing at the time, and that these have never been found.

The numerous cases covered on 'Incident Desk' and 'Photo Call' are reported, tallying the number of calls received for each and the current state of progress in apprehending the perpetrators. We are even told that the aggravated burglary brought in two responses, one stating that the culprit is 'the son of a neighbour'. Further reports are then given on the follow-up to responses on previous *Crimewatch* programmes, including the unsolved murder of a young woman, and a series of rapes in London.

The *Update* closes with a final appeal to viewers to contact the programme or the police if they have any information on the crimes shown. Sue Cook states: 'Remember, the sort of serious crimes that we show on this programme really are much less common than a lot of us might think they are, and the whole purpose of *Crimewatch* is that with your help we can perhaps make them even more rare.' This is followed by Nick Ross telling viewers 'Do sleep well!', before the closing credits and theme tune.

How the respondents reacted

As noted in Chapter One, *Crimewatch* (along with other such programmes and the popular press) has been the focus of recent concern about the media's role in increasing fear of crime. We were interested in investigating how our viewing groups would evaluate different types of crime covered by the programme. Of crucial concern was the rape and murder of the young woman. But we were also interested to see how our groups assessed crimes against property compared to those against the person, and how they might view the different types of violence presented in the programme (see Appendix III, Guiding Questions for Discussion, *Crimewatch*). The main findings show group members drawing a clear distinction between crimes against property and those against the person, with the latter defined as far more serious. Fear of crime was discussed both in general and in terms of *Crimewatch* itself, with those who had experience of crime being more likely to express apprehension about becoming victims. Discussion of the police focused on how they are represented and appear on *Crimewatch* as well as expressing more general orientations to policing. Finally, the programme itself was discussed in terms of its educational and entertainment value, portrayal of women and ethnic groups. Interestingly, the question of confidentiality when reporting on viewers' telephone calls was raised by the women. Responses to and interpretations of *Crimewatch* were often affected by women's experience of violence and their ethnic background.

A considerable proportion of women in this study told us they were 'occasional' or 'regular' viewers of *Crimewatch* (69% of the entire sample). Women with experience of violence were more likely to be 'regular' viewers (31%) than women with no experience (8%), although almost the same proportion from both categories, about 65%, said they 'always' or 'sometimes' watched the *Crimewatch Update*. Most Asian women (93%) said they 'sometimes' or 'always' watched the *Crimewatch Update*. By contrast, 67% of the Afro-Caribbean and 42% of the white women said they 'never' watched *Crimewatch Update*. A considerable proportion of Asian and Afro-Caribbean women (around 40% of each) had seen the particular episode of *Crimewatch* screened in the study, while only 17% of the white women had seen the programme. Nearly the same percentage of women with experience of violence and those with none (about 65% of each category) had not seen the particular programme.

After the screening, the vast majority of women indicated that they found *Crimewatch* 'believable' and 'realistic' and that they treated the programme seriously (see Figure IV and Figure V).[13] The following quotation illustrates the impact that it can have on some:

> I do take *Crimewatch* seriously, because when I have watched it in the past, it's made me nervous, like when I've had to go upstairs, thinking 'God, I'm not safe', because they have shown a lot of scenes where things have happened within your own home. Where people have come when you could be in bed and that, so I mean, I take it serious. And I don't like the programme.
> [English Afro-Caribbean woman, with experience of violence]

Overwhelmingly, the women endorsed *Crimewatch* as an important programme, yet most found it difficult to describe as 'entertaining' or 'exciting'. About 25% of those with experience of violence rated it as 'entertaining' or 'very entertaining', although almost half of the women who had no experience of violence rated it in this way.

There was also an important difference to the response of women from the three ethnic backgrounds. Over half (55%) of the Asian women in the study thought the programme was at least 'entertaining', whereas only a quarter of the other two groups responded in this way. Whether women had experience of violence made little difference in how 'exciting' they found *Crimewatch*; an overwhelming majority in both categories indicated that it was not exciting. Again, Asian women stood out: while 44% felt the programme was 'exciting' or 'very exciting', only 6% of the white and 7% of the Afro-Caribbean women agreed.

The programme content was not considered to be particularly violent, although women with experience of violence were more likely to judge the programme as such. A small number of the women who had experience of violence (17%) felt the programme was 'very offensive'; only 3% of the women without experience made the same assessment. A number of Asian women, about a quarter, also found the programme 'very offensive' in contrast to white (6%) and Afro-Caribbean (13%) women. A similar proportion of white and Afro-Caribbean women, around one-third, found the programme 'disturbing' or 'very disturbing', while slightly fewer Asian women (23%), made this judgment. Asian (65%) and Afro-Caribbean (50%) women indicated that they felt the programme was 'upsetting' while only a quarter of white women (27%) reported the same. Experience of violence appeared to make little difference to the proportion of women reporting that they felt that *Crimewatch* was 'upsetting'.

For all participants, the most salient programme content was the 'featured' crimes. When asked to record the three crimes they recalled from the programme, all but four women listed the rape and murder of the young woman. They were also very likely to remember the bank fraud (75% of those with experience, 92% of those with none) and the car thefts (73% and 94% respectively). The women who had experience of violence were also likely to mention the child assault case (15%), a crime which was not featured but relatively briefly covered on 'Incident Desk'. Other crimes were not as likely to be remembered. Obviously the most salient crimes were those featured in the reconstructions. About 95% of all the women agreed that the most serious crime for them was the rape and murder of the young woman. They also thought the wider society would make the same assessment. Importantly, however, nearly a quarter of the women with no experience of violence and one-tenth of those with experience thought the bank fraud would be rated of greater importance by the public. Another reason for singling out the rape and murder may have been identification with the victim. Half of the women who had experienced violence, and 30% of those who had not, indicated that they could identify with the young woman who was raped and killed.

> It's sort of, like, you know, you could feel, like, this could happen to me in your own space.
> [Scottish white woman, with experience of violence]

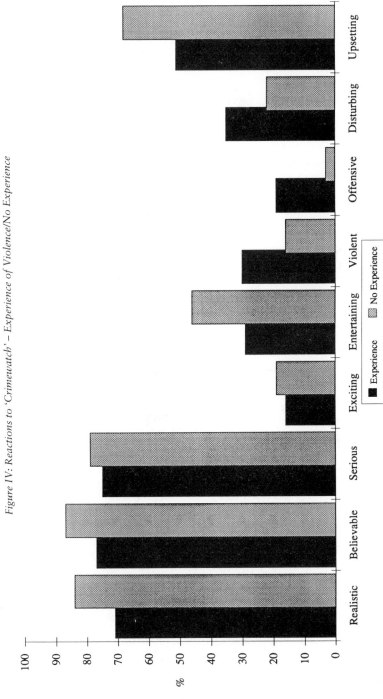

Figure IV: Reactions to 'Crimewatch' – Experience of Violence/No Experience

■ Experience   ▨ No Experience

53

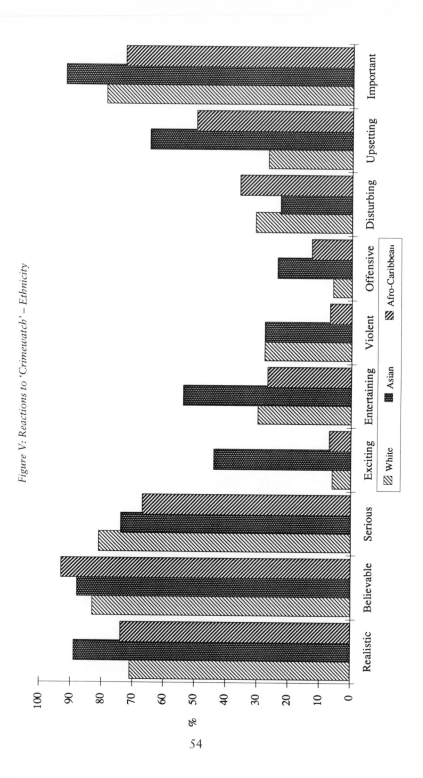

Figure V: Reactions to 'Crimewatch' – Ethnicity

White　Asian　Afro-Caribbean

54

The differences in respondents' ability to relate to the victims in *Crimewatch* are illustrated in Table 1. The Yule's Q of .45 demonstrates a moderate association between experience of violence and ability to relate to the victims portrayed.[14]

Table 1: Relating to victims in 'Crimewatch'

	Violence			
	Experience		No experience	
Relate to victim	N	%	N	%
yes	25	51	11	30
no	24	49	26	70
Total	49	100	37	100

Yule's Q= .45

Over half of all the participants said that the programme 'increased' their fear of crime and, in both groups, one-third said that it made them 'feel afraid', although about a third said it had 'no effect'. Only five women out of the ninety-one participants said *Crimewatch* made them feel safe. Ethnicity made a difference to the effects of *Crimewatch* on women's fear of crime. Significantly, none of the Afro-Caribbean women said the programme decreased their fear of crime or made them feel safe. Asian women were more likely than white or Afro-Caribbean women to say that the programme decreased their fear of crime (31%) and made them feel safer (12%).

> When I did the first thing [filling in a questionnaire including questions on fear of crime], and it said 'which crime programme' [made you afraid of crime], I put *Crimewatch*, because I don't like it because it makes me nervous. Living on your own ... if you go outside you're not safe, and even in your own home, you're not safe. I'm aware if I have to walk home and it's sort of dark, I'm sort of looking everywhere, I'm always nervous. Even to go round, to go and shut the entry door, you know, I sort of look in. ...
> [English Afro-Caribbean woman, with experience of violence]

Experience of violence was not related to women's assessment of the way the programme affected fear of crime. We shall return to this topic later.

Reactions to crime

Crimes against property

Although the official purpose of *Crimewatch* is rather high-minded – to enlist public help in solving crimes – occasionally some of the crimes amused the audience: this was the case quite uniformly with the Mercedes thefts. The bank fraud produced some admiration for the audacity of the criminal mind or merely left respondents cold because an institution was not perceived as a victim:

> See the wee bits they have like the video. ... They walk in, they rob the building society, and they walk back out the door and nobody sees them again! These bits are just fascinating. That's the best bit I like, I really think this is brilliant. They can actually walk in there, rob it, and walk back out. I mean, look at the guy! And then four minutes later he was in another building society. And I think that is brilliant. ... You've just got to sit there and laugh at it! I mean, like when the building society's entered and they all hand over the money to him!
> [Scottish white working-class woman, with no experience of violence]

Although some property offences were sometimes seen as amusing or entertaining, and not taken too seriously, crimes of violence were never taken lightly. Relatively few identified strongly with the victims of property crimes. At times there was a feeling that the Mercedes owners who handed over their car keys had more money than sense, a point that came across especially from working-class women:

> It's the middle and upper class that's going to own a Mercedes. They're the only ones stupid enough to give somebody their car keys. You know what I mean? The working class – you've worked all your life, you've bought a car, you're going to give somebody your keys!
> [English Afro-Caribbean woman, with experience of violence]

However, this point could also be made, in a rather different register, by middle-class women:

> Oh, it's difficult, isn't it? Somebody with too much money and too little sense, I think.
> [Scottish white middle-class woman, with no experience of violence]

> They were the right sort of people to do it though, weren't they? They were all sort of upper-class. Used to handing things out to other people, letting other people do it. They've got to be rich enough to own a Mercedes, haven't they? So they were just used to sort of saying, '[James], take this over here', and they were doing the same there. And when somebody comes along and goes, 'I can make your car go', they think, 'Thank God for that', you know, somebody else can get their hands dirty.
> [English white middle-class woman, with no experience of violence]

Views of the criminals portrayed in *Crimewatch* could not be said to be uniform, and varied with judgments as to the seriousness of the crimes concerned. In the case of the Mercedes thefts there was widespread agreement that the criminals had been quite clever. On one occasion they were likened to Arthur Daley, a well-known television character of a slightly shady kind, and another not untypical view was that they were good actors.

The financial fraud was also treated in a somewhat distanced way by most of the women. Once again the criminals were widely seen as clever and cunning, and, to some, as somewhat frightening. There was no point of identification with the defrauded bank:

> I don't think there are any victims there really. I think it's all such a game to these people, this sort of wheeling and dealing. If people want to spend their whole time buying and selling this concept of money, I don't think there is any victim there. I think there is just a great illusion and not a lot in it.
> [English white woman, with experience of violence]

The bank was widely condemned for simply not taking enough precautions to safeguard its security, and the con-man who walked into the office was depicted by some as vicious and clever, although some believed that they would not have been so gullible:

> *Speaker 1:*   The con-man is a very vicious character.
> *Speaker 2:*   Very clever, though. I couldn't have made people believe that.
> *Speaker 1:*   Right smoothy! ... But then the man who spoke to the cleaner, I'd never have let him in.
> [Scottish white middle-class women, with no experience of violence]

A note of admiration frequently crept into perceptions of this reconstruction; it was seen as an ingenious 'sting':

> I should imagine we're all quite law-abiding citizens, and to have a brain that could think that up, I mean, I don't know who the hell thinks them up. It's as if ... you've just watched a detective story or something and you're all laughing at the end. But, the brain! – it's such a waste really.
> [English white working-class woman, with no experience of violence]

There was widespread agreement that the criminals were clever and the victims stupid, although even here there are quite interesting nuances in the ways in which this story is interpreted, particularly in respect of differences to be found between women with experience of violence and those with none.

For instance, it was often observed that one or other of the couple in the Mercedes theft story could have stayed with their car rather than both go off on the wild-goose chase for spare parts. However, despite the general lack of sympathy for victims in this case, it was nevertheless recognised that one could quite easily fall into such traps. The range of views is aptly illustrated by the following exchange in which condemnation is mixed with an understanding of how one can easily fall victim to an audacious con:

Researcher: What do you think of the car theft victims?
Speaker 1: Stupid!
Speaker 2: Idiots. They got what they asked for.
Speaker 3: Well, everybody could be caught out, whoever they are. Everybody. If you're in a state, you could be caught out.
Speaker 1: It's like watching a comedy: 'Here, have my keys.'
Speaker 2: 'Have the keys, that's fine, you know, bring it back when you've finished.'
Speaker 1: 'You can have the log book and all if you want it.'
Speaker 3: But everybody could do it.
Speaker 1: Yeah, easily.
Speaker 3: I mean, in a certain situation.
Speaker 2: I suppose at the time it wasn't really actually like that. It was just the way it came across.
Speaker 1: Yeah, just the way it came across. It was hilarious.
Speaker 4: Those two men got it down to an art.
Speaker 5: It's easy to criticise. Relating back to my situation [when beaten by my husband] I'd think I was a right mug. Now I do, but I didn't at the time.
Speaker 2: No, you get taken in. Yeah.
Speaker 5: Looking back on it you can think, 'Oh, God!' But it wasn't until he'd done it to somebody else, until it happened to somebody else, I could accept that, perhaps I'm not such a mug, and perhaps I'll do something about it.
Speaker 6: Well, I can't really accept that somebody would actually hand over their car keys.
Speaker 2: No, it seems ridiculous.
Speaker 6: You know, I mean, I just ...
Speaker 2: Especially that second couple, there were two of them, and they both went off. One of them could've stayed in the car. To me, I would've thought, 'I'm not going to go off and leave my car keys with that ...'
[English white women, with experience of violence]

So far as robbery or fraud were concerned, quite often personal experiences of being robbed or conned in a minor way were invoked. When speaking about their experience of thefts or robberies, this was couched in terms that could afford some women a measure of identification with individual victims:

> It was my car alarm, you know, it goes on and on. I couldn't stop it because the battery had gone. So somebody who was passing by said, 'Can I help?' I said, 'Yes please.' [Laughter] ... One went inside the car to open the boot. The car was fairly new, I didn't know how to open the boot. But that was another thing, and he just took out my purse from the dashboard and he took money. The purse was there and seventy-four pounds and an Access card. And everything went missing.
> [Scottish Asian woman, with experience of violence]

Women with experience of violence were apt to judge the bank fraud as not very serious, as no violence against persons was involved. However, and this again testified to their heightened sense of danger, some underlined the *physical threat* to the victims of the Mercedes con trick, a point completely absent from the perspectives of women with no experience of violence.

> I think the woman would've been in more danger staying with the car than going with the taxi. I think she'd have been in more danger. He was really desperate for the car, and the woman was there. I think there's such a thing as getting into the car and the lassie, you know, the woman hanging on, but then you never know what could happen.
> [Scottish white woman with experience of violence]

Crimes of property vs. crimes against the person
A value universally held across all groups was that crime against property was much less serious than crime against the person and that sentencing policy ought to reflect this view. The point was expressed with epigrammatic succinctness thus:

> Money can be replaced. Cars can be replaced. Toys can be replaced. Lives cannae.
> [Scottish white woman, with experience of violence]

However, it was pointed out most vociferously that this perspective was by no means reflected in the programme time accorded to different items. Repeatedly it was affirmed that murder and sexual assault were much more serious than fraud and robbery. Car thefts were not very serious because insurance could be claimed, and for a bank to lose money was quite different from the harm occasioned to an individual:

> And I [wrote] it down 'most time given to offences against property'. ... I think the whole atmosphere of the programme was that serious crime is the thefts against property. And that's given much more

time, much more attention, this is much more serious. And as about the bloke who is presenting it, he sounded much more sympathetic when he was talking about the stolen Mercedes, than at the end when he was talking about giving the phone number and things, you know, 'If you've got information, have you seen this car or this van, if you think you saw this young woman.' I thought his voice was a lot less sympathetic at that point. And also that they focused a lot more on the victim in the murder case than they did when it was fraud and stolen property.
[English white woman, with experience of violence]

This comment also revealed considerable insight into the different discourses used to describe crimes against women. They do tend to focus on the victim to a greater extent than in discussions of other types of crime, as will be further demonstrated.

However, the comments about the rape and murder of the young woman tended to be of a quite different order from those about property. We shall concentrate on the sexual crime here because it is of the greatest centrality to the group discussions and the aims of this research. However, there was a significant difference in *when* this crime came onto the agenda of group discussion. In the case of groups of women with experience of violence, almost invariably it was seized upon immediately discussion began, underlining their sensitivity to violence against women. Among the groups of women with no experience of violence, the running-order of the programme, or the structure of the questioning during group discussion, tended to determine when this crime was discussed. By contrast, in groups of women with experience of violence, members could draw upon their experiences of physical assault, whether sexual or domestic, and this provided a strong point of identification with the victim. That is not to say that the murder victim always evoked widespread sympathy or understanding. But we shall return to this point later.

Interestingly, however, in group discussions, for most the second-worst crime and for some the first among equals was the very brief 'Incident Desk' item concerning the assault with a knife on two young girls. This was a key example that brings out exceptionally clearly the potential for divergence between audience members' own values and perceived programme values. Many group members stressed that crimes – not least sexual crimes – against children were especially disgusting. The view that this item had been underplayed was particularly apparent among the groups of women with experience of violence, once again indicating a special sensitivity to the vulnerable and their predicaments.

The following comment illustrates how the argument was put over and persisted with, in the face of speculation that the programme-makers and police might not have been able to release more information:

I also feel that because they just seemed to skim over it, it seemed as though they were saying it wasn't important. But it was dodgy – the children's information. I think you find that with a lot of things, they won't believe the children, even in sexual abuses and that. It is very difficult, you know, they don't want to believe the children, they'd rather believe an adult.
[Scottish white woman, with experience of violence]

For some, the argument took the form of a more general attack on broader social values which, it was felt, were reflected in the priorities of *Crimewatch*. This view could be heard elsewhere, but it was voiced with particular frequency by women with experience of violence:

Because I just felt that the beginning of the programme was put on to the materialistic things. And then you got this little girl, who was indecently assaulted, and she has got to live with that for the rest of her life. Her family have got to live with that. Fraud they can, well, there's nothing they can do. They're just hoping to catch somebody. Hopefully they will. And the Mercedes car, it's very distressing, it's very upsetting to have anything stolen from you, but it can be replaced. But that little girl can't be.
[English white working-class woman, with no experience of violence]

Hitchhiking
The fact that Rachael Partridge was murdered when hitchhiking served to focus many anxieties about personal safety. Among all the women there were worries about their own general safety and that of their children, especially daughters:

Well, it's an act of violence against a person where – it's awful. I've got a daughter of seventeen, so I can relate to that. I mean she's not allowed out unless she's got a bodyguard with her. But if she goes out, she has to have money with her for a taxi home. She can only go to one taxi rank in town because we know them, and come back with them. And she has to be put in a taxi by the people she's with. If she's by herself then we have to know, because there's no way I'd let a seventeen-year-old wander round the town – I could've done it at my age years ago, because it seemed 'less violent'. I say that in inverted commas because it seemed to be. But the thought of my daughter hitching a lift and anybody hurting her is just awful, just awful! Well, she rings me up and I come out and fetch her. She's walked once with a friend – she got blasted from here to eternity by me.
[English white middle-class woman, with no experience of violence]

A restatement of this view came from some other women, in this case commenting from a different angle on the perilous values prevalent in male culture:

> *Speaker 1:* I'll say one thing, men think that if you go out hitching on your own ...
> *Speaker 2:* You're asking for it!
> *Speaker 1:* Yeah, you're asking for it. Because my husband said it to me, and a lot of his friends said it to me. He says if a woman goes out hitching on her own, or a woman walks down the street with a mini-skirt on, tarted up to the eyeballs, they're asking for it. I think that's wrong.
> [English white women, with experience of violence]

This formed an ideological critique of masculine privilege and aggressiveness, and was widely shared among women with experience of violence of whatever background:

> Why should women be restricted? The very question you ask in the questionnaire: 'Do you think men have a privilege?' Yes, they're privileged. They're privileged to walk about wherever they like, at whatever time of the night, at any time, it doesn't matter. Nobody says you shouldn't be doing it, he shouldn't be doing it, if anything happens to him.
> [Scottish Asian woman, with experience of violence]

> People will say 'Oh, she watches too much telly', but I don't even watch the telly, it's just 'my imagination'. I know what these people are like, men are out there. Yeah, but I mean, they do do these things.
> [English Afro-Caribbean woman, with experience of violence]

This criticism strikes at the heart of the social arrangements that make public places dangerous for women – a point that is of special relevance in our later analysis of *The Accused*. For instance, among the groups of women with experience of violence, one could hear the call for safe and convenient public transport to be made available, thus obviating the need for risk-taking by women. For others, it was the unfairness involved in these dangers that made them so unacceptable:

> I mean, what they actually said about the hitchhiking was wrong. ... The first thing they said is 'This is what happens when you hitchhike' basically. Why should we be the ones to stop hitchhiking? They should be catching the people that are murdering these people that are hitchhiking. I've done some hitchhiking in my life and you meet some nice people. It's not us that are at fault because we hitchhike. It's them; it's their minds. They made you think, they made you think that you shouldn't hitchhike because this is what will happen

to you.
[English white woman, with experience of violence]

Underlying all these comments was a vivid sense of the risks involved in hitchhiking. In fact, the activity of hitchhiking, and the meanings that it embodies, crystallise and even symbolise many currents of anxiety about personal safety. Equally strong is resistance to the idea that women should be prevented by men from moving around freely. For older women, there was a strong sense that conditions of safety had deteriorated since their own youth, as is encapsulated in the following observations:

> I think most, more than twenty years on from the days when I hitchhiked, we are much more aware of crimes. We're much more aware of these things. All kinds of ills of society are much more out in the open than what they were in the idealistic late 60s, where you did what you liked and you just never – it was there at the back of your mind, but you thought it was so remote that the risk was worthwhile taking. Whereas now, I have a daughter who is nine, and in another nine years there is no way she – if I have any say in it then – that she would be allowed to hitchhike.
> [Scottish white middle-class woman, with no experience of violence]

This comment about social change reflected the views of many of the older women in our sample. The parental fear for the safety of children was reiterated time and again, and focused most strongly upon girls and young women, although occasional mention was made of the vulnerability of boys and young men as well:

> I've got a daughter who is coming up to seventeen, and you know, saying to her, 'Now, if you're stuck somewhere, phone us.' If we're out, she can stay at a friend's, leave a message, but she's been told never to go in a taxi on her own. There always must be two of them together, either to our house, to a friend's house. Obviously, her parents were very caring, they'd been to pick her up and so I could relate [to that].
> [English white working-class woman, with no experience of violence]

Much of the concern about the vulnerability of women and children derived from general anxieties about public safety, sometimes fed by direct references to cases made well-known by media coverage; on other occasions women would talk about the experiences of friends. What these observations tell us is not only how anxious women may be about the safety of their children but also the extent to which a culture of peril is sustained and transmitted by impressing women in general and particularly young women (and sometimes young men) of the need to pursue a continuous strategy of avoiding danger. Although safe forms of transport were advocated, concern was expressed by some that women might be attacked by taxi drivers, by neighbours in a position of trust, or when standing alone awaiting the arrival of public transport.

Discourse about victims and causes
There is a tendency when discussing violent crimes against women to focus on the victim rather than on the perpetrator when seeking explanations and causes. This has the effect, often unintended and unnoticed, of implicitly making women the 'cause' of their own victimisation. It becomes a type of discourse which actually 'blames the victim' for male violence. The perpetrator often remains a shadowy figure left undiscussed as the focus upon the female victim becomes sharper. Explanations of male violence often serve to excuse the violence by citing others' actions, often women in their roles as mothers or wives, as will be seen in the later discussion of *EastEnders*. This form of discourse about crimes of violence against women, while expressed throughout our culture and learned to varying degrees by everyone, is, nonetheless, problematic for women in general (who may experience some discomfort at such explanations) and women who have been the victims of violence in particular (who must deal with the real contradictions of this accepted view of their 'blameworthiness' while at the same time rejecting it and the injustices associated with it).

These tensions were evident in the discussions about the rape and murder victim and the role of her mother in the event. Since no clear suspect was identified by the police, little mention was made of the possible perpetrator in the course of the programme. This was limited to talking of a suspect in a white van. There was also no discussion or even speculation about the murderer or rapist in the groups' discussions. Instead, the entire focus was on the rape victim and her mother. A range of judgments was offered concerning the young woman's behaviour, particularly concerning the perils of hitchhiking, and her personal appearance. There was also considerable speculation about what should and could have been done by the young woman and by her mother to avert the dangers of attack and what our respondents might have done in similar circumstances. Given the deep-rootedness of this framework of interpretation in our society, these themes are to be expected and are repeated in discussions about the other programmes as well.

Attention was drawn by many of the women to Rachael's *non-provocative* way of dressing. In so many words, it was said that she was not 'asking for it':

> I think it probably highlights that even though you're not wearing provocative clothes or anything, the dangers are still open to you. Because like the usual stereotype that she was being very provocative

– 'that's why she got raped'. But the person who did the show there, she wasn't even – she had got jeans on and everything.
[English Asian woman, with no experience of violence]

This line of interpretation was widespread, with the victim being described as 'respectable', 'normal' and as not 'suggestive'. It could therefore be said that the idea that women are 'asking for it' if they dress in a certain way, and then go out hitchhiking, was widely diffused among the respondents. In a particular cultural slant on the question, members of the Scottish Asian group of women with no experience of violence linked modesty in dress in a highly distinctive way to other norms in their communities, highlighting the positive value for them of familial restrictions on women's freedom of movement. These were seen as making a positive contribution to their safety from attack:

Speaker 1: I think the Asian women are more careful than the white ones. Especially in late night, we don't go out alone.

Speaker 2: We are not allowed, that's why.

Speaker 3: Yes, we are brought up like that and that's why we can't go alone. ... [If] we should go [there are] two women, and sometimes a man and woman go, sometimes sons and mothers go. We can't go alone after eight o'clock; we are brought [up] like that. You [white women] are not brought up like that. You always go [out] alone.
[Scottish Asian women, with no experience of violence]

There were contradictions and tensions in the discussions about the arrangements for travel, the dangers of hitchhiking and the problems of mobility for young people in rural areas without proper public transportation. Women from different groups expressed various sentiments:

She was a bit daft in hitchhiking. She should've had a bit more sense, not to do it. But at the same time she had no choice.
[Scottish Asian woman, with experience of violence]

Yes, because knowing there was no arrangements made for the girl, she had a six-mile journey, no lights on the road, I mean that was really ridiculous to expect a seventeen-year-old to walk, you know, and take the chance of being picked up.
[Scottish white woman, with experience of violence]

But I don't think it's fair that she should be restricted.
[Scottish Asian woman, with experience of violence]

You've got this all the time, whenever she's away from me. ... Well, I'm not the best mother in the world, well, I try, but we can only do so much. We can never fully guarantee one hundred per cent that she will be safe for the rest of her life. We can't, but we will do what we can.
[English white middle-class woman, with no experience of violence]

So far as Rachael herself was concerned, there were also differences of opinion about her actions. For some women she was foolish for putting herself in danger. However, for the most part, her actions were put down to naïvety and her resistance to her mother's suggestions as simply the kind of thing that teenagers do. Many group members pointed out that she should have made alternative arrangements, such as telephoning her boyfriend for a lift or hiring a taxi, or staying overnight at her friend's house.

There is almost a sense of a desperate attempt to will the event away, to suggest any possible means by which the extraordinary outcome of this ordinary action of hitchhiking could have been avoided:

I think it was all wrong. I think if she was really desperate for a lift, she could've gone to the police station and said that she couldn't get a lift home, and that some way they could arrange for her to get home.
[Scottish white woman, with experience of violence]

The tension in the following comment – which comes right to the edge of blaming the victim – is obvious:

I think it's like, she asked her mum – she's seventeen – she asked her mum if her mum could take her to her friend's house, yeah, she asked her mum if her mum could take her to her friend's house and her mum said 'No' and she persisted and persisted. For ten minutes on the sunbed! Yeah, she persisted for ten minutes on a sunbed, and then she had to hitchhike home. You know what I mean? She got what she – not that she got what she deserved, but like there was a lesson to be learnt and she just ended up like. ...
[English Afro-Caribbean woman, with experience of violence]

When asked to discuss the scene in which the young woman is shown in her underwear lying under a sunbed at her girlfriend's house, a scene which was also repeated in the *Crimewatch Update*, some had little adverse reaction to this segment whereas others saw it as a gratuitous display of near-nakedness:

... she was trying to get herself a tan, which I suppose a lot of us do if we're going away – save getting burned – and it's just that extra personal thing to show that that was what she wanted to do and she

was determined to do that before going away.
[English white middle-class woman, with no experience of violence]

But this contrasts with the following:

You could ... just show the head upwards, or just the girl talking to her while on the sunbed. ... You don't need to see the fact that she was in her underwear, on a sunbed. I think that was a bit of titillation, which you don't need. ... I can't see the logic [of showing it again on the *Update*]. I mean surely the scene of her standing hitch-hiking again would focus people on the fact that that's where people would have seen [her] – they wouldn't have all seen her on the sunbed; there's only one person that saw her on the sunbed.
[English white middle-class woman, with no experience of violence]

A much more frequently aired opinion on the part of women who had experience of violence was that the programme ought to be far more explicit about violence and the impact of rape, since this could serve an educative purpose from which they and others might benefit:

Speaker 1:   That's what you could think about after, it's like watching a film with no ending, you put your end. That girl was either unconscious or she was conscious, you don't know, they haven't said. That girl could've gone through hell, so your mind then – if it's gonna upset you – is gonna think what that girl went through. ... Well the TV have to say what can be put on and what can't. I mean, they're the ones that say, 'You can't put that on, you can only use the words there, can't you really?' I mean, we're saying we'd like to see sort of what happened to that girl, but really they can't put it on.

Speaker 2:   Yeah, but they could've illustrated it a bit more.

Speaker 3:   I thought it could've been stronger.

Speaker 2:   Yeah, it could've been a lot stronger.

Speaker 1:   I agree, but they won't put it on.

Speaker 2 :   No.
               [English white women, with experience of violence]

In another group the following was said:

Speaker 1:   One minute it was green fields and the next minute there was a body in the barn and that was it. ...

Speaker 2:   Yeah, but some people it offends them to see it, you know what I mean? So they can't win can they? ...

Speaker 3:   That's the point that they're putting, they portrayed the violence in the hold-up thing, the guys with the

guns. And they portrayed a lot of the action by the perpetrators in the other crimes, but in the one in the rape and murdered girl, there was no attempt at reconstruction of anybody actually doing anything to her. There was just – she was on this road hitching a lift and the next thing, there was this body found. There was no, I mean, there was no, well I mean, because it would be so offensive, wouldn't it, to actually show that? And the same with the knife attack, there was nothing at all about that.
[English white women, with experience of violence]

Despite doubts about the feasibility, these views were expressed with considerable consistency by women with experience of violence. It is interesting that those closest to the experience of violent physical attack by men should call for even greater openness as a means of public education. Some women, and particularly those who had experienced violence, went on to suggest that such depictions should not be sensationalist in nature, should not trivialise the violence, should not blame women for men's violence, and should not minimise men's responsibility for their behaviour. What was wanted was an accurate and realistic depiction of their lives, the horror of violence and its negative consequences. Thus, the purposes of showing violence should be to educate the general public in order that they may become more enlightened and, therefore, more sympathetic and helpful, and to impress upon violent men the true nature of their actions with a view towards deterrence.

Crimewatch and fear of crime
Overall, women with experience of violence were more likely to stress the ways in which *Crimewatch* was a disturbing programme. What came across with great force in group discussions was the *generalised* sense of danger that they felt as a result of their experiences of violence. Echoing the results of the Background Questionnaires concerning these groups, the question of fear of crime as a settled and pre-existing part of their thinking was much more apparent than among women with no experience of violence. Hence, to the extent that *Crimewatch* aroused fears in the case of women with experience of violence, it was addressing viewers already highly sensitive to the dangers of everyday life and also aroused considerable sensitivity to this among women without experience of violence.

However, although the programme was seen as 'raising awareness' in a general way rather than as offering participation, so far as our sample of women was concerned it hardly needed to do so. It was apparent that fear of being attacked was deeply entrenched in women who had experienced violence against them as well as among those who had not. There was a widely diffused and lively sense of the social danger posed to women by predatory males, of which many could talk feelingly in terms of either the experience of being subjected to direct physical attack or measures that they had taken to avoid such an eventuality.

This brings us to the general issue of fear of crime, and *Crimewatch* itself. As noted earlier, programmes such as *Crimewatch* have aroused official concern about whether or not they cause fear of crime and some women in this study spontaneously mentioned the programme as increasing their fear of crime. The programme's producers have from the very start taken on board the likelihood of stoking up public fear. The presenter's 'pay-off', stressing the statistical infrequency of the crimes featured and asking viewers not to have nightmares, is intended to reassure. From this research it is clear that at times this effort to take the sting out of the programme's impact is neither entirely convincing nor even acceptable:

> Especially the programme which we just watched, which really more or less they say, 'Don't go to bed and have nightmares. You've got nothing to worry about if you don't let your children sit outside shops, if you don't go hitchhiking and if you remember to lock your car and about three hundred other little additions for it. Then nothing will happen to you. Unless, of course, you happen to work in the Midland Bank, but don't have nightmares about that.' I mean, that's the kind of the ethos around it. Because they're putting a lot of the blame for the crimes on the people who are actually the victims of them.

> The ending of the programme really annoyed me, you know, 'Don't have nightmares or anything.' Ha, ha ha, let's joke about this. Somebody's just been violently murdered, but you can still go to bed and sleep. I thought it was disgusting.
> [English white women, with experience of violence]

> I didn't like the bit where she says the cases are rarer than – what? Because it's not really [true]. Because you lift the papers, you get it in the papers day in and day out. You get it on the telly day in and day out. I don't know how they can say it ... if that was true why do they have that programme? Because it's not a rare occasion. I mean, none of those things are rare occasions, they're happening every day. So how are they rare?
> [Scottish white woman, with experience of violence]

Television articulates with fear of crime in highly complex ways, it would seem. Programmes may become integrated into a pre-existing complex of anxieties about safety:

> I think [*Crimewatch*] still frightens you, really. But I do watch it. I

mean, my husband's on nights when I watched it this week ... and my alarm is on. That's the only thing that reassures me, I've got real brilliant alarms in the house. That's the only way I feel safe in my house.
[English white working-class woman, with no experience of violence]

Once again, although fear is attributed to *Crimewatch*, this has to be seen in the context of a woman at home alone in a house which is heavily secured against intrusion. Yet another way of dealing with the question was to consider what impact it might have upon others:

It doesn't frighten me but I think that I can relax if I'm on my own and I'm the responsible person. ... But it does heighten your perception of everything, I think – if you are on your own. Which is why I think with old people, they're going to be more aware as well, people living on their own. I think that those sort of people, say little old ladies who go around with a walking frame, those sort of people, it probably would frighten them more than an able-bodied [person] for instance.
[English white working-class woman, with no experience of violence]

Finally, it is worth noting that for some, at least, the *Crimewatch Update*, apart from offering a reminder of crimes committed, can function to reassure as well as to meet the desire for the solution of unsolved crimes. Some group members talked of their minds being 'put at rest' by the flow of information from the public to the police or of being made to 'feel better'. The *Update* was also described as showing results and therefore offering evidence of effectiveness. If there is little response to the call for help from the police some can feel disappointment. We might conjecture that this desire to have a good ending for the story is rooted in long exposure to having a positive resolution to narratives. It is certainly a wish that surfaces in our studies of *Closing Ranks* and *The Accused*.

The police
There were mixed responses to the programme's 'call to action'. About half of the ninety-one women said they would be willing to report someone to the police, but about a quarter were unsure, saying that they did not know what they would do in such a situation. Fourteen per cent of the women with experience of violence and 3% of those with none said it would depend on the nature of the crime. When asked whether they 'would like to be able to help solve the crimes' presented on *Crimewatch*, only about half said 'Yes'. Afro-Caribbean women were even less likely to want to act to assist *Crimewatch*. Although most Afro-Caribbean women sympathised with the victims portrayed

on the programme, 79% saying they felt sorry for them, the highest figure for any group, they were unlikely to say that they would report someone who had committed one of the crimes presented on *Crimewatch*. Only a quarter of the Afro-Caribbean women said that they would take such action. Around three-quarters of Asian and white women said they would report known perpetrators while 15% said they would not. The majority (54%) were just not sure, saying they did not know what they would do in such a situation. Over three-quarters (79%) of the Afro-Caribbean women also indicated that watching *Crimewatch* did not make them feel willing to help solve the crimes reported, whereas 44% of white and 73% of the Asian women said it made them feel willing to help.

Crimewatch failed to increase our respondents' confidence in the police. Only a quarter of all the women, despite their experience of violence, indicated that watching the programme gave them more confidence in the police. Ethnicity, however, did make a difference. About the same percentage of Afro-Caribbean and white women (85%) indicated that the programme *did not* increase their confidence; nearly half of the Asian women (42%) said it *did*.

It could not be assumed that all viewing groups shared an identical view of the police cause. There was a noteworthy scepticism, among some women with experience of violence, of the availability of the police when they were most needed, but this was not universal:

Speaker 1:   I mean, I have actually seen them standing in shop doors, calls coming through and they totally ignore them. I've actually seen it. ... And just last night there was a guy got his head kicked in and the police are sitting watching it. Now the police are only fifty yards away; they're sitting in the van watching it.

Speaker 2:   In [our town], if you're looking for the police, if you can't get them at the police station, you'll always get them down in the [pub-cum-restaurant]. And that's where they all meet every Friday night. Now that's at the weekend; it's normally when the crimes were all committed. You can never get a policeman in [our town]. You phone the [pub-cum-restaurant] and ask to get somebody from there, 'Oh yes, no problem.' And yet there's supposed to be one sergeant or whatever on duty at all times.

Researcher: What does this programme make you feel about the police, then?

Speaker 1:   To me it makes the police look really efficient.

Speaker 2 :   And they're not.

                 [Scottish white women, with experience of violence]

Disenchantment with the police based on a variety of personal experiences was also to be found among some of the Asian respondents, although the ethnic dimension remained unarticulated here:

> And I thought the experience about the police, because I have dealings with them through my work [as a social worker], referring women who come to us because of marital violence and everything and referring them on. In my experience, the women have had such bad service because of the type of attitudes that they get from the police. When they get there, they're sent back home. They're not taken seriously: 'Oh, what did you do to provoke?', that sort of questions. They're always asking them what happened. 'What provoked your husband to beat you?' You know, the type of questioning which shows that they don't really see it from the woman's point of view. They always try to see it that she did wrong, that justified her getting beaten about. So we always tend to be very reluctant about the police, although ... I've got mixed feelings because when you do need help, you do have to call them. They are the police force, so you have very little choice but to turn to them. But when the response you get doesn't meet your needs then it's a sad state of affairs, and I think it meets the needs less and less as time's going on in terms of the way they actually treat [abused women]. Because you can't argue with them in terms of the law, they will operate within the law and do what's necessary, but it's their attitudes that are supposed to be part and parcel of getting that law into action. They stop the law helping people because they could encourage women to have an injunction, because they could do a lot of things. They say 'Oh yes, you can have an injunction but that won't keep him away.' The poor woman's thinking, 'If it's not going to keep him away, what can we do?' ... So on the one hand they say, 'These are your rights', but on the other hand – well, you know.

> And I've had so far a very good opinion about the police force. But for the last two years, something personal – a family matter – my husband and I've seen the police from a very different angle, and all the things that I thought the police force would never do, I know they do now. And all these things about being absolutely fair and honest all the time – I have been completely disillusioned. I hope I get my faith back, but I didn't want to believe that at all. The things that I know if somebody else had told me, I would've said, 'Oh, they're biased, they're prejudiced, something must have happened, it couldn't have happened'. I mean, things like police saying, 'OK you admit to something small and we'll drop everything else.' I mean, why would a police force in a civilised society say this to an individual? [English Asian women, with no experience of violence]

These comments, based upon direct experience of dealing with the police, offer considerable insights into how the representation of law and order is open to sharply varying interpretations. It should be said that among some women with experience of violence as well as some with no such experience, there was a good deal of scepticism about police effectiveness and honesty. It was noteworthy that both Asian and, as reflected in the quantitative results, Afro-Caribbean group members were the most disenchanted, which doubtless says something of their wider experience as members of ethnic minorities and their often tense relations with the police:

> In reality, when you do try to help the police, like if you phone the police and you think there's a crime being committed, or you're a victim of a crime or whatever, the police never turn up until the crime's been committed.
> [Scottish Asian woman, with experience of violence]

> But they don't catch them, do they? Half of them they don't catch them. You know what I mean? The police, half the time they sit down drinking tea. They put their sirens on when they want to go home early, you know, just to get back to the station to dump the car.
> [English Afro-Caribbean woman, with experience of violence]

The programme
The programme itself was discussed in several respects, most notably its education and entertainment value, its public service role, police-public relations and its depiction of women and ethnic groups. *Crimewatch* is presented on television as having an educational and motivational intent. Its format, style of presentation and call to action are all intended to increase the empathy of viewers for the victims of crime and to lead to greater co-operation between the police and the public. The members of our viewing groups, however, responded in a more mixed and ambivalent manner. Although very few women (eleven) felt that the programme sensationalised crime, only around 60% in both categories thought it actually increased their knowledge of crime. The programme did generate empathy; three-quarters of women in the sample said that they felt sorry for the victims and about the same proportions (76% of women with experience and 65% with none) said the programme made them angry about crime.

There was a pronounced ambivalence among the viewing groups about whether *Crimewatch* should or should not be categorised as 'entertainment'. The dilemma was typically expressed in the following way:

> To be entertained is something that is pleasurable, really. I find it interesting and informative really, but I wouldn't say it was actually entertainment.
> [English white working-class woman, with no experience of violence]

73

The notion that it is a 'public service' programme that needs to be taken seriously was prevalent in all groups. However, at another level, *Crimewatch* was frequently talked of in terms of its attention-grabbing qualities or entertainment value. Analogies were also drawn at certain points with television drama and the narrative tensions that this creates. The desire to know how the crimes are solved is what makes the *Update* interesting to an audience and plays upon the narrative drive inherent in the programme, a point already alluded to:

> *Researcher:* And do you, shall I say, enjoy that side of it? The solving of the crimes?
>
> *Speaker 1:* Yes, I like thrillers and Agatha Christie, but I like any sort of thriller.
>
> *Speaker 2:* It's seeing it come right through, isn't it? ... To know that there are people ringing in, and that there's a good chance that they might catch the creep who did it.
> [English white middle-class women, with no experience of violence]

However, for some women who had experienced violence, the 'public service' claims of the programme were simply dismissed and, contrary to other groups, it was stressed that *Crimewatch* engaged in trivialising for the purposes of amusement, lacked sensitivity and glamorised crime. Nevertheless, for the most part, *Crimewatch* was seen as a specialised television programme aiming to help the police. The image of the presenters was relatively neutral, evincing only very occasional comment. The programme was not, for the most part, seen as a piece of police public relations, although as already noted, questions were raised about police effectiveness (not usually judged to be great – sometimes on the basis of how they had intervened in domestic disputes) and some concern was expressed about the guarantee of confidentiality for those who choose to inform through the programme's hotline.

Some rather damningly held that the police ought to do their own work themselves and that the programme was really there to make them look good:

> Yes, and another thing that annoyed me, the police were sitting there answering the phone. We're the ones that are supposed to be doing all the work; we're the ones that are supposed to be saying, 'Right, we're giving the information; there's a name, there's an address.' They don't have to do anything, just get the guy. They're like saying, 'Oh, we'll sit here, we'll take your calls and you've got good information, we'll go and get them.'
> [Scottish Asian woman, with experience of violence]

Running throughout much of the discussion was a sense that, in many of the cases screened by *Crimewatch*, women are presented as weak and stupid whereas men, including the criminals, are clever:

> I noticed the way the people who were presenting the programme were dressed and the way they were presenting themselves. The men were all in suits and looking very formal, and the woman presenter was in a pretty dress and she'd got this frothy blonde hair. She had all this make-up on, and the women in the background were doing similar things. They were doing sort of side issues and all the little bits, and when you see a woman in the background she'd be answering the phone and the men were looking very serious. And I thought [in] the reconstruction of the fraud they were focusing on the women a lot. And the women: this woman – she was a cleaner; and then the secretary; and the women were shown to be very vulnerable. And the women were all talking in very soft voices. They were all presented as very soft and sweet and powerless and easily conned. And they're presenting these men as being quite clever. ... And another thing I noticed was that the woman police officer had no jacket on, she just had this white shirt on. The men were in jackets.

> I thought the whole programme made the general public, but particularly women, look like absolute idiots. The cleaner, I mean, I'm sure more conversation went on than that before the cleaner let that man in totally unconcerned. The car theft, the woman handed over her keys without any question and I'm sure there would have been a much deeper conversation than that going on before you hand anything over. And the hitchhiker, she was made to look the fool for leading herself into a situation where she gets murdered.
> [English white women, with experience of violence]

For English Afro-Caribbean women with experience of violence, ethnicity played a major role in influencing the interpretation of *Crimewatch*. It was stressed that the programme was biased against blacks, a view coupled with an intensely hostile perception of the police and their relationships with black people:

> Well, the thing is, say the difference between watching [*Crimewatch*] and something like *Police Five* is this makes me more conscious of the police being involved all the time. Like you get little inserts of the police officer and stuff like that. And because they're really famous for arresting more black people in proportion to how many are in the population, I just don't really believe them at all, ever. So when you get a programme like that, and you're also seeing black people being associated with the crime, it doesn't make me feel very comfortable. Because I'm aware that black people commit crimes, like white people, but if you were a white person and you were watching that, you would zoom in more on the things that have been done by

black people. And so it doesn't do anything for me.
[English Afro-Caribbean woman, with experience of violence]

Very occasionally, this perspective was endorsed elsewhere:

I thought they were very racist as well. When they were talking about the suspects, one of them referred to a black man and they hadn't already referred to anybody else by colour apart from when it was a black man, and then they referred to 'the white man' when it was in comparison to the black man.
[English white woman, with experience of violence]

A point made by some women who had experienced violent attacks was that, apart from raising awareness by portraying criminal activity, *Crimewatch* also carried a risk of causing emulation (although this was not a widely held view):

I think for one that I, I watch it and I hope that it's highlighted that particular risk area. I watched it and this woman has been murdered and hopefully her life hasn't been lost, somebody has learned something from it. But on the other hand, there's the negative aspect, in that there will be somebody else thinking, 'Yeah, perhaps this is something that I can do and it shows me examples of how I can go about abducting a woman.'
[English Afro-Caribbean woman, with experience of violence]

A number of women expressed concern about whether or not *Crimewatch* really ensured the confidentiality of its informants, a concern most marked among those who had experience of violence:

The bit where he said about the son of a neighbour. ... Well, the next-door neighbour's going to know that it was her next-door neighbour that told, isn't she? I mean, they say it's supposed to be – your information's confidential. Well, he just let out there who it was. If that man gets caught, then his mum's going to know that it was her next-door neighbour that – although he shouldn't have done it. It's supposed to be confidential.
[Scottish white woman, with experience of violence]

This thing about confidentiality, I thought that was a laugh ... like that son of a neighbour, is that confidentiality? They shouldn't have said that ... that's a neighbour that said that, you know – 'Go bash your neighbour.'
[Scottish Asian woman with experience of violence]

And when the callers are calling up, they're saying, 'We'll take your calls in confidence.' One call was from somebody's neighbour. ...

Well I mean, they might not have wanted that to come out, mightn't they? When it does come out and if it is that person, they're gonna get into trouble.
[English white working-class woman, with no experience of violence]

The programme's importance in alerting the public to the dangers of hitchhiking was a point frequently made. We have noted earlier that this connected with broader fears about personal safety among women. Such coverage could be interpreted as helpful:

I think there are lessons to be learnt from it, I mean, as for hitchhiking really, nobody should hitchhike, but people do. Watching these programmes perhaps it might bring it home to them. I know I definitely wouldn't hitchhike.
[English white working-class woman, with no experience of violence]

An important general issue about how *Crimewatch* is to be interpreted arises from this. The taking of such a broad moral lesson from the tale of a particular incident of crime is really the only possible reaction for the vast majority of the audience, for only a tiny minority can and does respond meaningfully to an appeal for information. In effect, everyone is quite literally a spectator rather than an active participant in crime-fighting. In other words, direct engagement with the time and place of the crime, or the victims and perpetrators, does not afford a point of entry into the programme's stories for most viewers.

Conclusion
The main findings that emerge from the analysis of reactions to *Crimewatch* fall into two categories: some are specific to this programme alone and others reflect more general patterns also found in responses to the other programmes studied. One point of considerable importance is that the women in our viewing groups unequivocally held that violent crimes against the person were far more important than any form of crime against property. Almost all agreed that the most serious crime was the rape and murder of the young woman. The discussion of the rape and murder focused substantially on her, and there was great concern to understand how the event had occurred and how it could have been prevented. The responses revealed a tension between popular forms of explanation, often referred to as 'victim blaming', and arguments that, by contrast, rejected women's responsibility for male violence and viewed the constraints upon women's independence and mobility as unjust. This is a common theme in debates about violence against women and reappears in the discussions of subsequent programmes.
Group members also discussed fear of crime in general, using *Crime-*

watch as the springboard for this. The quantitative results revealed that women who had been victims of violence were more fearful and apprehensive about crime than those who had not been. In group discussions this difference was less apparent. The programme's 'pay-off', which stresses that the crimes shown are unusual, and urges viewers not to have nightmares, was sometimes viewed with derision and dismissiveness.

There is a general desire to believe in the police and in *Crimewatch*'s stated purpose of assisting them with catching criminals. However, the programme does not seem to be viewed as unambiguously as might be expected. Women with experience of violence who have needed to use the police service are among the most critical of *Crimewatch*'s presentation of the police, but such scepticism was not limited to that group. Ethnicity was particularly important in shaping responses, with many Asian and Afro-Caribbean group members believing that police practices are racially discriminatory.

To conclude, criticisms were made of the negative portrayal of women as victims of crime, of the perceived negative portrayal of ethnic minority groups, of the way that crime is sometimes sensationalised, and of the breach of confidentiality revealed in this particular programme.

4

EASTENDERS

About the programme

EastEnders was launched by the BBC as a bi-weekly prime-time soap opera in February 1985 and rapidly acquired a large following, challenging Independent Television's long-running *Coronation Street* in popularity. Alongside *Coronation Street* it is the most widely viewed of British soap operas. At the time of writing its regular audience is between seventeen and eighteen-and-a-half million. The initial programme concept envisaged a community in the East End of London 'populated by a healthy mix of multi-racial, larger-than-life "characters". It also has an inbuilt culture: a past. ... The East-end community – as personified by the "Cockney" – is lively, tough, proud and sharply funny.'[1] This conception has been elaborated ever since the programme's launch.

EastEnders was devised as part of the BBC's ratings battle against its commercial rival, the Independent Television network, in the mid-1980s (one that continues today). Its prominent place in the schedules as popular television, often controversial because of the issues with which it deals, has ensured it more than its fair share of controversy. From its inception, *EastEnders* has had to navigate between the BBC's 'public service' responsibilities and what in some quarters has been seen as an illegitimate quest for a mass audience. This has been complicated, in many respects, both by the considerable marketing effort that has surrounded the programme and by the obsessive interest of the popular press in poking into the private lives of its actors, and in predicting (or more often inventing) future twists and turns in the plot.[2]

Faced by outbursts of criticism, *EastEnders*' producers have cautiously resisted the idea that it is in some sense a 'social issues' programme – a label apt to attract attacks from the right of the political spectrum – arguing instead that it is high-quality entertainment that explores dramatic conflict. However, in a detailed study of *EastEnders*, David Buckingham has argued contrariwise that it 'was intended from the outset to be a programme which would be committed to representing the realities of inner-city life, and which would therefore inevitably confront "social issues".'[3] This tendency, he goes on to suggest, has on some occasions tended to didacticism, although these have been 'comparatively rare and short-lived'.[4] One might see the episode of domestic violence discussed below in this wider context of social concern, one in which the programme has taken up a number of controversial issues – such as teenage pregnancy, cot death, unemployment, mental illness, prostitution, suicide, AIDS, racism and homosexuality. For present purposes, it is also worth noting that violence against women has been part of the storyline previously, with episodes in which a number of female characters were threatened. Buckingham has commented that 'This storyline ... provoked widespread criticism: it was felt that the repeated (and commonplace) use of violence against women as a narrative "tease" was tasteless and misogynistic. ...'[5]

What the respondents saw

Two themes dominate this episode of *EastEnders,* which was transmitted on 13 July 1989. Several minor sub-plots add to the narrative. The episode centres upon the relationship between Matthew and Carmel. Matthew is a white Englishman in his late twenties, tall, good-looking and of muscular build. His employment is not quite clear, though he does have a job. Carmel is a social worker, also in her late twenties, of Afro-Caribbean origin and slender in stature. The second major storyline concerns the decision by the publican and second-hand car dealer, Frank, and his second wife, Pat, to take Frank's youngest daughter Janine into their home. There are a number of additional sub-plots concerning various *EastEnders* regulars. These include Pauline's health problems which cause her to give up her job behind the bar at the local pub, the *Queen Vic*; Dr Legg's difficulties in accepting retirement and handing responsibility for his surgery over to his nephew, Dr Samuels; disagreements between Dot Cotton and Frank's mother, Mo; Cindy's possible pregnancy and her jealousy over Sharon and Simon's relationship (previous episodes have suggested that Cindy is pregnant by Simon); Rod's deliberations upon how to earn himself some money; and Trevor's comical efforts at building work for Mr Kareem.

The aim of using this episode of *EastEnders* was to gauge how our groups responded to the violent relationship between Matthew and Carmel. Therefore we have concentrated on the scenes involving this couple. However, it is important to note that the build-up to the violent moment that concludes the episode is part of the wider narrative flow of *EastEnders.* In other words, as with the other programmes screened, it is violence *in context.*

The episode runs for thirty minutes, of which seven minutes and forty seconds focus on Matthew and Carmel. Slightly over a quarter of the programme concerns the theme of domestic violence and this focus exceeds that upon any other single theme. Six scenes involve Matthew and Carmel, some very brief, although as the episode progresses their scenes become longer. The couple are married and act as parents to Carmel's brother's children, Junior, who is approximately twelve years old, and Aisha, who is about six. Both the children are Afro-Caribbean.

We first encounter the couple in the opening minute, as they leave their house in the morning to take Aisha and Junior to school. This twenty-two second scene portrays a happy couple enjoying being with the children. (Regular viewers of the programme, however, would know that all is not well between Matthew and Carmel.) Carmel warns Junior to return straight home after school, but he jokingly comments that he might in fact run away as he is getting his school report that day. They bump into Mo on the street, who then becomes the focus of the following scene as she goes in search of her son Frank.

We next encounter Carmel when she is talking to Frank outside his second-hand car lot. Frank greets her with a definite undertone of sexual innuendo. Carmel has information for Ali, who works at the car lot, about his son's nursery school placement. She leaves the message with Frank. Carmel then bumps into Dr Legg, whom she criticises for getting involved with a patient of Dr Samuels.

As Carmel continues on her way through the square she notices Matthew in the street. Carmel asks him what he's up to. He's taken the day off work, he says, and then asks her what she is doing. She says she couldn't concentrate on her work so was going home to have a sandwich. Carmel asks Matthew why he has taken time off. In a firm and serious voice he replies, 'I thought I'd check up to make sure you're behaving yourself.' Carmel looks tense. 'It's a joke,' states Matthew sarcastically as he equally sarcastically kisses her, and puts his arm around her as they walk off together. Twenty-one seconds in length, the scene then cuts briefly to Pauline preparing lunch for herself and Arthur in their home, before cutting back again to Matthew and Carmel.

Now in the couple's house, Matthew has made a sandwich for Carmel. At two minutes and forty-four seconds this lunchtime scene is the longest to involve Matthew and Carmel. At this point the viewer sees Matthew begin to intimidate his wife.

As Carmel sits working at the table, Matthew asks what she is doing. She replies that she is working on courses to keep up to date with new trends in social work, so that she can change direction in her career. Matthew, attempting to cuddle her while she works, asks why she didn't tell him that she was thinking of a change. He stands up and picks up one of her books, throwing it back on the table when she suggests that she only *might* change her direction. 'Thanks for discussing it with me,' remarks Matthew. Carmel replies, 'There's nothing to discuss yet', and that she has to keep up to date with the work as her opinion is increasingly sought on matters by doctors and other professionals.

Matthew picks up yet another book, looks at the spine and asks, 'What, like violence against wives?' 'Yes,' she replies. Carmel begins to look flustered, and Matthew stalks round the room taunting her: 'Oh, so you're an expert now, yeah? An expert on domestic violence. So what do you do then, darling? Get in a huddle with Dr Samuels, do you, tell him about your home life, straight from the horse's mouth?'

Carmel explains that domestic violence is just one topic that she has to read up on. Matthew accuses her of winding him up and treating him as if he were stupid. He then reads chapter headings while reclining on the settee. Reaching the chapter titled 'Family Therapy', he rests the book on his chest, closes his eyes and mockingly remarks, 'I've beaten my wife, doctor, not a lot, just now and again. OK? No big deal.' He looks directly at Carmel and continues: 'Now what makes me do it?'

Carmel tries to get him to stop by pointing out that she has work to do, but Matthew is insistent, and claims he is testing her knowledge. He asks whether it could be his upbringing. Carmel replies that it could be. 'Maybe I saw my dad beat my mum,' Matthew suggests. Carmel asks, 'Did you?' Matthew replies, 'Maybe', and continues with a further example from the book which suggests that his mother might have rejected him as a child, making him bitter and angry. He then laughs. Carmel comments that that is possible. But Matthew retorts, 'Oh yeah, so when I became a big boy I felt this terrible compulsion to smack my wife, that about the size of it?' Carmel looks nervous, saying that any of these explanations was possible. Matthew throws the book at Carmel shouting: 'Middle-class do-gooders, do me a favour will you? Find me the page where it says it's the woman's fault, where she lies, and cheats, and goes on relentlessly provoking and winding him up until the only answer is a smack in the mouth.' He has jumped up from the settee and stalks around behind Carmel's back. With the final few words he leans in front of her, staring into her face. Carmel leans away, avoiding his gaze, then turns and looks at him, asking, 'You're not serious, are you?' 'No,' he replies, 'I'm just testing, that's all.'

Carmel begins to pack her work away. Matthew asks whether she got the books from Dr Samuels and Carmel says she can't remember exactly. As she gets ready to leave Matthew states that he will pick up Aisha from school and cook the tea, saying, 'That's why I took the day off work, ain't it? You need looking after.' Carmel looks at Matthew almost in tears and leaves the house. The action shifts to Ethel and Dr Legg in the *Queen Vic*.

There follow five minutes and twenty seconds of scenes in which Matthew and Carmel are not involved, and in which the programme foregrounds characters in the *Queen Vic* and the launderette. The action then returns to Matthew for a one-minute extract. He is preparing a meal at home ready for Carmel's return from work. He talks to Junior, who wants to know why Matthew is trying to put on a show for Carmel. Matthew asks Junior about his school report, which is not terribly promising, though Junior does remark that he has been praised for his athletic abilities. Junior is then sent off to buy some flowers, signalling a change of scene, this time upstairs at the *Queen Vic*, where Pat is preparing a tea-party to welcome Janine to her new home.

The tea-time scene involving Matthew, Carmel, Junior and Aisha has two moments. The first, of one minute and fifteen seconds, begins with Matthew putting the tea he has prepared onto the table. Carmel is delighted, commenting, 'It smells delicious.' She then goes on to ask for Junior's school report. Matthew suggests she should look at it later and he and Carmel mock-wrestle on the settee with the report. Carmel succeeds in getting hold of it. She makes fun of Junior's disappointing grades, which Junior defends. The scene appears to be that of a family enjoying themselves. Carmel shows her appreciation for Matthew's cooking with 'What did I do to deserve all this?' Matthew, pleased with himself, smiles. There next follows a parallel scene involving Frank and Pat. Janine's tea party, and her welcome to her father's home, much to Pat's delight, has been a great success.

The storyline returns to Carmel and Matthew. Apparently all has been forgotten about the lunchtime fracas, until Carmel mentions her work and Dr Legg's treatment of Dr Samuels. Matthew points out that Dr Legg is unhappy because he has been pensioned off, and she should understand how he feels. Carmel says that she wouldn't mind being pensioned off, and Matthew suggests that if she was she could stay at home and cook him fancy meals, and then he'd 'know what she was up to'. Matthew, seated, puts his arms round Carmel's waist as she stands next to him. Junior chips in that he'd like that too, as she could make 'some of that pepper stew like you made for Dr Samuels'. Carmel anxiously remarks to Junior, 'Don't be silly.' Matthew, now gritting his teeth and having let go of Carmel, asks Junior to repeat what he has just said. Carmel picks up Aisha, telling her that it's her bedtime.

Matthew persists in demanding to know what Carmel cooked when Dr Samuels came round for dinner. Junior is apprehensive. Carmel, having put Aisha in her room, states that Dr Samuels came round to discuss work. 'So you cook him a fancy meal?' Matthew questions angrily, as he stands up clenching his fists. Carmel repeats it was a working meal: 'We worked solidly all evening; I was exhausted.' Matthew violently pushes her backwards repeating, 'Exhausted! What, both of you? Well, we know there's only one thing that exhausts you, and we both know what that is.' Carmel tries to reason with him: 'Look, Matthew, I thought we'd got to the point where we could start to talk things through in a rational way.' Matthew shouts that he can't be rational when he doesn't even know what is going on under his own roof. Again he pushes her backwards, and now accuses her of having an affair with the doctor and of talking about his and Carmel's relationship behind his back. Carmel denies it, but Matthew wants to know why Dr Samuels gave her the books on domestic violence. Carmel backs away from him, but Matthew pursues her. He throws over a chair and jabs his hands at Carmel's face.

With the camera close up on Carmel's face she looks terrified and screams that her relationship with the doctor is 'purely professional'. Junior shouts at Matthew to leave Carmel alone. Matthew tells him to 'shut up and get out'. With Carmel backed up against a door Matthew's clenched fist is thrust into Carmel's face. We do not see the fist make contact with Carmel, as the scene immediately cuts to Frank and Pat with Janine. This final scene between Matthew and Carmel lasts one minute fifty-four seconds.

Frank, Pat, Diane, Ricky and Janine are watching television, contented after the tea-party for Janine, who is evidently enjoying herself with her brother and sister. An ambulance siren is heard. On the street an ambulance is seen stopping outside Carmel and Matthew's house and the episode closes to the familiar theme tune.

How the respondents reacted

As has been described above, the episode selected portrays scenes of domestic violence between a young married couple, culminating in the husband striking his wife, although the blow itself is not portrayed. There is a gradual build-up to the violence, and we were concerned to identify those points at which our respondents saw the relationship as violent. What were group members' interpretations of the context of the violence and of the relationship between the man, the woman and the violent event? The female victim of domestic violence is Afro-Caribbean, whereas her husband is white. We investigated reactions to this. The domestic scenes involving families in which there is no violence stand in possible contrast to the violent relationship. Such variation offers a range of points of potential identification for the audience.

A further issue was the extent to which the viewing groups found the episode to be realistic, particularly those scenes involving domestic violence (see Appendix III, Guiding Questions for Discussion, *East-Enders*). We anticipated that some women in the viewing groups were likely to be more familiar with *EastEnders* than others, therefore having extensive prior knowledge of the characters which others lacked. It was felt that such differing levels of familiarity with the programme could have a bearing upon the perceptions of the violence portrayed.

A surprisingly large number of participants, thirty-four women (37% of the entire sample) indicated that they remembered seeing the selected episode, and they were about equally divided between those with experience of violence and those without. Given that many group members indicated that soap operas are their favourite form of programme, it is not surprising that three-quarters of the women with experience of violence and just over half of those with none regularly or occasionally viewed *EastEnders*. An additional quarter of the entire sample described themselves as infrequent viewers. This 'intimacy' with the series was important for the subsequent discussions in which our sample often invoked their background knowledge when interpreting scenes and characters from the screened episode.

Some very strong differences in reactions emerged, based on whether or not the women concerned had experienced violence. A majority of women in the study thought that this was a violent episode, rating it from 'somewhat' to 'very violent' (see Figure VI). However women with experience of violence were much more likely to indicate that they took the programme 'seriously' or 'very seriously' (51%); only a quarter of women with no experience made the same judgment. Women with no experience of violence were much less likely than women with experi-

84

ence to consider the programme to be 'believable' or 'very believable' (41%) or to think it 'realistic' or 'very realistic' (36%). Having been a victim of violence meant that one was more likely to interpret the *EastEnders* episode as 'believable' or 'very believable' (64%) and either 'realistic' or 'very realistic' (59%). Consequently three-quarters of the women with experience of violence found the programme 'disturbing' or 'very disturbing', while only half of the women who had not suffered violence made the same assessment. Experience of violence also led a greater proportion of women (34%) to judge the episode 'offensive' or 'very offensive', whereas only one-tenth of women without experience judged it similarly. Possibly because of the disturbing and realistic nature of the programme, few women from either category evaluated it as 'exciting' (6% and 20% respectively), although rather more found it 'entertaining' (33% and 24% respectively).

This did not mean, however, that women rejected *EastEnders* and the role that soap operas might play in addressing social issues. On the contrary, all the women with experience of violence rated it as either very (56%) or moderately (44%) 'relevant' to daily life. By contrast, only 10% of women with no experience of violence rated the programme as 'very relevant', although 74% thought it was 'moderately relevant'. Many women in both categories, about one-quarter, indicated that they were unsure whether *EastEnders* portrayed 'a fair picture of life', but those who did express an opinion overwhelmingly thought that it did.

EastEnders was also judged to be 'doing a good job of handling social issues'. About three-quarters of those who held an opinion made this assessment, although a quarter said that they did not know. As far as these women were concerned, soap operas are a highly appropriate genre for addressing social issues, with only a tenth dissenting.

As with *Crimewatch*, ethnicity was an important factor in responses to the programme. Women from Afro-Caribbean backgrounds tended to interpret this episode of *EastEnders* differently and to exhibit a greater intensity of feeling than women from white or Asian backgrounds. They were just as likely as women from Asian and white backgrounds to relate to the characters and situations depicted in the programme, and all of the Afro-Caribbean women related to Carmel. All of the Afro-Caribbean women indicated that the programme was 'moderately' or 'very relevant to everyday life', and most of the women from the other two groups expressed similar feelings. The important differences were evident in the *strength of feeling* about the programme. Afro-Caribbean women were more likely than the other two groups to describe the programme as 'believable' and 'realistic' and to find it 'disturbing' and 'offensive' (see Figure VII). Four-fifths of the Afro-Caribbean viewers (80%) thought that the programme was 'violent' or 'very violent'; this compares to 64% of white and 32% of Asian viewers. Very few Afro-Caribbean viewers (14%) found the programme 'exciting' or 'entertaining' and they were much more likely than the other two groups of viewers to describe it as 'not at all entertaining' (whites, 29%; Asians, 34%; Afro-Caribbeans, 60%). It should be noted that the direction of these trends is the same for all groups, but that Afro-Caribbean women expressed a greater intensity of feeling about these issues.

Although a substantial majority of Afro-Caribbean women thought the programme was 'realistic', 'believable' and 'related to real life', many did not think it portrayed a 'fair picture of life' or handled social issues in an effective manner. A fair proportion of white (20%) and Asian (43%) women were equivocal on this point, saying that they did not know. Somewhat fewer Afro-Caribbean women were unsure (15%), and, of those who held an opinion, a greater percentage criticised the programme's handling of social questions. A smaller percentage of Afro-Caribbean than of white and Asian women indicated that they thought this episode of *EastEnders* handled social issues well or that it portrayed a fair picture of life. This is in contrast to the other two groups, in which most women who expressed an opinion thought that *EastEnders* was doing a good job in these two areas. Around 93% of white women and 80% of Asian women felt that *EastEnders* handled social issues well, and 86% and 80% respectively thought that the episode painted a fair picture of life.

Why these differences? Although the numbers in each group are fairly small, and the results should therefore be viewed with caution, the qualitative results provide additional information for understanding these responses, and the final question on the programme questionnaire points to an important reason. When asked whether they thought 'that television soap operas like this should be made', two Afro-Caribbean women and one Asian woman said 'no'. In giving a reason, one Afro-Caribbean viewer said that she thought there should be no violence portrayed in soap operas and another told us she thought they tended to depict racial stereotypes. Some of the thinking behind these formal responses is explored later.

Characters and scenes
One of the most important findings from the quantitative data is the way in which the women who had been victims of violence identified with the character and scenes associated with the domestic assault; the other was the significance of ethnicity in shaping responses. Over 90% of the women with experience of violence said that they could relate to the characters portrayed, particularly Carmel. About a quarter of the women who had no experience of violence identified with the characters, mainly Carmel but also Pauline. These dramatic results indicate that there is a strong and significant association between the experience of being a victim of violence and the ability to relate to the character. As indicated in Table 2, the Yule's Q of .94 demonstrates a near perfect relationship between experience and the ability to relate to Carmel.

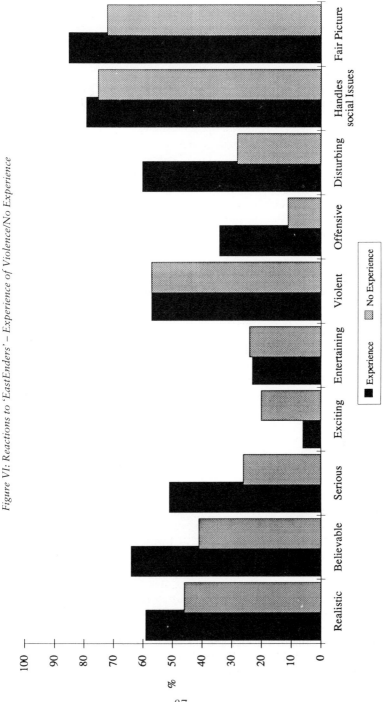

Figure VI: Reactions to 'EastEnders' – Experience of Violence/No Experience

■ Experience   ▨ No Experience

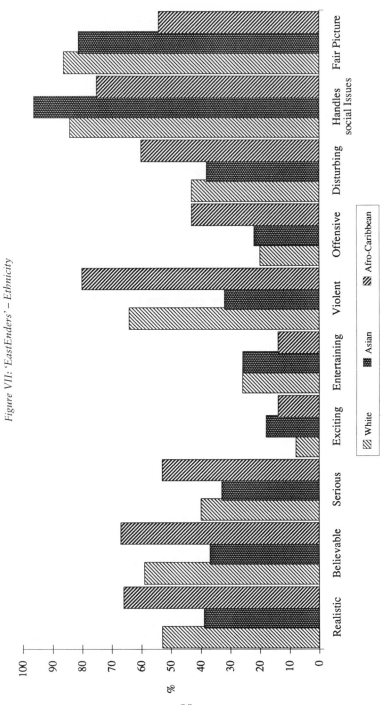

Figure VII: 'EastEnders' – Ethnicity

88

Table 2: Relating to characters in 'EastEnders'

| | Violence | | | |
| | Experience | | No experience | |
Relate to characters	N	%	N	%
yes	47	90	9	23
no	5	10	30	77
Total	52	100%	39	100%

Yule's Q= .94

Women who had experienced violence also strongly identified with the situations depicted in *EastEnders*, with most (89%, N=46) saying they could identify with the situations portraying domestic violence and the predicament of the victim. By contrast, only 31% of women who had no experience of violence related to the televised scenes, but they were just as likely to identify with the situations depicting the marital argument and with Pauline's problems as with the violence and/or the victim. Table 3 presents these results and indicates another strong association, Yule's Q .89. What is noteworthy is the extraordinary strength of the difference between the two groups. Clearly, experience makes a tremendous difference to how group members read this episode of *EastEnders* and the depiction of violence against women, although it is important to distinguish the extent of identification with the *situation* portrayed from that with the female *character* who is subject to violence.

Table 3: Relating to situations in 'EastEnders'

| | Violence | | | |
| | Experience | | No experience | |
Relate to situations	N	%	N	%
yes	46	88	12	31
no	6	12	27	69
Total	52	100%	39	100%

Yule's Q= .89

The qualitative data provide further elaboration of the reasons behind this general pattern of reactions and more specific insights into some of the responses. Many of the women studied reveal the depth of their identification with Carmel, their belief that Matthew is ultimately responsible for his violent behaviour despite his deforming background experiences, a profound concern about what children might learn from viewing such a programme, and perspectives on the educational value to be extracted from the episode. Less frequent, but nonetheless recurrent, themes in the discussions follow lines familiar from the literature on domestic violence and common within our society. These include looking for provocations committed by Carmel and attributing blame to her for her victimisation. In addition, Matthew's violent behaviour is explained or excused either in terms of his treatment as a child by his mother and/or his treatment as an adult by Carmel.

Social issues and 'entertainment'

In group discussions, responses to the *EastEnders* episode varied considerably. Whereas groups of women with no experience of violence related to it as a social issues soap opera, those with such experience tended to single out the portrayal of domestic violence as *the* crucial scene. Although class did at times affect perceptions, it was by no means an overriding factor in the interpretations offered, while ethnic background played an important part in group positions taken towards *EastEnders*.

Almost all of the women, irrespective of their class and/or ethnic backgrounds, saw the episode as demonstrating the emotional dilemmas of a victim of domestic violence at the same time as it was covering other issues:

> Well, this episode is going to bring out wife-battering. That's one of the main issues it's bringing out here. ... Also [the issue of] bringing a new child into the house. ... So it's making you think about a situation because I think with wife-battering, people would say, 'Oh, hit me once and I would throw him out!' and 'I would just go and that would be it.' But that shows you a situation where that's not happened – and she's a health visitor. I mean it's easy to say things and yet there you go, and she's a health visitor. She's the one that advises people and everything and she didn't do it [leave].
> [Scottish white middle-class woman, with no experience of violence]

Despite this widely diffused view, women with no experience of violence also focused, albeit to a lesser extent, upon other issues covered in the episode. In particular, for the Afro-Caribbean women, the fact that the couple were of mixed race clouded the issue of domestic violence. This will be discussed later.

The perception of *EastEnders* as a soap opera concerned with social issues meant that its entertainment value was seen as somewhat limited. The general recognition of its social realism led group members to emphasise that it was difficult to regard a programme concerned with everyday social problems as 'entertainment'. Its realism and the extent of its sensitivity and accuracy in portraying violence against women were deemed to be of much greater importance:

> I think it's realistic. I don't think it's an entertaining programme like watching, for instance, some sort of a show like *Sunday Night at the Palladium*. It's entertaining in so far as – I don't think entertainment's the word really. ... At the same time I suppose, well, I suppose that's life. I mean life's kind of depressing, let's face it.
> [Scottish white working-class woman, with no experience of violence]

Among white women, most discussion centred on the question of violence itself. By contrast, among both the Afro-Caribbean and Asian groups, the question of violence was closely linked to a discussion of ethnicity. Not surprisingly, for women with experience of violence the domestic violence was the focal point of discussion. The experience of viewing was not a comfortable one for many, for the tensions in the plot and the sense of the action's realism were enhanced as a result of what they themselves had lived through:

I think it was very real. ... the leading up to Carmel's beating, I mean, you could actually see it coming long before the beating happened.
[Scottish white woman, with experience of violence]

That episode I thought was quite realistic. In fact, very realistic because I think most of us here have been through it. Right? It does happen that way though, doesn't it? There doesn't have to be any particular reason and they can just turn round and strike us.
[Scottish white woman, with experience of violence]

Obviously she [another woman in the group] was upset because she related that to herself. I can understand her being upset because I went through that at first. See, you do, you just watch the very slightest thing and you become very, very upset. I know it doesn't give you advice and information on where to get help, but I think it's making people aware that 'look, this is happening'.
[Scottish Asian woman, with experience of violence]

Groups of women with experience of violence judged the merits of the episode in terms of what had happened to them personally. Dominating these discussions was how realistic the violence was. The realism of the episode was regarded by these groups as acceptable and mostly accurate and, although disturbing to watch, they found little difficulty in relating to the victim's circumstances. For this reason groups of women who had experienced violence tended to see the episode as much more centrally concerned with domestic violence than did the other groups. For them, the televised violence was foregrounded by its direct relation to their own lived experience. This is not to say that the women with no experience of violence were not affected by the domestic violence in the programme. Rather, the point is that they related to it quite differently. This response from an English middle-class woman is indicative of the shock of the unfamiliar:

I think it's very disturbing. ... The violence more than anything else. It was, well, I've never been in a situation like that, but I've found that believable, that it would just come out from nowhere and blow up, and it was quite frightening. ... I can remember when I saw it the

first time, I was at a loss what to do for half an hour after the programme, really. It frightened me. You don't expect that – I've just never come up against violence from parents or from family or whatever. In that situation I suppose home is a safe haven to me, and seeing it turn into something like that, especially in front of a child, it just frightened me, it really upset me.
[English white middle-class woman, with no experience of violence]

Such responses were generally confined to the middle-class women, and were not found among working-class women with no experience of violence. In these other cases, although there was no direct experience of domestic violence, for some it was plainly seen as just one step further in the kinds of difficulty that they had experienced with their male partners.

Characters
Most of the women, and particularly those with experience of violence, demonstrated sympathy for Carmel. Those with experience identified strongly with her predicament, were familiar with the patterns of male behaviour portrayed and brought many of their own experiences to bear in their judgment of the situation. The identification with Carmel as a victim of domestic violence was often expressed in very emotional terms:

> The violent bit made me feel quite sick. ... Because I knew exactly how the woman was feeling, and when the wee boy opened his mouth I could feel how she was then, and I thought, 'Oh, for God's sake, please don't, because I know what's going to happen next.'
> [Scottish white woman, with experience of violence]

Those with experience could relate to Carmel's anxieties, identifying the tensions in the relationship with much greater depth of feeling than those with none. Matthew's threatening and intimidating behaviour was an experience very familiar to them. Women with no experience of domestic violence had to rely largely upon the portrayal offered by the programme in assessing the problems of Matthew and Carmel's relationship. However, those who had experienced such situations judged the relationship, and Matthew's tendency to violence, by direct reference to their own knowledge of male violence. Therefore, although many women with no experience of violence could only hypothesise about what they thought was likely to be realistic, those with experience had no difficulties in making such judgments. Matthew's aggressive questioning concerning the meal that Carmel had cooked for the doctor was felt to be particularly well portrayed:

> Her reaction was instant and it was exactly the same as mine and any other woman's. It's get the kids out of here, because I know what's

coming. So I thought that was perfect.
[English white woman, with experience of violence]

Some, however, needed to distance themselves from any identification with either the woman who had been victimised or the situation, as the involvement with the television characters was just too painful:

> When I watch whatever, and the woman's been battered. ... I sit there – 'It's only make up' ... You have to just say to yourself, 'It's make up. It's make up.' Because ... I'm still frightened to death, because I think, yeah, that was me...
> [English white woman, with experience of violence]

Others who identified with Carmel expressed outright anger, again a feeling not expressed by women who had no experience of violence:

> I mean, I still felt for that character. Believe me, I felt anger, and if I'd been there I'd probably still try and stick a knife in him, or something. It got me worked up enough, you know.
> [Scottish Asian woman, with experience of violence]

Explanations of violence
Certain consistent patterns of interpretation were evident across the groups when discussion focused upon the young married couple, Matthew and Carmel, through whose relationship *EastEnders* portrayed the violence in question.

Before discussing this further, we should note that research has shown that in discussions of violence against women, the focus almost invariably turns away from a description of 'what happened' to an analysis of 'why it happened', and that in turn generally leads to explanations which excuse the perpetrator, and to victim-blaming. This may be illustrated, for example, by reference to the discussions about the various crimes depicted in *Crimewatch*, where talk about the bank fraud and the Mercedes scam left aside why the men concerned committed such crimes and concentrated instead upon what they actually did and how reprehensible that might be. Although there was an element of victim-blaming, particularly focused on the naïvety of the car-owners, no excuses were offered as to how others might have influenced or be somehow responsible for such crimes. By contrast, such discussions almost invariably occur when discussing violence against women, and women discussants reflect much of the widely diffused 'common sense' of our society.

There is an influential set of ideas concerning violence against women in the home. These popular beliefs are deeply rooted and it takes considerable probing to make them explicit. Those with experience of male violence are, for the most part, most likely to have been forced through bitter circumstances into reflecting upon the validity of such popular beliefs about who is to blame and what kind of behaviour can be justified. As a consequence they are often the most sensitive to the nuances of how to interpret the violence itself and to the explanations used to try to understand it. As might be expected, even they are not completely free from a tendency to offer excuses and blame victims. Such approaches are much more common among those with no relevant experiences that might cause them to modify what is taken to be 'common sense'.

In the discussions, several possible explanations were given for Matthew's violence but, for the most part, all of the women considered that the violence was wrong and held Matthew responsible for his own behaviour. Although most strongly articulated among the women with experience of violence, this perspective nonetheless characterised the conversation in all of the discussion groups. The exculpatory explanations so commonly offered throughout society were also given by some of the women and took the form of excusing Matthew's violence either in terms of past childhood experiences, usually with his mother as the cause (as suggested in previous episodes of *EastEnders*), or in terms of current experiences, usually with his female partner somehow being to blame. Both positions have the feature of blaming women for male violence and obscuring men's responsibility for their own actions. In the discussion groups such beliefs emerged as victim-blaming, where Carmel was the focus, and therefore her contribution to and responsibility for her own victimisation were stressed. It should be emphasised, however, that despite the victim-blaming and exculpatory explanations, the women unequivocally deemed the violence unacceptable and held Matthew responsible. There are contradictory tendencies at work, therefore, in the interpretations offered.

Although Matthew's childhood was recognised as a possible cause of his violence, he was by no means excused, particularly by women who had experienced violence:

> I just can't blame anybody's background for what they do as an adult. They're adults; they're responsible. They know, and their childhood has got sweet damn all to do with it ... I'm sorry, I've been through it all as a kid and I just can't believe in that myth. Because when you become an adult, you are responsible for your actions. You're not responsible for your actions when you were a kid. But [you are for] your actions when you're an adult.
> [Scottish white woman, with experience of violence]

Women with experience of violence expressed a great deal of concern that *EastEnders* itself might be offering excuses for the perpetrator of the violence, and that ultimately viewers would not consider the violence to be Matthew's problem, but rather one that he had inherited from his mother:

It's odd, portraying violence, really. Thinking about it, they'd built up to it. But it's not his fault in the programme. It's not his fault. Really, violence like a few of us have been through, it's a bit different. Because they built up to it by the sound of it. It's not his fault. Basically it's psychological. ... So, because what? His mother had, what? Deserted him? Perhaps, I mean, thinking again, perhaps his father was over-jealous and things. I don't know. But it's not his fault, according to this sort of programme.
[English white woman, with experience of violence]

For women who had experienced violence, there was an issue of considerable note here. Although they were sympathetic to the programme's goal of airing the issue of domestic violence, they were not happy that the onus of blame could be removed from Matthew and, particularly, placed upon his mother. It was felt that *EastEnders*, through its characterisation, should have promoted the idea that the perpetrators of violence are responsible for their own actions, and that they should recognise their moral responsibilities.

Some of the women were more willing to attribute the blame for Matthew's behaviour to a society which creates certain types of masculine identity:

I think society forces men, a lot of men, into it as well, because they are the ones in that situation. He's the one who is supposed to be the breadwinner, the one that's going out and being the man, and Carmel's doing it [instead]. So he watches the telly every day when Carmel's out working. And [on television] they're saying 'the man's off working and the woman sits in the house', and it's affecting his mind.
[English white woman, with experience of violence]

Interestingly, the above comment points out how television assumes that it has a day-time audience made up of women, and that because Matthew is watching day-time television, this is affecting his perceptions of his masculinity.

Explanations offered by other groups, both of women who had and had not experienced violence, located Matthew's aggressiveness in jealousy, his insecurity deriving from status differentials between him and Carmel, and his childhood experiences of his mother. This last explanation was introduced as a result of background knowledge of the programme. Those who were regular viewers of *EastEnders* knew that Matthew and his mother were supposed to have had a difficult relationship. It was widely agreed by such viewers that the couple's problems had begun when Carmel invited Matthew's mother to their wedding without his consent. From this point on he became a 'Jekyll and Hyde' character, a phrase repeatedly used by our respondents. However, it was much less clear why his mother's appearance on the scene should have culminated in his violence against Carmel:

> I wondered later on ... when his mother came back, and I wondered if there'd been some sort of incestuous relationship with his mother, because he wouldn't actually say what his mother had done. His mother had done something but he wouldn't actually say what it was. It was all hinted at.
> [English white middle-class woman, with no experience of violence]

> I've watched *EastEnders* before – I think it stems from his ... childhood. I can't remember the story, but his mum and dad were separating. I think that's a lot to do with it. It also brings up the subject of your childhood – the way you've been brought up – does it have an effect on you?
> [Scottish white middle-class woman, with no experience of violence]

> I don't know if he had [a] mother and father. Father was hitting the mother, and children picks it up, and that's why they do it when they grow up. It's sort of felt that he's sort of come from a background where it ... was happening.
> [Scottish Asian woman, with no experience of violence]

Among groups of women with experience of violence, it was accepted that Matthew's violence could stem from his childhood experiences. It was thought more than likely, however, that either he had been abused as a child, or had seen his father abuse his mother. Indeed, one woman who had experienced physical abuse as a child identified with Matthew:

> I really do have a strong reaction to it, because that has never happened to me as a grown-up woman. But, sadly ... I could've identified with the man's violent temper, because I received a lot of violence as a child and I've had to do a lot of work on my own behaviour. Not that I'm physically violent, but I can really feel whatever it is that he has suffered as a child, whatever's made him behave like that.
> [English white woman, with experience of violence]

Carmel's occupation as a social worker was a central point of discussion in all groups' assessments of the relationship. Her professional life was frequently cited as the core of the problem between Carmel and her husband. Many women who had not experienced violence found it surprising that a social worker could not deal with the problem of violence in her own relationship:

> I think she's a together sort of person, until it comes to her husband. That's – I can't say too much – I can't remember what happened

now. But I remember she sort of, that's right, she sort of covered up for him a lot. But she'd come across, as, really sort of over-stressed because of her work. But generally her heart was in the right place, and she was a together sort of person. She didn't know what to do for the best there, because she did make mistakes, and you think because of the job she'd know what to do.
[English white middle-class woman, with no experience of violence]

That's what I kept thinking. You should be aware of all these things. You know, you are a social worker, how come you let yourself get in this situation?
[English Afro-Caribbean woman, with no experience of violence]

Across all groups, it was felt that at the heart of the violence was a problem of unequal status between the couple, which led to Matthew's insecurity and his subsequent violence. Afro-Caribbean women who had experience of violence felt that difference in status was a further problem for other reasons as well:

I think we looked at it from the point of view of saying that here's a woman he's with, not just a woman, but a black woman who's achieving and he's not achieving.
[English Afro-Caribbean woman, with experience of violence]

Many women in groups with no experience of violence held Carmel partly responsible for Matthew's behaviour, in that she did not give him enough attention and put her work before her family. This argument was particularly strong among Asian groups:

Probably because she's coming from work, she's talking about work, work, work, and he doesn't like that sort of thing.

See ... like my husband, if he comes from work and you question him about the work, he gets annoyed as well. Because he says, 'I want to make my mind free from work because I'm home. I want to be relaxed and everything.' Some people want to be relaxed at home. Rather than talking about the work all the day.
[Scottish Asian women, with no experience of violence]

Among groups of women with experience of violence however, this argument was turned upside down. Sensing Matthew's portrayed inferiority complex, they felt he was incapable of giving his wife any freedom outside of the home environment, and that this was symptomatic of his possessiveness and jealousy towards her:

It was her career as well, I mean, it was obvious he didn't want her to have such a good career, wasn't it? ... Yeah, it gave me the

impression he wanted the little woman at home, and not wanting her to have a career and her own viewpoint.
[English white woman, with experience of violence]

Carmel was perceived as a weak character by a majority of women who had not experienced violence, because of her inability to take issue with Matthew's behaviour and leave him. Though she was regarded as a tough character in terms of her career, her weakness lay in her love for Matthew, and in letting these emotions overpower her rational thinking. It was also suggested that Carmel may have provoked Matthew:

> She was the sort of person ... say poor old Pauline had been battered, you could have related it more to that. ... She wasn't a person that you could sympathise with. I know it's a terrible thing to say, but I don't know. ... She was such a confident person that, not so much there, but sometimes she did antagonise Matthew. ... Sometimes she did wind him up – she did do stupid things that – not that she deserved a beating, because she didn't, but you know, she was, she was quite a forceful character. She was.
> [English white working-class woman, with no experience of violence]

Some women felt that Matthew's suspicions of her flirtatious behaviour with other men were justified:

> I think that her... she's having an affair behind his back and not telling him the truth. And she's doing this just to please this doctor and not to please him.
> [Scottish white woman, with experience of violence]

The range of interpretations of the nature of the violent relationship portrayed in *EastEnders* demonstrates that there is no single reading of exactly who or what has to take responsibility for the difficulties within the relationship. Although none of the groups condoned Matthew's behaviour, to a degree women with no experience of violence were more prepared to hold Carmel at least somewhat responsible for Matthew's lack of security, finding motives for his behaviour which were outside his control. But among those who had experienced violence, although there was criticism of Carmel, identification with her predicament resulted in far less sympathy for Matthew. Indeed, while some could identify with the possible social causes of Matthew's behaviour, this was seen as no excuse.

Ethnicity
For Afro-Caribbean women, regardless of their experience of violence, the issue which dominated discussion was the programme's portrayal

of the black community. Indications of the importance of this dimension have already emerged from our discussion of the quantitative findings. Equally, the English Asian women with experience of violence took issue on the basis of what they perceived as the negative stereotyping of ethnic minorities by *EastEnders*. By contrast, the question was not expressly addressed by any of the white groups, which is a curious silence. It is our belief that awareness of Carmel's colour did operate in some of the views expressed about her. In sharp contrast, both English Afro-Caribbean and English Asian groups sensed that the episode was not an innocent portrayal of domestic violence, but one that was attempting to pass a broader, negative, comment on mixed-race relationships:

> ... as soon as you knew that there was a black and white couple, you knew that it wasn't going to work.... So you sort of look out for them, things to go wrong, and as for that being the violence part and him beating her up, I mean, not that I was expecting the violent part ... But you just knew from day one it wasn't going to work. So you were just looking out for the bad points.
> [English Afro-Caribbean woman, with no experience of violence]

Both English Afro-Caribbeans and English Asians supported their arguments with extensive references to ethnic characterisation in other episodes of *EastEnders*. However, the Scottish Asian groups did not draw upon such referents. Here, irrespective of whether or not they had experienced violence, group members tended to state that the episode's portrayal of domestic violence was relevant to Asian culture. Domestic violence was a social problem highly familiar to them, and one which affected Asian women no less than any other ethnic group. As one Asian woman stated: 'There's some women, like Asian women, it happens to them all the time, and they just sit at home and take it. Programmes like that help them.' *EastEnders'* attempts at portraying ethnic minorities, however, were viewed in a very poor light by the ethnic minority groups.

Afro-Caribbean women found it difficult to regard the programme as a discourse on domestic violence. Their point was that the mixed-race relationship confused the issue of domestic violence, and that by using a black woman as a victim, the programme was distancing white society from the issue:

> I really wished when I saw it, that instead of making it a mixed couple, they just made it the same colour. Because you can look at it nakedly as a man doing this to a woman. But if you've watched it in context. ... She's not typical. I mean she's, like, the one that's born in England, been educated in England, so you've got a different perspective from a black person who's been born outside England. To a degree there's a certain amount of trust of white men, right? And, like, the white men who consider themselves quite liberal tend

to have these underlying feelings about black women, you know, like there's a real kinky feeling about going out with a black woman and that they're really into sex. And he was losing out in his conversation with her. And there is the threat that she is a black woman and she's doing better than him, because he only works in a record shop. And she's meeting all these people and it's obvious that her career is progressing and his isn't. And he has got a problem in terms of how he relates to women. But all that is almost clouded by the fact that he does beat her up. ... They're not tackling the fact of how people view black women or mixed couples and all that kind of thing. So I would've preferred it if they'd just kept it two white people or two black people. To actually do a mix caused a bit of aggro in the sense that it wasn't dealing with it properly.

I sort of felt that by using a black woman, it was making it more acceptable to white society. Well, you know, it's that one step away from too close to white women, white women's experience of violence. And it's more like viewers, white viewers, perhaps feeling '... well she's a black woman, anyway'. And I think if they'd used a white woman in that scene, in the story, it would have hit a lot of women more.
[English Afro-Caribbean women, with experience of violence]

Embedded within the episode for one Afro-Caribbean group was a white man's domination of a black woman through force. This was not only domestic violence; it had the added dimension of being a racist attack. One Afro-Caribbean woman who had been raped by a white man explained the ambivalence of her feelings:

I know that physically, whether it's a black or white man, what I'm going to be able to do is pretty limited. Because ... I was raped by a white guy, the fact is, at the end of the day, because of the way the police perceive black women and the way they perceive rape, there was no way on earth that I was going to run to no police officer and tell him. Especially when it came to classes, because this guy was a middle-class guy and he was a teacher, so I was going to be the one who looked like a fool. ... So I'm going to be the one who looks as if I was provoking it and all that kind of business. Especially as it was my birthday, especially as he was drunk and I was drunk, but he knew what he'd done. ... But I see the historical thing.
[English Afro-Caribbean woman, with experience of violence]

No other groups identified these racist undertones in Matthew's violence towards Carmel, in the portrayal of the characters in the programme, or in the potential response of others.

Since ethnicity has proved so important in this research, it is worth considering David Buckingham's related evidence on responses to *East-*

Enders. This derives from a study of sixty young people in London, aged between seven and eighteen, conducted in 1986. Although some of the groups he interviewed were almost exclusively black and others ethnically mixed, his work was not sufficiently systematic to afford a full-blown comparison with the present analysis.

The presence in *EastEnders* of black members of the cast did provoke comment. Buckingham was evidently surprised at 'the lack of explicit reference to ethnicity in the children's discussions of these characters. Their responses might be seen as a consequence of the programme's tendency to *suppress* ethnic difference in its attempts to provide a positive representation of a "multicultural" community.'[6] Nevertheless, he did find that where white characters evidenced racism this was condemned by some of his respondents and that there was also a certain recognition of the programme's multiculturalism. Our own research among adult Afro-Caribbean and Asian women has raised the issue of racism much more sharply. Yet at the same time, there was an undoubted reticence among white women about the representation of ethnic difference in the episode, which parallels Buckingham's findings.

In fact, although *EastEnders* has stood out from other British soap operas in giving central dramatic roles to black characters, there have been controversies among the cast, with some black and Asian members leaving amid accusations against the scriptwriters of racist script lines and inadequate knowledge of their communities.[7] In a popular guide to soap operas, Hilary Kingsley has rather flippantly commented that:

> *EastEnders* tried to make itself *EthnicEnders*, the soap opera which reflects the cosmopolitan mix of races and nationalities in poor parts of London. It wasn't too successful. By early 1988, it was as though the Ku Klux Klan had held rallies in the Albert Square Gardens. There was hardly a non-white face to be seen.[8]

Judith Jacob, who played Carmel, has expressly taken up the issue of negative stereotyping in interviews, and has been interpreted as saying that 'it is important for black women to secure positive representations of themselves in mainstream popular culture in order to alter the image of black women held by themselves, by black men, and by white people – even if such representations may not be entirely "realistic".'[9] In line with this it has been suggested that Carmel's role is actually 'a positive representation: she is a professional woman, a responsible adult, who is in a position of some authority in relation to the predominantly white population of Albert Square.'[10] In her soap opera guide, Hilary Kingsley has likewise commented that 'Carmel is a good caring citizen and, to date, the only West Indian in *EastEnders* to be portrayed sympathetically. The others have been either weak, crooked or just downright nasty.'[11] Among the Afro-Caribbean and Asian respondents in this study, however, it is negative rather than positive impressions that have predominated.

Possible effect upon children

The possible effect of showing domestic violence to children was a matter of general concern. It was suggested that exposure could desensitise them to violence and that it would upset them because they could not understand it. In groups of women with experience of violence, there was the added worry that children's memories of violence encountered within their homes could be activated:

> In [my daughter's] case, it, the whole situation screwed her up so much that I wouldn't want her to watch that because I'd know that it would bring back what she was getting in the past now. And I think that would bring it back. ... She's nearly fourteen, so she's older. ... I mean, personally I wouldn't want her watching that because I think it would bring back something that now is receding into her past. Do you know what I mean? I would prefer her not, not to actually see it.
> [English white woman, with experience of violence]

There was a strong belief that children needed protection from viewing such violence. This was the most frequently cited reason for censorship in this area:

> Ah, but the thing is adults understand that these things do work out and that when two adults are shouting it's not going to end up in fisticuffs and somebody ending up in hospital. Whereas kids, they believe what they see on television. It might wash over them, but when they see a Disney one where the parents get divorced, they ... say, 'Oh, are you going to get divorced?'. ... You know that that's obviously going through their minds, that if it can happen on telly it can happen here. It'd worry me sick if mine had seen that.
> [English white middle-class woman, with no experience of violence]

Numerous respondents who had not experienced violence, then, were anxious that by tackling the issue of domestic violence, *EastEnders* could well create the wrong impression in the minds of children.

Value of the programme

Despite concerns expressed over the characterisation of the domestic violence in this episode of *EastEnders*, it was felt by most groups that the programme was of value. The portrayal of a social worker as a victim of domestic violence was noted as significant because it underlined the fact that this could happen to any woman, whatever her status in the community. Many of the groups pointed to the programme's potential for making contact with women who were being abused by their husbands. This point of view was widely acknowledged by women who had experienced violence, among whom it was additionally felt that the programme could educate those who did not fully understand the nature of such attacks:

> I think there's some people watching it, right, and it's actually happened to ... the wife in the house, right? It's just making her realise how it's happening to other women.

> Because a lot of them feel that they're on their own, when it's happening to them. 'This isn't happening to anybody else. Why am I getting this?' And there you are, it's on the telly, and ... you think you're on your own a lot of the time, and you don't want to discuss it with people.

> Well, I think it's not just the people that experience it. I think it shows the people who think it's just a flash in the pan that it really does happen.
> [Scottish white women, with experience of violence]

Despite being painful for many women to watch, it was argued that where there was a background of domestic violence, the programme could have taken a more explicitly positive stance against it. It was felt that more 'positive images' would have resulted if *EastEnders* had shown that this form of violence occurred outside the confines of a given class. Afro-Caribbean women argued that the programme was maintaining the notion that this was a working-class problem, not only through its characterisation, but also because they felt that *EastEnders* was targeted at the working-class. It was also argued that the programme did not give confidence to women in violent situations:

> What I'm saying is, people who ... haven't said to anybody ... 'God, I'm in the exact same position', they don't learn anything from it or feel the confidence the person should have or sort of gain. Something like that should be used to give people confidence who don't have the confidence to get out of the situation they are in. I think all it does is highlight it, I don't think it helps.
> [Scottish Asian woman, with experience of violence]

There was concern among all the groups of women with experience of violence, and within some of the others too, that *EastEnders* did not draw attention to agencies that could offer women support and advice. It was strongly argued that the programme should have shown Carmel taking such action, thus producing a more positive effect:

> And considering she never had anyone to talk to, I'm surprised they didn't want to show her picking up the phone and phoning a wife-battering centre and saying, 'Can you help me?' ... But she was just literally left there to get on with it, with no one around her.

She could have phoned up ... you know, someone independent [to] seek help, but she never. And it would have helped other women as well who [were] watching the programme at the time and they'd say 'Oh, I never thought of these', you know? They could've got on the phone about their husbands or their boyfriends.
[English Afro-Caribbean women, with no experience of violence]

It was also argued that a help-line telephone number should have been provided after the programme which might have encouraged women in such situations to seek help.

Among all groups there was some scepticism about the motives for the inclusion of domestic violence within the programme. For some it was seen as a way of attracting viewers:

In an idealistic world obviously you wouldn't use violence that way to get you to watch. But human nature being what it is, that's what brings people back, and they are running a business and they're using it.
[Scottish white middle-class woman, with no experience of violence]

They're just doing that to increase the ratings.
[English Afro-Caribbean woman, with experience of violence]

Others felt that the programme could actually encourage violent men to abuse their partners. For example, one woman was concerned that some men might regard such violence as justified:

Perhaps it was just that ... it was done in that particular way, with the woman who was about to be beaten actually being a professional woman and an articulate woman, and a woman with a degree of power. Not very much, but she was probably one of the more powerful women in that episode. With her actually being subjected to the abuse and the violence. There's men that I can think of that would've firstly said, 'Well, she deserved it', and feel justified in saying that. ... I also think that some of the men that I've known would feel, if it was raised, if it was actually spoken about afterwards – I actually think that it could make them violent ... I could just see him standing up and saying, 'You say a fucking word and you'll have it, right? Just shut your fucking face and get the kettle on, now.' And I can see it and I can hear it. ... And I can feel that man being so defensive about that.
[English white woman, with experience of violence]

Alternative viewpoints, however, suggested that the programme could demonstrate to violent men how destructive their violence is and the impact it could be having upon their children:

104

I think it's good to show on the telly, so people think when they do this sort of thing, violent men, so that they do realise when they're doing it. But they don't realise – the children – what they are suffering from what they are seeing.
[English Asian woman, with experience of violence]

Still others were concerned that the portrayal of the violence within the context of an entertainment programme might make it more acceptable to the general public:

I mean, I think it's good that programmes do address violence and things like that. But I don't know to what extent the fact that it's an ongoing series and people watch it, and it's very well known, actually makes that situation more acceptable. … I think it's right that these things should be shown, but whether they should be shown in the context of a programme that is actually for entertainment is another matter, because if it's showing this thing that it's entertainment, it becomes more acceptable. Therefore it's not actually addressed properly.
[English white woman, with experience of violence]

Despite these concerns, in all the groups it was felt that *EastEnders* provided useful insights into the nature of domestic violence, and for the most part, because the soap opera attracts many women viewers it was regarded as beneficial for the topic to be screened. Those with direct knowledge of male violence, however, frequently argued that a soap opera such as *EastEnders* could not deal adequately with the issue of violence in the home, being constrained by the need to please the audience and maintain high ratings, and that the documentary form would pursue the issue to much better effect:

Because the documentaries are, to me, are [where] … you're getting a true answer … the people are not play-acting. It's facts, and that's what you need to go on. Whereas the likes of a soap … they've got a script in front of them and it's how they portray the character they're playing. But the documentary, it's true to life.
[Scottish white woman, with experience of violence]

EastEnders, however, was widely considered a useful means of reaching women affected by such violence since they might be encouraged to realise that they were not alone in their experiences. It was also regarded as an issue relevant to all ethnic groups within Britain.

Conclusion
To conclude, the main findings show a strong identification with the woman portrayed as the victim of violence and a general rejection of the violence *per se*. The programme's realism was crucial in the groups'

evaluations of its overall value to potential audiences. For instance, it was argued that women who had experienced violence might therefore feel both vindicated and less isolated by a realistic portrayal of their circumstances. It was also suggested that men might realise the detrimental nature of violent behaviour and that the general public could become more knowledgeable of, and therefore more understanding about, domestic violence. The issue of ethnicity was highly salient, particularly for the Afro-Caribbean women for whom it evoked and reinforced negative racial stereotypes, which additionally would have the effect of clouding the central issue, namely male domestic violence.

There was some concern about explanations that excused men's violence and that blamed the victim, particularly among women with experience of violence. These reservations were given substantial relevance by the fact that precisely such victim-blaming ideas *were* expressed by some women, notably among those with no experience of violence. There were also worries about the possible effects upon children of viewing such violence. To a lesser extent, there was some anxiety about whether some men might actually feel vindicated in their violent actions as a result of viewing this programme, rather than be deterred from it. This related to much broader conceptions of male culture and how women might, in certain circumstances, represent a threat to masculinity. This theme was addressed more centrally in the responses to *Closing Ranks* and *The Accused*, as will be seen.

5

CLOSING RANKS

About the programme

Closing Ranks was broadcast by ITV in January 1988. A Zenith Production for Central Television, it was devised and directed by Roger Graef. Graef had previously produced for television the factual BBC fly-on-the-wall series *Police,* on the Thames Valley police force, which caused considerable controversy, particularly in respect of the police interrogation of an alleged rape victim. Graef has subsequently written about his investigations into the police in his book *Talking Blues.*

The making of *Police* and of *Operation Carter* – this time about Regional Crime Squad No. 5 – gave Graef considerable insight into the current state of policing in Britain. His investigations were conducted during the 1980s, a period when there was increasing controversy over such issues as police corruption and racism as well as major confrontations with the trade union movement (notably, the miners and print unions). This was also the decade that saw major inner-city riots and much concern in civil libertarian quarters about the political uses of the police by Mrs Thatcher's administrations.[1]

Published in 1989, Roger Graef's book, *Talking Blues,* was based upon interviews with 500 police officers in twelve different forces, and intended to offer 'an emotional mosaic' of their voices.[2] His film, *Closing Ranks,* picks up many of the themes of the book, although, of course, in fictionalised form. While it does not purport to be a drama-documentary as such, both the characterisation and elements of the plot can be seen as derived from the tales told by Graef's police informants – and their wives.

Graef's own view is that law enforcers in Britain have an embattled mentality in which 'the aura of violence, the imminence of it, informs much of police feeling about the job'.[3] In *Talking Blues,* he dismisses the view that it is 'rotten apples' in the force that behave exceptionally badly, pointing rather to a culture of violence among some officers and observing that 'it is group attitudes and lack of supervision' that foster this.[4] The behaviour depicted in the film is clearly linked to cases discussed in the book. In particular, there was a notorious case in Holloway in North London in 1983 when, for two years, officers covered up a brutal assault on a mixed-race group of youths, a case that resulted in action only after one of their number broke ranks and confessed.[5] In one section – actually headed 'Closing Ranks' – Graef makes the following comment:

The process of closing ranks presents PCs [police constables] with the greatest moral dilemma. The British ethos is all about people being loyal to their friends. The police culture reinforces that. The remoteness of senior officers throws young officers into the arms of their relief, their day-to-day working colleagues. Only the training instructors and such Olympian figures as the Commissioner or Chief Constable speak of the need to stand up for what they believe is right.[6]

Hence, from this point of view, the pressure is to conform and cover up, despite the misgivings of decent officers – precisely one of the plot lines in *Closing Ranks*. The other central theme in the drama, that of domestic violence, is also dealt with in the book. To put this in context, Graef writes that 'many police marriages are under permanent strain. The reasons are obvious: long, unpredictable hours, shift patterns that destroy normal social life, drinking after work, sexual distractions, money pressures and more.'[7] From the testimony of his informants, it would seem that 'violence in the home' is not unknown in police marriages, although it remains a taboo topic. Once again, although the particular scenario enacted in *Closing Ranks* is not to be found directly retailed in the book, the loss of intimacy it depicts, the empty sex lives, the wife's attempt to make a life for herself and her child and the physical destructiveness of the husband are all themes rehearsed in *Talking Blues*.

It is evident, therefore, that the film has its roots in the stresses and strains of the lives of police officers as told to its director, and in that sense it certainly has a documentary (and well documented) origin. According to publicity for *Closing Ranks*, 'The really disturbing aspect … is that all of the events in the film are based on real incidents.'[8] Graef himself said: 'I don't want people to think the film's central character, PC Rick Sneaden, is typical. He is a heavy individual, a bully who takes his stresses out on his wife. But the problems his attitudes produce for other coppers are typical.'[9] One critic has observed that, despite the drama's strengths, its central weakness is precisely the weight placed on the Sneaden character, using him 'to write the encyclopaedia of police crimes'.[10]

It was precisely this last point that was made by Roger Birch, Chief Constable of Sussex Police, in *Closing Ranks – A Discussion*, a special programme produced by Central Television that followed the transmission of the film. This treatment is rare for televised drama and was an indication of the considerable sensitivity of the programme's themes, demonstrating the broadcasters' evident desire to forestall hostile criticism for putting the police 'on trial by television'. The discussion was chaired by the well-known presenter Mavis Nicholson, and, apart from the Chief Constable of Sussex (then President of the Association of Chief Police Officers), those present were Roger Graef, another senior policeman, Deputy Assistant Commissioner Peter Winship of the London Metropolitan Police's Complaints Bureau, and Janine Turner, founder of 'Lifeline', a telephone counselling service for battered women and their partners.

What was most interesting about the discussion was that it tended to treat the film as though it were a documentary rather than a drama. The two police officers argued that the Sneaden character was a composite of bad qualities that were scattered across many individuals and that in any case current selection procedures were tending to screen out and eradicate such misfits from the force. They did stress, however, that the increasingly hostile environment that faced police officers did tend to produce a bunker mentality and some unprofessional behaviour, and to that extent they quite straightforwardly accepted the film's premise. Peter Winship argued that brutal officers must be ousted but that the police had to have sympathy for their domestic problems. Roger Birch drew attention to the growth of stress counselling to try to cope with the rigours of contemporary policing.

For her part, Janine Turner noted that police officers and their wives were increasingly among those who sought counselling. She maintained that to understand the roots of aggression against women at home it was essential to look at the early learning experiences of male perpetrators of violence, and noted the attraction to positions with uniforms and power of such personality types. She also underlined the fear of stigma of police officers regarding their domestic problems.

The televised discussion, then, in effect treated *Closing Ranks* as the starting-point for testing out documentary claims, with the fictionalised narrative being almost entirely ignored. Roger Graef's own observation that the film should be treated as a 'cautionary tale', and his recurrent appeals to his own research, underlined the documentary origins of the storyline. Whether *Closing Ranks* should be read as a drama or as a documentary (or as a drama-documentary) bears closely upon audience perceptions of the film's credibility and realism, which, as we shall see, were rather divided.

What the respondents saw

The central figure of *Closing Ranks* is PC Rick Sneaden, a 'rotten apple' of the police force, who leads his colleagues into corruption through an act of intentional violence. A tall, thick-set man in his early thirties, Sneaden has no respect for authority and a very low opinion of women. He is racist, violent, and has no regard for attempts to treat the public with either diplomacy or sympathy. At home Sneaden proves to be no better. He regards his wife as an instrument for sex who should put his needs before her own. Inasmuch as his wife does not conform to his ideals, she is forced to suffer both mentally and physically. In the end Sneaden's wife Shirley, also in her early thirties, is subjected to the ultimate degradation when Sneaden rapes her. The couple have a young son, Billy, of ten or eleven years of age who emulates Sneaden's attitudes to Shirley, showing every sign of developing into a copy-book image of his father.

The play opens dramatically at night in London when a group of three CID officers in an unmarked police car observe, give chase to, and arrest a man for committing armed robbery. The scene cuts to a long shot of a block of flats. Inside, a small boy wearing an American football helmet sleeps huddled up on a settee; his mother looks at him; near to tears, she shakes her head. Following a brief scene during which the CID officers, returning to their station, harass a group of Rastafarians on the street, the woman picks up her sleeping son and takes him to bed. As she does so, she bursts out sobbing. Sneaden, in the police car, suddenly remembers that he has forgotten his son's birthday.

At home, as Sneaden scavenges through the remains of his son's birthday meal, his wife enters. Sneaden swings round and she sharply jumps as if terrified. Sneaden explains he thought she 'was a bloody burglar', and apologises for missing his son's birthday. His wife Shirley looks upset. Sneaden dismissively enquires what is wrong. Shirley hesitantly replies that she has come to a decision, she wants to leave her husband and take her son with her. Sneaden is totally unsympathetic and questions the legitimacy of her taking his son away. Shirley, holding back her tears, tells Sneaden that she doesn't see how she and her son can be happy living in London, that they will leave, and that he can get a transfer to another force if he wants to go with them.

The scene immediately shifts to a rural landscape and semi-detached house on an estate. Shirley is excited by having a garden, but for his part Sneaden describes it as a 'bloody mess'. Shirley responds: 'Don't you know nothing about nature, planting the little seeds, the birds and the bees?' Sneaden's comment that 'It's been such a long time, Shirley, I've forgotten about it, maybe you should remind me', signals his sexual frustration.

Sneaden attends an interview with his new superintendent, who takes an obvious dislike to his cockiness. In the police club, Sneaden holds forth to his new colleagues with tales of policing in London when he is told that his wife is asking for him at the front desk.

Shirley and her son could not get a bus back from the school, resulting in a long walk home. She has broken the heel on her shoe and asks her husband how long he is going to be. Sneaden tells her that he is now on a case. Realising that he is lying, Shirley observes, 'A case of beer, was it?' Sneaden gives her the taxi fare home and tells her to 'Clean yourself up, coming down here like a bleeding gippo, Jesus God.' Shirley buys a pair of wellingtons and an old bicycle with the taxi fare. To a cheerful piano solo, Shirley rides her way through the rural setting.

Walking the beat at night with his new partner Albert, Sneaden asks about the local 'crumpet situation' and enquires about a WPC. Albert's tentative reply indicates that he is having a relationship with her; he reluctantly admits that she wants to get married and for him to take exams for a promotion. Sneaden laughingly tells Albert to 'give her the elbow' if she aggravates him about promotion.

Following night duty, Sneaden sleeps as Shirley talks to a neighbour while she cleans the windows outside. The neighbour enquires how they are settling in. Shirley comments that as long as Rick is happy then she is happy. As the neighbour goes indoors, she tells Shirley to pop round for a chat because 'moving never solved any of my problems'.

Shirley visits the local doctor to enquire about a job vacancy. She successfully persuades him to employ her.

Following a further night's duty, during which he harasses some local men over the unroadworthy state of their car, Sneaden returns home. Shirley, in her dressing gown, cooks his breakfast. When she tells him there is no bacon and that 'eggs will have to do', he retorts, 'Oh well, yeah, yeah, sure, eggs will have to fucking do, won't they?' When Shirley gives him coffee without milk, Sneaden gets increasingly angry and with his face inches from hers, he yells, 'Look, you! I've just come in after being out all night with the naffing zombies and you tell me there's no milk, there's no bloody bacon, you've given the milk which I paid for to the naffing cat.' Sneaden finds the cat, grabs it and throws it outside. Shirley protests, saying the cat is Billy's, but Sneaden retorts, 'Listen, you, cats are for pigging poofters and little girls, right, got it? Now, that is my son and I will buy him a dog, right?' Billy sits on the stairs listening.

Another night duty and Sneaden and Albert are again out on the streets. Sneaden tells Albert that Shirley has a job. Complaining that the money she earns is not enough to feed the cat, and that she does not now have time to do the shopping, Sneaden remarks, 'There's only one job a woman's good for, know what I mean?' They come to a school vandalised by local children. When inside, they receive a call from the station reporting a domestic violence incident. Sneaden replies on his radio that they are investigating an intruder at the school, which is not true. Sneaden tells Albert: 'Listen, domestics are poison, my son, pure poison, I'm telling you.'

Shirley, working with the doctor, asks after his family, and learns that his wife and daughter were killed in a car crash. She is sympathetic and understanding when the doctor tells her that sometimes he finds things difficult as she also has 'bad days', which 'are the story of my life'.

Sneaden, Shirley and Billy go shopping together on one of his days off. It is an unusually happy day for the family. At home, decorating, Sneaden tries to persuade Shirley to have 'a little bit of heaven upstairs'. Shirley is resistant, however, insisting that they finish the work. Sneaden suggests that they go out together for the evening to a restaurant. Shirley looks pleased at this, though when he suggests 'an early night' she becomes tense, but concedes.

As Sneaden and Shirley are about to go out, the telephone rings. Despite her entreaties he answers it and then says he has to go to an armed siege. Sneaden drives off and Shirley begins to cry.

Sneaden takes control of the situation at the siege, an incident involving a man holding his mother at knife-point. While the man's attention

111

is distracted, he and Albert enter the back of the house. They surprise the assailant and Sneaden wrestles with him while Albert, at his behest, administers two severe punches to his abdomen. As the mother pleads with the two policemen not to hit her son, Sneaden observes: 'See what I mean about domestics, Albert, they are poison.'

Shirley is asleep in bed when Rick gets back home. 'Are you awake, darling?' he gruffly enquires, intentionally trying to wake her. He tries to kiss her, but Shirley tells him to 'leave it out'. She lies with her back to him, with her eyes open.

On Sneaden's day off, he takes Shirley and Billy out for a drive in the country. Shirley points to the cows in the fields, but Sneaden sarcastically remarks that they are not cows but sheep. Billy takes sides with his father, treating his mother as childish and stupid. As they drive along, Shirley notices an elderly woman she has met at the doctor's surgery and asks Sneaden to pull over. Setting up a CND stall by the roadside with friends, the woman comes over, greeting Sneaden with 'You're a civil servant, I understand.' He replies, 'Well, not exactly' and drives off. Shirley is angry, but Sneaden tells her to be careful whom she befriends in future: 'Listen, Shirley, I know what those women are like, a lot of bloody loony lefty lesbos ... what they need is a good stiff dose of ... housework, that's what they need.'

Shirley and Billy go ice-skating. He helps her into the middle of the rink but then speeds off, leaving her stranded. A woman bumps into Shirley. They sit chatting and the woman invites Shirley to a CND demonstration at an air-base, but Shirley explains that she's married to a policeman. The woman asks: 'Does he bring his work home or something?' Shirley replies, 'He is his work.'

The action cuts to scenes of police riot training for the CND demonstration. During the training Sneaden steps out of line and kicks one of the 'rioters' in the ribs.

Sneaden arrives home that evening wearing his riot helmet. Shirley comments on the dangers of nuclear weapons, showing him a leaflet the CND woman had given her. Grabbing the leaflet, Sneaden shouts that she shouldn't have anything to do with the CND women. Shirley goes into the kitchen and cries.

At the air-base, Sneaden and his support group colleagues sit in the police van playing cards. Shirley arrives concealed under a scarf and a large anorak. The CND women are pleased to see her. Sneaden gets increasingly frustrated and bored in the van. Two women taunt the policemen in the van and Sneaden swears and threatens them.

The support group are called to investigate a reported intrusion into the air-base. As the van speeds away with siren blaring, Sneaden catches sight of Shirley. 'That's my fucking wife,' he shouts.

In the speeding police van a young graduate sergeant starts singing 'Here we go, here we go, here we go', and is joined by others. One policeman, Walter, looks on disgusted. Sneaden bangs the roof in time to the song. They find an old painted ambulance, with a young 'hippy' man fixing one of its wheels. Sneaden tells the man to move the van and when he replies that it cannot be moved, Sneaden grabs him and smashes one of the side windows with his truncheon. Albert throws belongings out of the vehicle and destroys a guitar. The hippy tries to stop this and Albert punches him in the stomach, at which point the man pulls out a knife. Both Sneaden and Albert pound the man with their truncheons. Eventually the sergeant intervenes. The man falls to the ground and Sneaden tells him he's under arrest.

The hippy is examined by the doctor in Shirley's presence. The doctor realises that the man has been unnecessarily beaten by the police, and submits a complaint to the local superintendent. Shirley discovers that her husband was one of the perpetrators of the attack.

At the station, the group of policemen, led on by Sneaden, fabricate evidence. There is little the superintendent can do to challenge their story as Sneaden forces the men to stick together, warning them of the consequences of breaking ranks. Walter reluctantly supports the story to save the younger officers' jobs.

Shirley is painting when Sneaden returns home drunk after a party at the police club. 'If it ain't the enemy within,' he taunts her, leaning back against the wall. Shirley tells him she's just finishing the painting. 'Of course you are, 'cos you didn't have time to do it this afternoon, did you, eh? You was too busy because you was with your scumbag dyke friends, weren't you, Shirl?' Shirley, standing on a stepladder turns to Rick saying, 'And I bet I know what you was doing, you was out giving somebody a pasting.' She carries on painting. Sneaden protests: 'He tried to kill me. *He* tried to kill *me*.' 'No, Rick, you did 'im over while his wife and kiddy looked on. ... What do you think I am, some thick tart that cooks your dinner?' Shirley replies. Sneaden argues, 'You have got me wrong, Shirl', and pulls her from the stepladder. Sneaden grabs her hair and bangs her head severely against the wall several times while she screams 'You bastard'. He then takes his trousers down and rapes her from behind. A tall shelving unit crashes to the floor and Sneaden trips, dragging Shirley down with him. He grips her with one hand by the neck pressing her back to the wall as he squeezes her throat. Shirley gasps for air and crumples to the floor. Sneaden, kneeling on the floor, looks at her, gets up, slaps her affectionately on the face, saying, 'Come on, you, beddy-byes.' Shirley is left in a sobbing, shaking heap.

Sneaden, in the bathroom, looks at himself in the mirror. Stuck on the mirror is a picture of the couple, embracing happily, and a separate picture of their son Billy. Sneaden stares at himself, the camera moves into an extreme close-up of his face in the mirror. A sombre haunting piano solo plays and the picture fades.

How the respondents reacted

This television drama was of particular interest to the research team as a rare example of the portrayal of a police officer abusing his wife. In contrast to *EastEnders,* it dealt with the issue of domestic violence within a single programme, as well as with the uses of violence by those in authority in society. Additionally, as the drama portrayed a marital rape, and violence in excess of that demonstrated in the *EastEnders* episode, it thereby opened up somewhat broader scope for discussion.

Closing Ranks presented an extensive range of issues: for instance, women's place in the home and in society, the influence of a violent husband upon his son's attitudes, police reactions to reports of domestic violence, and corruption and violence within the police force. The programme portrayed not only violence in the domestic setting, but also a case of police violence against an innocent male member of the public, and introduced the issue of police attitudes to demonstrations and non-violent public protest.

Viewing groups

Four groups viewed *Closing Ranks*, two of women with no experience of violence and two of women with such experience. Two of the groups were based in Scotland, the other two in England. Of the groups of women with no experience of violence, one was drawn from middle-class women, the other from the working class. Difficulties in recruiting middle-class women with experience of violence meant that no such women viewed this programme. Possibly because of the constitution of the groups and the substance of *Closing Ranks,* group discussion often reflected the importance of class in shaping interpretations. Therefore, in contrast to the presentation of findings for the other programmes, we explicitly consider the importance of class as well as the significance of experience of violence in determining reactions. Further, as all the groups consisted of white women, we could not investigate how ethnicity might affect reactions to *Closing Ranks*. Of the twenty-four women concerned, only two had seen *Closing Ranks* when it was originally televised.

All of the women with no experience of violence and 92% of those who had been victims of violence judged *Closing Ranks* to be 'violent' or 'very violent' (see Figure VIII, Reactions to *Closing Ranks*). Although most women felt that it was disturbing, a small number of women did not react to it in this way. The vast majority of women (68% with experience and 80% without) found the programme 'offensive'. Only a small percentage of women with experience of violence rated the film as 'exciting' and 'entertaining', and only a slightly greater percentage of women without experience felt the same (see Figure VIII).

A third of the women from both categories told us that they would not have chosen to watch *Closing Ranks* if they 'had seen it advertised in a newspaper or on television', primarily because it was too violent, disturbing and/or close to their own experiences. Yet all but one of the women who viewed *Closing Ranks* said that similar television dramas should be made.

114

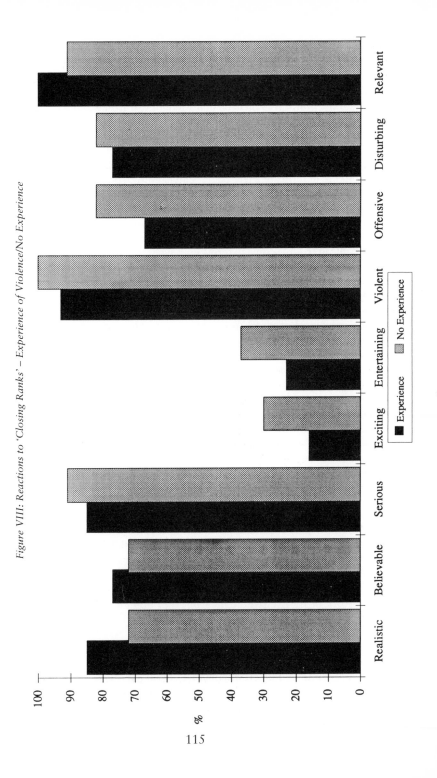

Figure VIII: Reactions to 'Closing Ranks' – Experience of Violence/No Experience

Women with no experience of violence

Approximately 70% of women with no experience of violence judged *Closing Ranks* to be 'realistic' and 'believable' (see Figure VIII). However, in group discussions, middle-class women resisted the idea that the picture of the police was realistic and found it disturbing and narrowly conceived. They began from a position of sympathy for the police and a consequent tendency to discount the negative portrayal offered by *Closing Ranks*. For their part, however, the working-class women were far more inclined to judge the programme as 'realistic', although at times talking in terms of there being 'bad eggs' or 'rotten apples' in the force. They found the idea of police cover-ups entirely plausible.

Middle-class women stressed how shocking they had found the programme and tended to see *Closing Ranks* as overdoing its various depressing themes, as well as expressing scepticism about its ability to help people in trouble come to terms with what was happening to them. At times, they were particularly concerned about the portrayal of the police.

Discussions of Shirley revealed that, so far as the working-class women were concerned, she was in a difficult predicament and she had made a great deal of effort to escape from it. However, she was perceived as a flawed character, as 'going about in a trance', with weaknesses as well as strengths. In one bit of folk wisdom it was observed, 'Move to a different area does not solve the problems, though, does it?', evincing agreement on these lines: 'The problems go with you; the problem's your husband; he's the big one.'

This view of Shirley was echoed by middle-class women, who dismissively evaluated her as 'half-soaked', and this was linked to her class position:

> I'm not saying she's soft, I'm just saying she's lower intelligence. There's something about her ... you wouldn't look at her and say she'd been to grammar school and university. Just the way they portrayed her in very, very high-heeled shoes, very tight skirts, no matter how they looked. ... Everything was made to make her that sort of working class ... it was just that image they gave her. Then he was as well. They both sort of came from that sort of class, where the grandparents are in Sheffield, the men are men, and the women are women. And women cook and mend clothes, and men go out and work or they're redundant – but they don't do the housework. It's that sort of working-class environment where there are two different worlds if you like, and they don't cross. And you have your man's dinner down on the table when he comes in or you're in trouble and you're a bad wife. You do what they tell you to do.
> [English white middle-class woman, with no experience of violence]

Her mentality, and that of Sneaden, the violent and corrupt husband, were thus interpreted through the framework of class differences understood as cultural differences. By contrast, working-class women brought a sense of familiarity to the kind of household in which Shirley lived. The culminating violence against her was seen as already implicit in her daily relationship with Sneaden, who was described as aggressive and intimidating when he did not get his way – for instance, when there was no milk or bacon for his breakfast. Working-class women felt that it would be rational to take this on board and simply avoid situations that might cause such domestic tension. These perceptions were shared by middle-class women, who talked of Sneaden as a 'macho man' beset with self-doubt. In a very similar characterisation, he was described by working-class women as a 'chauvinistic' male. Within the household, women from both classes agreed, the couple's son was being set a very negative example by his father and would grow up reproducing the established pattern of violence against women:

It goes back … I'm saying, 'Look Donna, don't get married and don't do this, and don't do that. Have a good time. They treat you bad – get shot of them. Don't put up with any snash.' Now that's the kind of thing I've instilled in her early, so that she'll not make the same mistakes I made. Like my mother went to work, she came in and my dad's dinner was there – my dad slept on the couch! My mother went to work, she went and got the messages. … But the old values are still there. It's new when we're starting to say, 'Oh no, that's not good enough.'
[Scottish white working-class woman, with no experience of violence]

Despite some agreement, views of Shirley varied as between the two classes. For the working-class women, she was seen as a gaudy dresser (and therefore not a serious person). However, at the same time she had gone out and found herself a job with the doctor, judged a highly sympathetic male because he was kind and gentle. Shirley also showed her mettle, it was held, by going to the demonstration despite Sneaden's veto:

She had a right to participate if she wanted to. But I quite understand from a policeman's point of view … that it's all right as long as it's a peaceful demonstration. … If my husband was a policeman and I went to a demonstration, I would go, I wouldn't necessarily get involved in any violence – don't believe in violence – violence doesn't get anybody anywhere, but if I wanted to go on a demonstration [I would], irrespective of whether my husband was a police officer or not.
[Scottish white working-class woman, with no experience of violence]

Some respondents also thought that Shirley showed a lot of determination in trying to change her life, beginning with the pressure on Sneaden to move out of London into a country force:

> But she was trying to make a life for herself, I mean, she was taking her son roller-skating, something she'd never done before in her life. That was something new for her. Then she went to that demonstration because it was something she wanted to do, not because of what he wanted her to do, she done it for herself. ... And she got herself a job. It was nothing to do with him she done it. ... And she went out and bought her son a cat because he wanted it. Not because the husband wanted it. He said he'll get the boy a dog because cats are for girls and poofs. ... Because she did it all for her and her son. And that's how it goes. You've got to work for yourself or you're never going to get anywhere.
> [Scottish white working-class woman, with no experience of violence]

However, the problem for Shirley was that she could only assert herself so far before she was trampled on in the most humiliating form possible – by being raped at home by her husband. Working-class women pointed out that for women to have ambition was a good thing. Sneaden's sense of resentment at Shirley's wish to better herself and her pressure on him to better himself were cited as causes of his violence towards her.

But the discussions by both working-class and middle-class women focused upon Sneaden's evident sexual frustration as a possible factor in the rape. A typical sentiment was:

> During the film it was any time he wanted to have a relationship with her she was too tired. ... Obviously he was frustrated, looking at it from his point of view. He thought, 'Right, I'm having it' sort of thing. I still think it's wrong, it doesn't matter – it's still rape.
> [Scottish white working-class woman, with no experience of violence]

In the reactions of middle-class women, there was a definite tendency to see Shirley's denial of sex to her husband as more of a *justification* for his behaviour than as simply an *explanation*. There was also some condemnation of her attendance at the anti-nuclear demonstration in disobedience of his orders. Nevertheless, there was no doubt that the rape had been used as a way of degrading and disciplining Shirley:

> He'd come in expecting to have a big row with her, get her to say she was sorry, and then she turns the tables on him. And the look of disgust on her face, he just knew he was in the wrong, and he couldn't get out of it any other way than to degrade her in the only way – possibly the worst way. It also stopped her power over him.

He'd done the thing to her that she'd been keeping him off for months, and he did it in the worst way possible.
[English white middle-class woman, with no experience of violence]

Middle-class women also made an excursus into conceptions of male and female sexual pleasure, in which Shirley's refusal was understood as rooted in 'most women's' desire to have sex in the context of a relationship, whereas as one group member put it, 'Men can have sex with a doormat if it looked attractive enough, as a release.' In this context, Shirley was seen as trying to exercise control through denial.

Overall, there was a tendency for the working-class women to view Shirley more sympathetically than the middle-class women, although not without reservations. Middle-class women found it difficult to identify with Shirley and the situations depicted, and it was this distancing effect which probably accounted for the great measure of ambivalence about the gravity of the rape when compared with the use of arbitrary violence by the police.

Indeed, it was this corrupt use of police power that occasioned most discussion after the question of sexual violence. Working-class women thought the depiction of the police cover-up was realistic. Although accepted by middle-class women as well, this notion was a good deal more troubling for them.

For both groups, the antipathy of the police to both hippies and female peace-campaigners was comprehensible and plausible. Some working-class women observed that Greenham Common 'type' women were often dirty, smelled, and such demonstrations attracted those who broke the law. As one woman put it:

To be suspicious of them and that because, well – we're going back a few years ago when they first started – they were, like, camping outside places like Helensburgh, and that, in the Faslane, and living like gypsies. I know that's a bad word to say, but they were living in tents and what have you, weren't getting bathed and they were, having, like, drugs and things among them. So it put the police off.
[Scottish white working-class woman, with no experience of violence]

In similar vein, the police's view of hippies was seen as understandable, without thereby justifying any violence that might be meted out.

In this context, middle-class women spoke of Sneaden as a man who enjoyed violence, and who in some respects also had the redeeming quality of bravery, shown by his tackling of an armed man in the siege scene. However, overall, he was viewed as a flawed character who had no respect for either 'deviants' or for women. Both his masculinity and his class identity were seen as threatened by middle-class anti-nuclear campaigners. As one middle-class woman observed: 'When they come across a better class or educated person they feel quite inferior to them and, rather than feel inferior, they get aggressive.'

To sum up, for working-class women with no experience of violence, *Closing Ranks* was a realistic portrayal both of how the police function and of marital relations. Underlying much of the discussion was a fundamentally disenchanted view of gender relations, and a broadly sympathetic identification with the victim's predicament. There were no reservations about such dramas being shown; on the contrary, the programme's perceived connectedness with lived experience was seen as offering something of value to those women in the television audience who might be experiencing such difficulties.

By contrast, middle-class women with no experience of violence took a broadly negative view of the programme, which they felt was aiming to shock, and which attacked treasured views of the police and of how relations between the sexes ought to be conducted. Although it was highly regarded as a piece of compelling drama, there was little belief in the value of *Closing Ranks* as a help to women in difficulty and also a considerable resistance to explicitness in sex and violence.

Women with experience of violence
Women with experience of violence offered strong reactions to *Closing Ranks*; almost all of them told us that they took the drama 'seriously' or 'very seriously' (see Figure VIII), and they offered immediate reactions to the drama in terms of their personal experiences. Anger against the Sneaden character and his treatment of Shirley was well to the fore. In the group of white Scottish women with experience of violence, Sneaden was denounced as 'a bigoted sadistic pig', terms which commanded widespread assent. For their part, members of the English group felt the play was very accurate, that it 'hit the nail on the head' and therefore produced a 'downer'. Because of its depressing effect, it was observed, such a drama was easier to watch in a group setting than alone. In both groups, there was the shock of recognition and identification with the problematic central relationship.

Around 45% of women with experience of violence considered domestic violence the main theme of *Closing Ranks*, with another 18% citing family relations. Twenty-seven per cent cited police corruption as the dominant theme. By contrast, whereas 80% of women with no experience of violence cited police corruption as the main theme, only 10% cited domestic violence. Around three-quarters of women who had experience of violence stated that they found these themes to be both 'realistic' and 'believable', with all of them indicating that the story of *Closing Ranks* was relevant to everyday life (see Figure VIII).

In discussion, women focused first upon the police, with which all had had some contact. For the Scottish women with experience of violence, the play was highly realistic, given that at least some police officers, in their experience, were capable of behaving in that way. For instance, cases of people being kicked about and slapped 'in the back of the van' were referred to; in one instance a Scottish woman with alleged experience of police violence spoke of making a complaint about it to the Procurator Fiscal. The idea of 'using the uniform' to get away with assaults on the public was generally accepted as a fact of life. However, in both groups it was also made clear that by no means all police could be tarred with this brush and that some group members had had very positive experiences of being helped, as in this case:

> Don't get me wrong when I says it was spot on. I didn't mean by the whole force. I wasn't talking about them all, because before I moved through to [this town] I came from [a village], and I couldn't praise the police in [village] up any higher than what I did. I mean, they were really good, and they stuck by me and done everything for me in [town]. So I'm not saying they're all like that, but the ones that are, that film is spot on.
> [Scottish white woman, with experience of violence]

There was an unusual twist, however, in one instance, when an English woman with experience of violence talked of how she had been helped by a local policeman: 'Without his help really, I don't think I would have made a stand and stayed there, even though I'd made the effort and gone home.' However, in a revelation that brought together both the themes of the play, she disclosed that this helpful policeman was himself alleged to beat his wife.

The programme was perceived as having two central messages among the women with experience of violence. First, that the director was attempting to show the nature of police corruption, and second that *any male* could be involved in domestic violence, irrespective of his background, hence the choice of an authority figure. As regards the second theme, one point made repeatedly and with force was that violent behaviour by men towards women could be transmitted from generation to generation: here the point of focus was the upbringing that Sneaden was giving to his son, and the inability of Shirley to make any serious inroads in disciplining him and offering an alternative model.

Both the principal themes – police corruption and domestic violence – were intertwined in discussion, but it was the experience of the latter which provided the principal framework of interpretation. This is perhaps best conveyed by illustrating the vivid expression of fear of male violence that was encountered. One Scottish woman spoke thus of her terror:

> Women in the refuge, we will band together. Now I'm terrified of my man. If my man suddenly appeared I would crap it, I really would. But the fact that I knew there were other women, that I can maybe stand back, the other women would take my place, if you get my meaning. The same thing would happen if it was somebody else – if it was [Joan's] man, I'd make sure [Joan] was out the road and I'd

121

go in there, no fear. But your own man is entirely different. That fear is there of that one particular man.
[Scottish white woman, with experience of violence]

And another gave this insight into the tensions that arise prior to experiencing a physical assault:

It was never the beatings that bothered me, it was the roaring. And he'd keep me awake for hours ... going through the house, and that. Stereos getting broke on your head, and all that. That was what got to me, not the hitting. Once the hits came I knew I was getting it over quickly.
[Scottish white woman, with experience of violence]

In this kind of context, the breakfast scene, where Shirley fails to provide what Sneaden wants, was seen as simply part of a relationship in which the woman is tortured by continuous aggressive demands by her husband. There was an extreme sensitivity to the nuances of what might, or might not, really happen in such a situation. For instance, the Scottish women with experience of violence believed that Shirley would have been battered. The English women with such experience observed that, in her general position, she would have made sure that there was milk and bacon available for fear of the consequences.

Table 4: Relating to Characters in 'Closing Ranks'

	Violence			
	Experience		No experience	
Relate to characters	N	%	N	%
yes	9	69	4	36
no	4	31	7	64
Total	13	100%	11	100%

Yule's Q= .72

Table 5: Relating to Situations in 'Closing Ranks'

	Violence			
	Experience		No experience	
Relate to situations	N	%	N	%
yes	10	77	4	36
no	3	23	7	64
Total	13	100%	11	100%

Yule's Q= .70

It is not surprising, then, that the women with experience of violence who saw the drama stated that they could identify with Shirley and the situations of domestic violence and mental cruelty portrayed in *Closing Ranks*. As one Scottish woman with experience of violence observed, it was not simply the situation with which she could identify so much as the way 'she was feeling, aye, you know, saying try this and they'd move here, it'll get better and all that. Or if we start talking, try to talk, – [the man] he'll just roar in your face.' Around 70% of the women with experience of violence indicated that they could identify with the characters depicted in *Closing Ranks,* whereas only 36% of women with no experience expressed similar sentiments. Table 4 presents these results and the Yule's Q of .72 reflects a strong association between experience of violence and the ability to relate to the characters presented in the programme. These results must be assessed in the light of the fact that a majority of the women in the groups with experience of violence had been the victims of domestic assaults and/or mental cruelty, coercion and aggression. Significantly these women also related to the scenes of domestic violence and mental cruelty portrayed in *Closing Ranks.*

The strong association between experience of violence and the ability to relate to situations portrayed in *Closing Ranks* is reflected in the data presented in Table 5 and the Yule's Q of .70. Such results help explain the very nuanced level of interpretation which was brought to bear upon Shirley's actions by women with experience of violence, by contrast with that of the women with no experience of violence. For instance, discussion in the Scottish group indicated that the character would have been too afraid to go to the CND rally. However, in an interesting split of opinion, some argued that she was trying to assert herself despite her fear – as one woman put it: 'trying to keep a bit of yourself'. In the English group it was thought that attendance at the CND rally was broadly realistic and that Shirley should have tried to form relationships with the anti-nuclear campaigners who could have helped her. Indeed, it was precisely Sneaden's wish to impede the emergence of such solidarity that was seen as partly motivating his hostility to these women. Having one's wider friendships wrecked by a jealous and therefore rude husband or boyfriend was cited as part of the normal experience of such violent relationships:

> I used to sort of make excuses to my friends not to come round. Because they'd come round and he'd come in, and I'd be having a cup of tea ... and he'd be in the kitchen saying things like 'These people, haven't they got homes of their own?', and 'Don't they ever do any housework? Do they spend all day sitting in other people's houses, drinking tea?' I got so embarrassed. ...
> [English white woman, with experience of violence]

Members of the English group of women with experience of violence felt that Shirley should have stood up for herself to a greater extent, especially in the interests of her son. However, as is illustrated by the above quotation there was great understanding, based on direct experience, for her inability simply to leave such an untenable situation. In commenting on this, frequent reference was made to group members' own situations:

> *Speaker 1:* It wasn't that I wanted to go home, it was just that I couldn't cope with the whole thing, you know? It wasn't really that I wanted to go home, 'cos I didn't. No, I didn't want to, 'cos I couldn't cope with everything.
>
> *Researcher:* You were saying you think she should have stood up for herself more?
>
> *Speaker 2:* I think she should've done.
>
> *Speaker 3:* Yeah, but we don't. I lived with a man for ten years, and everyone thought it was a wonderful marriage. You don't say 'I'm not standing this' for years.
>
> *Speaker 1:* I put up with having his girlfriend living in my spare room for ten months. You don't stand up and say – you say you would, and you say people ought to, but you don't. It takes something to really get you like 'This is it. I can't take it'.
>
> *Speaker 4:* Suddenly you think, 'What the hell's happened to me?'
>
> *Speaker 3:* There's got to be a better life.
>
> [English white women, with experience of violence]

In similar vein, as with the women with no experience of violence, it was widely noted that Shirley was portrayed as finding Sneaden sexually repellent. However, while women with no experience of violence felt that Shirley was unsympathetic to her husband's sexual needs, women with experience of violence regarded her behaviour as an entirely comprehensible reaction to the situation. As one expressed it:

> They've put you through all this hell and then they come to you and they want sex off you. Oh, no! ... no, no. Mentally and physically they've made your life miserable and they can come to you and expect to have sex with you. No way!
>
> [Scottish white woman, with experience of violence]

The violent use of sexual power was perceived as central to the Sneaden character. In both groups of women with experience of violence, but particularly the English one, it was possible to discern an underlying rejection of male power – men in general being seen as repressive – which acted as a counterweight to the suffering that these women had undergone at men's hands. This was coupled with the view that traditional male-female relations reproduce themselves from one generation to the next. In this connection, the Sneaden character's routine degradation of his wife in front of their son was seen as part of such a pattern.

Turning to the discussion of Sneaden, we find that his conception of maleness was interpreted as requiring the domination of women.

Women with experience of violence saw in the gentle and kind doctor, for whom Shirley worked, a counterpoint to the macho male image. Indeed, they also indulged in the fantasy of wishing that Shirley would leave Sneaden and marry the doctor, thereby effecting a happy ending.

For the Scottish group, Sneaden was seen as obsessed with policing because it gave him power – such as the extreme violence that he could use against the hippy. One member summed up his view of women as follows:

> I think he expected women – their place was in the house at the cooker, at the kitchen sink. They had no other rights at all. That was their rights, if you like, lying on their back, and cleaning their house. And to me that was his attitude.
> [Scottish white woman, with experience of violence]

This instrumental view was linked to his inability to tolerate any challenges to his authority. Another Scottish woman with experience of violence put the point across with wry humour :

> When she was painting the wall and he brought through a cup of tea and he put a wee drink in it for her and then he put his arms round her, and he was whispering about going up the stair, and kissing, and that, she dented his ego when she said, 'No. Paint the house first.'
> [Scottish white woman, with experience of violence]

In short, Sneaden's relationship with others in his family was described as poor, with little communication and no spontaneous expressions of affection – including towards his son. It is precisely this rigid masculinity which makes him threatened by Shirley's desire to be independent, particularly by her going out to find a job.

The violence exerted during the rape scene was unanimously seen as far worse than that used during the other episode of major violence portrayed in the drama, the police attack on the hippy during the peace demonstration. A common view was this:

> And there again the beating of the hippy was uncalled for, but the bruises would've healed. ... But the rape never leaves you ... I mean, you can put it to the back of your mind, but there's always something ... it flashes, and you've got it back – and it's gory ...
> [Scottish white woman, with experience of violence]

The scene was found to be particularly upsetting:

> *Speaker 1:* I mean, after the violence, what stuck out to me was the fact that he slapped [her] on the face and says, 'Beddy byes'.

Speaker 2:	Says 'Come to bed.' Yeah, that really made me go 'Oh'.
Speaker 1:	As if they'd just made love, you know what I mean? ... I think that was too much for me.
	[English white women, with experience of violence]

Nevertheless, despite the distress caused to women who had experienced violence, there was only one woman who said such programmes should not be made. For most women, there was an emphatic desire that such dramas be shown because of their potential educative value. Indeed, some argued that *Closing Ranks* was insufficiently graphic in its portrayal of the impact upon women of having to live with a violent male. For a number of the women who participated in this study, it had taken up to one or two decades for them even to begin to talk about their experiences.

Conclusion

Reactions to the drama were largely divided according to whether or not women had experience of violence. Those with such experience were far more inclined to regard *Closing Ranks* as realistic and believable. Additionally, these women strongly identified with Shirley and her predicament. Women with no experience of violence were far less able to identify with this character and the situations in which she was portrayed. However, of the two viewing groups of women with no experience of violence, the middle-class women demonstrated a determined resistance to the drama's presentation of the police force. In effect, they denied the possibility that the forces of law and order could be flawed by corrupt and violent practices, and this led to a largely unsympathetic view of *Closing Ranks*. Members of the working-class group did not take this stance.

There are two points of particular note concerning differences between male and female cultures, a theme that emerged strongly in the discussions of *Closing Ranks*. One concerned the widespread view that Sneaden's dissatisfaction lay partly in a sexual frustration due to his inability to fulfil Shirley's need for a loving relationship. The second was the argument that the kind of violent relationship that Sneaden had with Shirley was bound to reproduce itself by virtue of the negative example that he set his son. Finally, and this is a point that also emerges in responses to *The Accused*, there were strong undertones of romantic wish-fulfilment for a clear-cut ending to the story. Some wanted Shirley to marry the doctor; others wanted simply to know that she had left the unhappy marriage and made a new life for herself; and yet another wish was for Sneaden to get his just desserts.

6

THE ACCUSED

About the film

The Accused (Jonathan Kaplan/Paramount Pictures, 1988) has occasioned considerable controversy, not least because it 'negotiates a fine line between social concern, feminism and exploitation'.[1] The charge of exploitation has been levelled against the lengthy scene of gang rape, which is extremely explicit. Much film criticism has focused on the way in which the audience in the cinema – or at home in front of the television, since the film is available on video and has been screened in Britain via satellite and terrestrial television – is invited to be voyeuristic. Some argue that the audience, in effect, is being put into the position of the rapists and their supporting crowd.

In the account that we have provided below, we have not tried to analyse the complexities of the film's construction, for, as we have made clear, it has not been our aim on this occasion to offer any elaborate textual analysis. The debate about *The Accused*, however, has been fuelled precisely by the ways in which different textual readings lead to distinct accounts of the director's intentions.

The benign view is that the film largely avoids the charge of exploitation and that it supports the right of the heroine to express her sexuality openly, without inviting male attack. From this standpoint, the film endorses the rape victim's right to be heard and believed and rejects a 'blame the victim' attitude.[2] It is those who stand by and observe the rape that are the guilty parties. The director's intention, therefore, is to shift responsibility from victim to perpetrator.[3] By some accounts, the aim is even broader: to ask citizens to be responsible *per se* and not to stand by, the rape being the means to promote this larger message.[4]

Even among those who see *The Accused* in a broadly benign light, there are still reservations about whether or not the rape scene is essential or is rather motivated by 'box-office intent'. As evidence, Jonathan Kaplan, the film's director, has been quoted as saying: 'The only difference between this and actual rape is that someone is yelling "cut".'[5] Whether explicitness of this kind is necessary, and whether or not the voyeurism of the audience verges upon the pornographic, are points that have quite properly been raised.[6] It has been suggested, for instance, that the rape scene could have been narrated as the witness's testimony in court, rather than being shown.

The malign view picks up from here and argues that *The Accused* makes a spurious claim to document reality in order to negate accusations of exploitativeness. Moreover, according to one line of argument, the film offers only the most negative view of men, as either rapists, or spectators of rape, or as totally inadequate beings. The film, it has been suggested, is really offering a view of male solidarity as a virtual conspiracy against women. Rape figures as a means of engaging in masculine group sport.[7] The consequence is to offer both male and female viewers only the most restricted ways of identifying with the characters: men as perpetrators; women as victims.

In the course of this chapter, we show the range of interpretations that respondents have brought to bear on *The Accused*. As will be seen, some of the themes considered by the critics are indeed taken up by the women who participated; but other, ignored, lines of argument are also explored.

Although clearly a fiction film, *The Accused* plainly claims in its postscript that it reflects the sexual condition of contemporary America as what some have labelled a 'rape culture'.[8] It is worth noting that much of its construction both of the legal investigation process and of the trial relates quite closely to some characteristic patterns of newspaper coverage of rape cases in Britain. We observed in discussing *Crimewatch* how the programme connected with the typical 'search for the offender' phase of news coverage in the press. In their study of sex crime in the news, Soothill and Walby have also noted how in trials for rape and other sexual crimes – the courtroom phase – the press's attention often shifts from the offender to the victim:

> From the widespread media reporting of the spectacular rape trials, women seem to have only two roles imposed upon them to play in a trial – a whore or a virgin – and yet, whether experienced or inexperienced in sexual activity, women are portrayed as 'asking for it'. … In seeking justice, the 'virgin' tag is still an important one. The message of these trials, as represented by the press, is that women may be culpable. There is little room for alternative readings of such reports.[9]

The convergence of these remarks with the subject matter and dilemmas of *The Accused* could not be closer. It should be remembered, though, that they concern the characteristic patterns of newspaper reporting, *not* fictional representations of rape. But to say this points to the ways in which cultural forms that we conventionally label as dealing in fact (such as newspapers) and those that we consider to be fictional (such as theatrically released films) do articulate with one another in complicated ways. This has been an underlying feature of all our previous discussions of given programmes, whether these have involved the drama-like reconstruction of a crime or the fictionalisation of well-documented social issues.

So far as *The Accused* is concerned, therefore, questions inevitably arise about relationships between the widely diffused ideas of women's own culpability for being raped, found in the popular press, and the possible interpretations to be made of the film itself. As may be seen, the women's reactions to the film analysed in this chapter are largely worked out in the context of such frequently rehearsed assumptions – but at the same time their responses often run against the grain of such dominant views. What men might think of how *The Accused* constructs its narrative remains open to conjecture, although we do provide some evidence on this below.

What the respondents saw

When *The Accused* was released in Britain in February 1989, it received extensive media coverage. The graphic portrayal of the gang rape of the character played by Hollywood star Jodie Foster assured the film of maximum publicity in its claim to have tackled the issue of rape and social injustice. In January 1992, the film was shown on UK terrestrial television. It was screened earlier on satellite television by B Sky B's 'Movie Channel' in April 1991. It is easily obtained from video stores and may be purchased over the shop counter. Directed by Jonathan Kaplan, the film co-stars Kelly McGillis as the Deputy District Attorney who fights the rape victim's case in court. It is classified '18' and runs for one hour and fifty-one minutes. The video version of the film has a number of cuts in it, and it was this version that was screened.

The film opens at a roadside bar under a fly-over, whose flashing red sign reads *The Mill*. Someone runs across the road from the bar, rapidly followed by a young woman bursting out of the door, screaming. Wearing no shoes, her clothing in disarray, the woman clutches a T-shirt to her chest. Telephoning the emergency services a man's flustered voice states: 'I'd like to report a girl in trouble.' He refuses to identify himself. The woman runs up the road waving her arms at cars which swerve to avoid her. The man, now in close-up in the telephone booth, states there has been a rape involving 'a whole crowd'. A small pick-up truck waved down by the woman stops for her.

Sarah, the rape victim, stands in a hospital gown while bruises on her upper legs, wrists and neck are photographed. Simultaneously, she is formally questioned concerning her use of contraceptives, when her last period was, when she last had sexual intercourse and whether she has ever had a venereal disease. A woman from the rape crisis centre enters and sympathetically offers to help the victim, an offer which is turned down. Sarah is then internally examined, lying on her back with her feet raised in stirrups. She winces and remains silent.

Katheryn Murphy, the Deputy District Attorney, enters the hospital room. In Sarah's absence, the lawyer remarks on blood tests which reveal the presence of alcohol and marijuana. With the rape counsellor's response: 'What difference does that make? She was raped by three men', the film germinates the seed of its plot – prejudicial perceptions of rape victims.

Sarah returns to the scene of her rape with the lawyer, a detective and a uniformed policeman. Here she identifies two of her attackers. The third rapist, a student, is no longer at the bar. Sarah spends a lonely night in her caravan home following her unsympathetic boyfriend's departure. During a phone call to her mother, she is unable to disclose the rape. The next day the third rapist is identified and arrested at his college, while the arrest is silently watched by the man who telephoned the police in the opening minutes of the film.

Sarah is alarmed when she discovers via television news that the rapists are to be released on bail. The news report carries an interview with the college boy's lawyer, who states: 'There was no rape. The so-called victim consented enthusiastically to all of the alleged acts. She put on a show pure and simple.' This same bulletin, watched by a group of college boys, is received with loud applause and congratulatory cheers for the accused student.

Sarah reacts with hostility towards the lawyer, Katheryn Murphy, when she appears at Sarah's home, her anger fuelled by the news report which 'made it sound like I did a live sex show'. The lawyer explains that Sarah will have to learn to put up with such accusations if she intends to pursue her case against the rapists, and she proceeds to question Sarah in a sceptical manner. Katheryn's doubts are fostered when she interviews Sarah's friend, Sally, who was present at *The Mill* on the night of the attack. Explaining that she did not see the rape, but can describe one man who was cheering on the attack as having a scorpion tattoo on his left arm, Sally tells the lawyer that Sarah was 'pretty loaded' after a fight with her boyfriend.

Katheryn Murphy explains the difficulties of Sarah's case to her District Attorney, stating: 'If I take it to trial they'll destroy her. She walked in there alone. She got drunk. She got stoned. She came on to them. She's got a prior for possession. She's a sitting duck.' The District Attorney suggests a deal with the rapists' lawyers that would 'put them away' for any crime to which they will admit. After some assertive bargaining with three male lawyers, Katheryn finally agrees to a plea of 'reckless endangerment', one she appears content with given the nature of the case.

That evening the television news reports that the three men have pleaded guilty to the reduced charge of reckless endangerment, and were sentenced to between two and a half and five years in prison. The report says that the charge was reduced because 'the young woman who was the alleged victim in the case would not have made a strong witness for the state.' Watching the report at her work in a cafeteria, Sarah is furious. She storms angrily into Katheryn Murphy's apartment, interrupting a dinner party, and accuses the lawyer of selling her out. Despite being told that the men's conviction for reckless endangerment carries the same prison sentence as that for rape, Sarah cannot believe the dismissal of her account.

Denied credibility by the courts, Sarah symbolically mutilates herself by cropping her hair with a pair of scissors. She then throws her boyfriend out of her home, following his attempts to caress her in a sexual manner and his lack of sympathy when she tells him to stop it.

Sarah drives to a record store. A man approaches claiming to know her. Despite receiving the cold shoulder, he persists and asks her for a date. Sarah continues to rebuff him, but as she gets into her car he then menacingly states: 'You're the girl from *The Mill* that night. Huh?' Sarah panics, frantically locking herself inside the car. The man laughs, taunting her with explicit sexual gestures. As she attempts to drive away, he blocks her exit from the car park with his pick-up truck. Slamming on her brakes to prevent a collision, Sarah bangs her head on the steering wheel. 'Hey! Wanna play pin-ball?' the man shouts. Sarah reverses and, in terrified anger, drives straight at the man's vehicle, into which she crashes. Although her car is severely damaged, she again reverses, and once more rams the truck.

In a hospital corridor, Katheryn Murphy sits waiting to see Sarah, and notices that a man arguing with the hospital staff has a scorpion tattooed on his left arm. It is the man from the record store. Katheryn finds Sarah, barely conscious in a hospital bed. Asked what happened, Sarah repeats the man's words: 'Wanna play pin-ball? He figures I'm a piece of shit. Everybody figures I'm a piece of shit. Why not? You told them that.' As Katheryn leaves the hospital, she pursues and questions the tattooed man. He says that he was minding his own business and 'she drove her car into my truck'. Asked if he knows Sarah, he replies: 'No, I don't know her. She's a whore. Last time I saw her she was doing a sex show.' Katheryn states that she thought Sarah was raped. 'Raped? She fucked a bar full of guys, and then turns round and blames them for it. Listen, lady, she loved it. She had an audience. She did the show of her life. Next time she does another show, tell her I'll be right there to cheer her on.' These words are to have a profound effect upon the lawyer.

The brief scenes which follow portray the transformation of Katheryn Murphy. Upbeat music underlines her new commitment to Sarah's case as she works through the night. She proposes to prove that Sarah was a victim of rape by prosecuting the men responsible for encouraging the attack for criminal solicitation, an intention ridiculed by her District Attorney.

Visiting Sarah's home, Katheryn explains that if they succeed in a charge of criminal solicitation, the rape will be formally recognised by the state, the rapists remaining in prison for a full five years. Although confused by Katheryn's change of heart, Sarah agrees to proceed.

Sarah's friend Sally, although initially reluctant to become involved, eventually offers her support, and attending an identity parade points to three men who encouraged the rape attack, one of whom is the man with the scorpion tattoo. Interviewed by Katheryn about the rape, Sally explains that she and Sarah had been drinking and 'joking around' with two college boys in the bar, and that Sarah had suggested that the best way of getting back at her boyfriend would be to 'take this guy home and just do it right in front of him'. Katheryn is astonished and reprimands Sarah for being dishonest, explaining that Sally could well end up standing as a witness for the defence.

Katheryn then drives to *The Mill*, where she discovers a vital clue which will lead her to an independent witness. Although very ill at ease in the tavern, she walks through into the games room. On a video machine, Katheryn finds a list of high-scoring winners alongside the date of their game. One such date, reading 2:14:87, corresponds with the night of the rape. The player's name is Ken. That night, scanning the young rapist's college yearbook, Katheryn finds a computer science student named Kenneth Joyce. It turns out that this is the man who telephoned the police at the opening of the film.

She locates Ken at his college. He claims to know nothing about the rape. However, Katheryn tells him that she knows he was there and that she is prosecuting the men who cheered the rape on. In turn, Ken replies that the men were doing nothing abnormal and that, given the chance, almost anybody would have watched the rape. He is persuaded that the men did more than watch and were thereby committing a crime.

The criminal solicitation case opens and Sarah is called to the witness stand. Embarrassed and near to tears, Sarah describes how, entering the bar at *The Mill*, she talked to a man named Danny. She danced with him and he kissed her. She then explains how, although she attempted to push Danny away, he pushed her down on the pin-ball machine, ripped her shirt and pulled down her underpants. Though she struggled, he held her down, kissing her and 'jamming his hand up my crotch'. She was then pinned down by a second man, Kurt, as a crowd of men cheered and clapped. Prevented from screaming by a hand over her mouth, she had shut her eyes as Danny penetrated her. Cheered on by the crowd, the college boy then took over Danny's position, and was followed by Kurt. She recounts the rape in explicit detail to the point at which she kicked free from the third assailant and ran out into the road.

A manipulative defence attorney questions Sarah, asking how she knew who was shouting if she had her eyes closed. He points out that she had been smoking cannabis and drinking alcohol, and that the room in which she was raped was noisy. A second defence lawyer asks Sarah whether at any time she cried 'help' or 'rape'. Sarah says that she kept saying 'no,' which the defence lawyer considers insufficient to signal that she was being raped. Katheryn again questions Sarah, asking what words came into her head as she was being repeatedly raped. Sarah replies that the only word which came into her head was 'no'.

During the trial, Ken Joyce visits his friend Bob, the third assailant, in prison, telling him that he is having to testify about the rape. Bob explains that if Ken testifies for the prosecution then he will have to spend a whole five years in prison and will be branded a rapist. Bob tells Ken to say that he cannot remember what happened. Ken is clearly torn between telling the truth and standing by his friend.

In Katheryn's office, Sarah explains that she has studied Katheryn's stars. Katheryn is not interested. The District Attorney enters with Ken Joyce, explaining that Ken is no longer willing to testify, and suggests that Katheryn move for dismissal. Leaving Sarah and Ken alone, Katheryn pursues her colleague. Sarah asks Ken why he will no longer support her. Realising that he is siding with his friend in prison, she tells Ken that he is just as bad as the other men for dismissing her as some 'low-life whore'. Ken denies this, and realises that his moral duty is to testify.

In court, Ken is asked to recount what happened at *The Mill*. As he does so, the film intercuts flashbacks leading up to and including the rape. Entering the bar dressed in a short mini-skirt and low-cut T-shirt with thin shoulder straps, Sarah attracts a lot of attention. She sits with Sally and flirts across the bar with several men until Danny, a tall fair-haired man in jeans and a leather waistcoat, joins the two women at their table. Danny then invites Sarah to accompany him into the games room.

Ken Joyce states that Sarah and Danny then started playing pin-ball and 'getting pretty loaded'. This is reinforced by a flashback which shows the couple smoking a joint. Sarah then dances alone in the middle of the floor to a record on the juke box. As she does so the straps of her T-shirt fall down. Danny joins in dancing, and other men gather round in the room to watch the spectacle. Danny then kisses Sarah, and as she tries to prevent things from going any further he forcibly lifts her onto the pin-ball machine and continues to molest her. Sarah starts to protest, but is forced to lie under Danny on the machine. The man with the scorpion tattoo whoops and encourages Danny to go further. Sarah begins to scream, but her mouth is then covered by Danny's hand. 'He's gonna fuck her right there!' exclaims the tattooed man. As the camera switches between Danny's and Sarah's perspectives, Danny calls for Kurt to hold her down. As Danny pulls down her underpants and his own jeans, the watching men cheer and gesticulate. Ken, standing near a video game, looks aghast at the scene. Bob is told that it is his turn next by the tattooed man. A glass falls from the pin-ball machine, smashing on the floor, and Danny's face is shown in close-up as he climaxes.

As Bob approaches Sarah, who is still being restrained and screaming, he unbuttons his trousers. 'Pump that fucking college arse,' shouts the tattooed man. Another shouts, 'Hold her down! Make her moan!' Kurt, who is restraining Sarah, is told he is next. 'Shut the fuck up, arsehole,' Kurt shouts to the tattooed man. The other men jeer at Kurt for not wanting to rape Sarah. They chant Kurt's name, and though momentarily appearing terrified, Kurt then pulls Bob off Sarah, spits in his hands and rapes her. Sally, who is now working in the bar, goes to the entrance of the games room to see what is happening. The tattooed man looks at her and suggests that she is next on the table. She draws back away from the scene frightened.

The cheering men chant, 'One, two, three, four. Poke that pussy till it's sore.' Ken and Bob's eyes meet, Bob staring silently at Ken, who rapidly exits. Sarah bites Kurt's hand as he continues to rape her. He screams out as he climaxes in a slow-motion shot and releases his hold on her. Sarah struggles free, falling from the table to the ground and running screaming through the bar. The rape scene, from the point at which Sarah is forced onto the pin-ball machine to the point at which she escapes, runs for five minutes and fourteen seconds.

The courtroom sits in silence following Ken Joyce's testimony. In reply to Katheryn's question as to whether he believes Sarah instigated the rape, Ken replies that he does not.

In the defence's summing up, it is claimed that Sarah's sworn testimony is worth nothing. It is pointed out that The People's (prosecution) case depends on Ken Joyce. The defence then implies that Kenneth Joyce was as guilty as the rest for watching the rape and, as for the three accused of solicitation, they had to know that they were committing a crime to be guilty of one.

Katheryn Murphy's summation contests the point that Sarah's testimony is worthless: she was a rape victim. She states that Kenneth Joyce was not as guilty as the other men; it was the men who cheered and clapped who 'made sure that Sarah Tobias was raped, and raped, and raped'. Katheryn emotionally asks the jury to consider whether they believe a rape is nothing.

As the verdict is awaited, and the jury continue to deliberate, Sarah tells Katheryn her astrological reading. This time Katheryn takes an interest in what Sarah has to say and asks her to sign the chart, a request that signals the solidarity between the two women.

In the courtroom, Sarah, Ken and Katheryn look nervous as they await the verdict. The foreman of the jury reads verdicts of guilty of criminal solicitation for all three defendants. Katheryn and Sarah face one another and smile, before turning towards Ken. As they leave the court they are mobbed by reporters. Sarah tells them that she just wants to go home and play with her dog.

The film ends with the following postscript. 'In the United States a rape is reported every six minutes. One out of every four rape victims is attacked by two or more assailants.' This signals the film's claim to be grounded in documentary realism.

How the respondents reacted

In certain respects, *The Accused* was quite distinctive when compared to the other programmes screened. First, of course, it is a major feature film which has been on general release, as well as shown on satellite and terrestrial television. In a number of cases, members of our sample had actually seen the film and, where they had not, its aura of publicity had frequently ensured that at least many had some broad image or prior knowledge of it. Second, of all the material shown, it was the only programme that had originated in the USA, which meant that it offered potentially distinctive points of either identification or distancing –

particularly in respect of judgments made about its 'realism' – for women living in Britain today.

Our intention in screening *The Accused* was to establish reactions to explicit scenes of sexual violence committed against a woman. We sought to remain within the bounds of what women could be expected to view in a formal situation. However, on those very grounds, it was considered necessary to inform members of the viewing groups that they would be seeing the film, that it contained an explicit rape scene, and that, should they feel unable to view that part of the film, they would be free to leave the room. Three women actually acted upon this warning and withdrew during the scene.

The Accused offered scope for assessing the emotional impact of a graphic display of sexual violence upon women viewers. For instance, one obvious concern was whether the portrayal of the rape was considered 'justifiable'. The characterisation of the rape victim was of particular interest to us: she is portrayed as 'provocative', unsympathetic, and involved in the consumption of alcohol and drugs, opening up a wide range of possible interpretations of her character and behaviour. It was important to assess the extent to which this victim might be held responsible or blamed for her fate, and whether this had any bearing on how the film was understood. Equally, we were interested in assessing varying reactions to the rapists portrayed in the film.

The viewing groups' perceptions bear directly upon debates about whether *The Accused* may be regarded as an 'anti-rape' film, as originally publicised. A further concern is whether *The Accused* might be thought to transgress the bounds of what should be screened on television.

Placing 'The Accused'
The fact that the film was American posed no difficulties for the women viewers and, in common with the other screenings, there were some strong and persistent reactions (see Figure IX, Reactions to *The Accused*). In contrast to *EastEnders* and *Closing Ranks*, there was considerable commonality in the responses of the two groups of women. Around 30% of both groups had seen *The Accused* previously. The vast majority of women in both groups rated it as 'realistic' or 'very realistic', and 'believable' or 'very believable'. It is of interest in this connection to cite the professional view of a rape counsellor who took part in the study:

> Very realistic right through, everything, her emotions, the rape in itself, the courtroom, the police, everything was very true to life. It was an excellent film. Very good portrayal of what actually happens in rape cases. I mean, it was horrific, the actual rape scene. I think every woman here was taken aback, but that's the way it happens, not necessarily gang rape all the time, but that's the shock they'll feel when they're going through it. It got it across and it didn't dwell on that action scene for too long because it was giving you all her

emotions and the courtroom drama, how no one believes you and guys think it's a laugh.
[Scottish white woman, rape counsellor, member of group with experience of violence]

Another professional judgment was expressed by a social worker, also participating in the research as a group member, who had the following (on the whole, minor) reservation about the film's realism:

Well, for me the damage would still be done, even though they won the case. I still felt prison wasn't enough, because the damage has already been done to her and it's like saying 'it's a film'. Somebody else said earlier that ... the effect on the victim wasn't enough, because she picks herself up out of a terrible rape and she goes out to fight a case. And the only bit is when she actually clips her hair off. Now a lot of victims do mutilate themselves because they tend to hate their own bodies, because ... they've sort of blamed themselves and they're still trying to commit suicide. All sorts of other traumatic things happen to rape victims. That didn't come through in that film. That wasn't shown. So to me that was the only bit that wasn't realistic about it.
[English Asian woman, social worker, with no experience of violence]

Only one woman out of all the participants said she did not take the film seriously. Most thought it was 'violent' and 'disturbing', and just over one half of the women in both groups thought it was 'offensive'. Women who had experience of violence were very unlikely to describe it as 'exciting' (6%) or 'entertaining' (26%). Nearly three-quarters of this group rated it as 'not at all exciting', and 58% rated it as 'not entertaining'. Only a small percentage (20%) of the women in groups who had not experienced violence rated it as exciting, although just over 40% found it entertaining (see Figure IX).

Entertainment?
An indication of the kinds of broad expectations held by those who had gone to see *The Accused* at the cinema emerges from the following quotation:

I must admit when I went to go and see it – it was the big thing – 'oh, there's this rape scene in it ... everyone's got to go and see it.' So I was going to see it anyway, because I go to see all the films that come out. But I especially wanted to see it just to see what it was like and I thought it was going to be about a couple of seconds, just guys cheering it on – I didn't expect it to be anything like that.
[Scottish white middle-class woman, with no experience of violence]

136

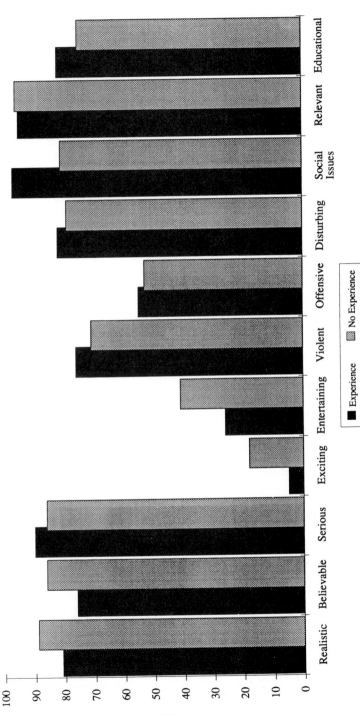

Figure IX: Reactions to 'The Accused' – Experience of Violence/No Experience

Such a comment conveys the interest aroused by the film for the cinemagoer. Obviously, enough knowledge of the central dilemmas had percolated into general circulation via media hype to arouse a motivating curiosity to see for oneself. But the impact upon the research groups was considerable. It was precisely the shock effect alluded to here that came across strongly in all of the discussions, albeit with variations described later. In fact, for the vast majority of group members, reactions encompassed shock, horror, disgust, distress and anger.

For the majority, the film's American setting was largely irrelevant, although this exchange indicates that its foreignness could very occasionally also be used as a way of distancing oneself from its message:

> I didn't really watch it as American or English. I was watching that film, and, see, the inside of me was feeling everything that that woman was feeling. I don't know why. That's how close I felt to that woman.

> I felt like that too. But I still felt that it was an American film and that the gang rape, it's not something that you see in the news or even in the newspapers about women being gang raped.
> [Scottish Asian women, with experience of violence]

As a major release, it might be expected that standard commercial assumptions about the pleasures of spectatorship would be applied, although in fact these were rarely used. The following quotation indicates how such criteria might quite exceptionally be invoked:

> I thoroughly enjoyed it. I thought it was entertaining and I really thought it was an excellent film, it was good acting and, you know, you have the good guys and the bad guys and I thought it was very, very, realistic.
> [English white working-class woman, with no experience of violence]

Much more common, though, in fact almost universal, were sentiments of repulsion, distress and shock. One can see from the following exchange how group members would typically try to devise the right kind of terminology for evaluating their viewing experience, and indeed for establishing a common baseline for holding the discussion at all:

Speaker 1: Even though I said – what I meant by 'not entertaining', I just think it's the wrong word. ... I enjoyed it in a way, but entertainment's not the right word for it.

Speaker 2: Gripping?

Speaker 1: No.

Speaker 3: Enthralling?

Speaker 4:	Riveting – something like that?
Speaker 1:	No, I just don't know. But it's not entertaining any-way.
Speaker 3:	Because entertaining sometimes is something that's humorous, amusing, jovial.
Speaker 1:	Yes ... that just grabbed you.
	[English white working-class women, with no experience of violence]

In general, it was simply not acceptable to define the experience of seeing *The Accused* as pleasurable, although at the same time its compelling qualities – a testament to the film-makers' skills – had also to be acknowledged. Interestingly, and this relates to how gender *differences* between masculine and feminine responses might be conceived, some made the point that certain kinds of men might find pleasure in viewing such a film because of the points of identification offered by the rapists:

> To women it can't be entertaining, I wouldn't think. I don't know about the women here, I certainly don't find it that way. To men, if it is entertaining it's because they maybe think along those lines, and think, 'Oh yes, that would be good' or whatever, or give them the incentive to go out and try it and see how it really is. Because they all look as though they're having a brilliant time, these guys, don't they?
> [Scottish white woman, with experience of violence]

As we shall see, this offers a pointer to the more general conceptions of masculinity and femininity that underlie such observations.

Aspects of identification
As with *EastEnders* and *Closing Ranks*, women with experience of violence were more likely than women with no experience to identify with the characters and situations depicted in *The Accused*, although this was not as strong as with the other two programmes. As shown in Table 6, 36% of women with experience identified with the characters in the film, overwhelmingly with the victim of rape, in contrast to 21% of women with no experience. The Yule's Q of .34 indicates that there is some association between experience of violence and identification with characters in *The Accused*, but much less than those revealed with respect to *EastEnders* and *Closing Ranks*.

However, there was a reasonably strong association between experience of violence and the ability to relate to the *situations* depicted. Over half of the women who had experienced violence (see Table 7) identified with situations depicting the rape, the victim's circumstances and her anger. Only 18% of the group without experience of violence related to the situations depicted, and none of them related to the portrayal of the rape. The Yule's Q of .64 indicates a reasonably strong association between past experience of violence and identification with situations in *The Accused*.

Table 6: Relating to Characters in 'The Accused'

	Violence			
	Experience		No experience	
Relate to characters	N	%	N	%
yes	14	36	6	21
no	25	64	22	79
Total	39	100%	28	100%

Yule's Q= .34

Table 7: Relating to Situations in 'The Accused'

	Violence			
	Experience		No experience	
Relate to situations	N	%	N	%,
yes	18	51	5	18
no	17	49	23	82
Total	35	100%	28	100%

Yule's Q= .64

Thus it could be said that the uncompromising depiction of the victim of rape in *The Accused* made it difficult to identify with her personally but not with the experiences and situations she faced. This may also have been reflected in the participants' overwhelming agreement that the film is relevant to everyday life, with only three of the viewers thinking it was irrelevant.

One aspect of the process of identification that needs to be stressed is the extraordinary depth of feeling that *The Accused* aroused among the groups. Just to emphasise the point further, it is worth noting that there was a widespread need for the film to end well, which offers a powerful index of how far the identification could extend in many cases. *The Accused* brought to the fore very strong sentiments about the need for justice to be seen to be done:

It has a predictable ending, because I think if they had been found not guilty I would've been furious. It gets to me in the sense that they got their just desserts if you like.
[Scottish white middle-class woman, with no experience of violence]

I would think if they showed a different ending it would have made it a different picture. It would have been like sort of glorifying it really. It wouldn't have been like saying, 'It was all wrong', it would have been a case of 'It's all right'.
[English Afro-Caribbean woman, with no experience of violence]

Ethnic diversity

Asian women had rather different reactions to *The Accused* than did Afro-Caribbean and white group members. Possibly they were more detached from the cultural context of the film because they did not find it as 'believable' and 'violent' as the other two groups (see Figure X). Very few women in the three ethnic groups described the film as 'entertaining', with none of the Afro-Caribbean women making this assessment although more Asian women found it 'entertaining'. Only 14% of Asian women said they could relate to the characters, whereas nearly half of the white and Afro-Caribbean group members identified with characters. Additionally, over three-quarters of the Asian women (77%) could not relate to the situations depicted, in contrast to just over half for the other two groups (52% whites and 57% Afro-Caribbeans). Perhaps surprisingly, 99% of the Asian women thought the film had educational value, whereas only three-quarters of the members of the other two groups felt the same. An indication of what Asian women meant by the educational dimension of the film may be judged from points such as these:

> If she's drinking too much, you know, that's why that happened. ... Drinking is bad and [we] learn [this] from that film.

> Yes, because then it's trying to show the girls, you know, that are upset and going to the bars like that, you know. It sort of gives them a lesson that things like this happen, you know, if you behave like ... that.
> [Scottish Asian women, with no experience of violence]

These remarks variously suggest that the film offers a warning about the dangers of drinking and of flirtation, viewed from within a cultural perspective which is relatively detached from the mainstream. There were also a few strong differences in the reactions of the Afro-Caribbean groups: a possible key to this distinctiveness is offered by observations made in the course of group discussions. One of these, which emerged with particular force amongst the group of English Afro-Caribbean women with experience of violence, concerned the ethnic dimension. The central challenge from them was: 'What if the rape victim had been black?':

> I found myself saying that in the film ... if I change that woman into a black woman, it would be even more painful for me. Because I know that the whole line of the story would've changed ... and I know that the verdict could have been different. And I know that the support ... the sympathy would've been very different. ... It is a very painful film. I sat here all the time ... sort of holding myself. I sort of felt the pain throughout the body. But I know if it was a black woman I would've felt – I probably would've been in tears, because

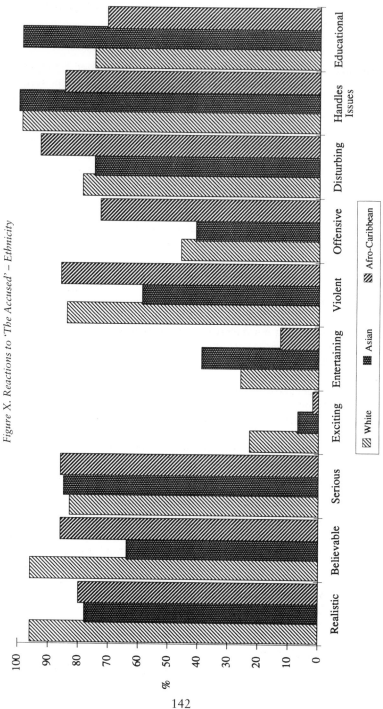

Figure X. Reactions to 'The Accused' – Ethnicity

White · Asian · Afro-Caribbean

%

100
90
80
70
60
50
40
30
20
10
0

Realistic · Believable · Serious · Exciting · Entertaining · Violent · Offensive · Disturbing · Handles Issues · Educational

142

I know that the verdict would've been different and I know that you wouldn't get the same level of sympathy.
[English Afro-Caribbean woman, with experience of violence]

This observation crystallised feelings widely acknowledged in the group concerned and brings out the identification felt with the rape victim. However, significantly, it also tempers this with reservations about equality of treatment between black and white that are based in the experience of racism.

The Accused was much more 'offensive' and 'disturbing' for Afro-Caribbean than for Asian and white viewers. Ninety-three per cent of them felt it was 'disturbing' or 'very disturbing', and 73% found it 'offensive' or 'very offensive'. An indication of the strength of feeling may be gained from considering the following views:

I think I was all right up to before the rape scene. I could handle that and that showed, up till then it showed me actually what women have to go through, if they are raped. But the titillation bit that the media's into was the scene when she was in hospital, and her legs were up, and they were doing the examination, and then the gang rape. And for me, that was unnecessary, there was no need for that. So for me, that bit wasn't catering for women, it was actually catering for titillation, for men to say, it's okay to rape. I mean it sort of glorified it for me.
[English Afro-Caribbean woman, with experience of violence]

Just over three-quarters of white and Asian women found *The Accused* 'disturbing' or 'very disturbing', and around 40% in both groups thought it was 'offensive' or 'very offensive'. Afro-Caribbean women were also twice as likely as the other two groups to say the rape scene should not be shown, and 66% of those Afro-Caribbean women offering an opinion felt the film should not be shown on television. This view was given particularly strong voice by one Afro-Caribbean woman with experience of rape:

I was gonna accept that 'OK' this is just like a film about rape and they're showing you how this woman has to stand up for her rights and everything. But once they showed the actual event, then they were endorsing it to me, because, like for a man, it's a cheap thrill. And if at the end of the day there's gonna be a big case and they're going to be dubious about whether he gets nine months or five years, then what's the big deal, you know? At least he'll remember it forever as something he did in his college days, risky but quite fun, you know, 'this was quite fun'. And that isn't good enough. Really, I don't want it on telly.
[English Afro-Caribbean woman, with experience of violence]

A third of Asian viewers and a quarter of white viewers thought the film should not be shown on television. Again, ethnic background appears to make an important difference in the interpretations offered of programmes with depictions of violence.

Was the victim to blame?

For the most part, immediate reactions after viewing centred upon the rape scene and the depiction of the victim, Sarah Tobias. At the heart of most discussion was the question of whether the rape could in any circumstances ever be justified and the relative responsibilities of the victim and the perpetrators. In addition, but to a much lesser extent, the roles played by other characters were also the subject of discussion.

One line of interpretation, very commonly articulated, stressed Sarah's risk-taking behaviour. At one extreme is as clear a statement as could be made that the victim was herself entirely to blame. The idea that dress, drunkenness and demeanour add up to 'asking for it' might be described as the archetypal macho male view:

> I thought she was asking for it, to be honest, the way she was dressed. That was pathetic. And the way she was carrying on, and the way she was dancing – that was number one that she was asking for it. To be honest.
> [Scottish Asian woman, with no experience of violence]

This attribution of sole responsibility was actually quite exceptional and is largely linked to conceptions of proper female behaviour held by many Asian group members. Much more common were views which in a variety of ways showed a nuanced understanding of Sarah's behaviour and which attempted to put her predicament into some kind of perspective:

> When I watched it first time round, I was a person just watching. ... Now, I'm looking at it with hindsight of having seen it before. But when I watched it last time, I was thinking, 'What actually happened in that club? Is she telling the truth? Was she really giving him the come on?' Yeah ... I was thinking, 'What else went on that made that happen?' But until I actually saw the rape scene, and I thought, 'Oh God, that was out of order! Nothing she did justified that the rape's happening to her.' So to me it was important to have the rape scene in there, to stop me giving her any blame, as the victim. This time round I knew from the beginning. But first time round, watching it, I was thinking, 'Oh, I want to know what actually happened in there.'
> [English Asian woman, with no experience of violence]

One frequently expressed point of view stressed the fact that Sarah had had a row with her boyfriend and that she wanted to get back at him.

This was often coupled with the recognition that she was somewhat drunk and also under the influence of drugs and, therefore, not entirely clear about the dangers into which she was placing herself. Crucially, however, this was commonly coupled with a denial that this warranted being raped:

> She was drunk, she'd been smoking them – funny tobacco, flirting. She'd fallen out with her boyfriend and, well, there was a couple of eligible men in the bar and she was going to have one of them that night.

> I think she was so high on drugs and a few drinks hadn't helped, had it? I don't think she really knew what she was doing, and I don't think that the state she was in should have led to her being raped, anyway.
> [Scottish white middle-class women, with no experience of violence]

The dangers, it was pointed out, stemmed from male culture itself, from the ways in which men might regard their drinking spots territorially and any woman who wanders into the wrong location as fair game:

> She went in there on her own, and they might not like the idea. But a woman walking into a pub on her own is labelled straight away, and always will be. Well, in this country you just get a label, you're there for a man and – a bit. Women, we know that isn't true, but no matter how much we say it isn't true, guys are still not going to believe it. And yet, I think that she should've just put a wee bit more thought into it. I mean she went out in an angry mood and all the rest of it, 'I'll show that bastard something, I'll just have somebody else.' And it fell about her.
> [Scottish white woman, with experience of violence]

It might seem extraordinary today, but quite clearly underlying this perception is a realistic recognition that women on their own in certain male preserves are simply not regarded as 'respectable' and therefore considered to be sexually available, and that no amount of refusing men's attentions will put them off.

A great deal of attention in discussion focused upon Sarah's dress as well as her demeanour. It is worth noting the fact that precisely the same issues arose in the case of the reconstructed rape and murder of the young female hitchhiker during the group discussions of *Crimewatch*, albeit in much less detail. The following exchange among a group of Asian women with experience of violence was typical of the kinds of observation made:

Speaker 1:   Aye, she was leading them on, I think, just then. She

145

	had too much to drink, and the way she was dancing, and her clothes as well ... her top, her shirt.
Speaker 2:	Her clothes have got nothing to do with it. I didn't want to say anything because my views are totally clear on this. ... The film for me, if I could give a quick summary of the film for me, it shows you how men portray women. It shows you how women think about women who wear short clothes and things like that, and think it's provocation. It's very, very, realistic. I mean, women do think that people wearing mini-skirts and low-cleavage shirts, you know, do provoke it, and in my eyes that's not right. And judges do it and jurors do it, and that's what the whole film is about. It's about pointing to the fact that she was doing all these things that people was saying provoked it. But she was still in the right. She was still raped and she was still a victim of criminal solicitation. You know what I mean? It doesn't matter what you wear. That's the whole point, that's the educational thing about it.
Speaker 1:	I say the same thing as her ... I mean, I think as well that she didn't provoke, but that's not what everybody will think. That's why most of the women don't go to report rape cases because they know they'll be on trial, not them. ...
Speaker 3:	... That one particular scene of rape. To me it was, you know, for the guys – it was like an easy game. Because of her condition. She had a drink, and she said she took the joint, and it was easy game and that's how I look at it. When I was watching that, I wasn't watching it saying, 'She was wearing a mini-skirt, she was dancing, and all that.' ...

[Scottish Asian women, with experience of violence]

It might be supposed that questions of immodesty in dress had received particular emphasis among these women, perhaps, because of their cultural sensitivity, as Asians, to this question. In fact, that particular line of interpretation could be, and was, expressed quite differently:

See, it's an Islamic point ... that women [are] not allowed to wear this kind of dress, so other men looked at her and fancy her. That's why they say you cover yourself with your clothes so that other men don't look at you, or fancy where he wants you. It's against our religion.

[Scottish Asian woman, with no experience of violence]

146

The above statement makes highly explicit the link between the culture of dress as a religiously regulated practice and its place in a specific set of relations between men and women. In fact, the views cited earlier, despite coming from a group of Asian women, were by no means discrepant with the majority line taken in our groups:

> Equally so, she was only dressed as the people of her age group would be dressed. I mean, my daughter dresses the same as all her friends, and equally so, I did the same when I was her age – hot-pants and shorts and boots up to here, and tops up to here, and a bare midriff. ...
> [English white working-class woman, with no experience of violence]

What this suggests is the obvious point that cultural norms about what is acceptable dress are quite deeply implanted into our everyday judgments about those we encounter and in media portrayals of everyday life. On that basis, rather standardised patterns of interpretation of particular forms of dress may be held. However, such patterns of interpretation are not uniform, nor are they uncontested. For some of the women studied, the problems resulting from the sexualised interpretation of dress lay with men rather than with women, and it could not be accepted that women should have to anticipate the adverse reactions that they might 'provoke':

> I don't know, I don't think it was stupid. I mean there was nothing wrong in her sort of, you know, dressing and dancing and whatever. It's the flipping men, isn't it? I mean, really it is a world where we can dress and really do what you like. But it's the men that cause the problem. It wasn't her, it was the men that think, 'Oh yeah!'
> [English Afro-Caribbean woman, with no experience of violence]

> I know there's this thing about how women dress. I think people have got a right to dress, and if they want to smoke drugs and be on a high, then that's entirely up to them. And it doesn't matter what she was doing. She was enjoying herself. She didn't say, 'I want to have sex with you.' She didn't say it. She didn't ask for it. So therefore, you know, I didn't see why they should've done that. Let her enjoy herself. She was on a low and she smoked, and she wanted to feel high and, you know. If he was a bloke, I mean nobody wouldn't bother him, would they? Many a bloke go out there and get drunk because they're fed up and nobody bothers them.
> [English Afro-Caribbean woman, with experience of violence]

Underlying both these comments is a call for equality of treatment for women and men. A distinctive twist was given to the argument by other women who interpreted the issue at one further remove, accusing the film of taking a stance on Sarah's blame by the way in which it represented her actions and demeanour:

> I think she's portrayed being provocative. I think she's portrayed as asking for it, that's how she's definitely portrayed. You know, the clothes and the dancing and the attitude, which would imply that a lot of rape victims are like that, which I don't think is true at all.
> [English white woman, with experience of violence]

> I think they deliberately did that. To play on attitudes like yours that 'God, what did she expect?' Yeah, I think that was a deliberate portrayal of her like that, because in the beginning she is a lonely person, you can tell she's, well, she had problems at home. She went out to talk to a friend. She didn't go out there for anything else. But the way they dressed her, the way they were saying 'She's pissed out of her brains and doped up', it's as if 'Yeah, well, she was just not in control or anything. She got what she deserved' attitude. That sort of starts coming through. They play on that. Because we do start thinking and making judgments about people.
> [English Asian woman, with no experience of violence]

Such comments, which address *The Accused* as a film that deliberately sets up its characterisation in certain ways, offer insights into just how much distance could at times be taken from the intense experience of viewing to analyse the film's very construction.

Impact

Many women who viewed *The Accused* felt that it had educational value (82% of the group who had experienced violence and 75% of those who had not). Most respondents (97% of the women with experience of violence and 81% of women with none) thought the film handled the chosen issues in a reasonable manner. However, a fair proportion were unsure about the inclusion of the rape scene. It was this that had the greatest impact. A quarter of the women with experience, and nearly a third of those without, felt the scene portraying sexual violence should not have been included for the following reasons: it should not have been seen as entertainment nor used for financial gain; it sensationalised sexual violence; and it served no useful purpose in the film. An even higher percentage of women from both categories rejected the screening of *The Accused* on television. Nearly half of the entire sample (40%) said that the film should not be shown on television because children might see it or be upset by it; it was too violent; and it might upset victims of rape. Women with experience of violence were particularly concerned that children might see *The Accused*. Despite these strong feelings, only six women who saw the film felt that it should not have been made. In part, it is likely that this was so because the overall message may be read as one of triumph over enormous adversity. This perception is embodied in comments such as these:

> She stuck to her guns and, I mean, she was flirting at the beginning, she could've been put off by that and thought, 'I'm not gonna win this case anyway.' I'm sure most women do do that. 'I'm not gonna win this case 'cos I was flirting with him', you know. Or because 'I took him back to my place, I'm not gonna win. I'm not gonna win the case 'cos they're gonna say that, you know, I encouraged him.'

> I think it did a lot to sort of lift the guilt from the person who was being raped and portrayed it as … you know, 'All I wanted was a good time. I'm not supposed to be guilty for this rape, because of that.'
> [English Afro-Caribbean women, with no experience of violence]

Much of the reaction to how *The Accused* achieved its impact crystallised around particular scenes and the roles played in these by different characters. Of particular note are Sarah's physical examination in hospital and the rape scene itself.

Profound feelings of revulsion were expressed about the entire business of 'victim-processing'. This centred mainly on the hospital scene when Sarah is taken for a physical examination to establish whether or not she has been raped. (To a much lesser extent, adverse comment was also forthcoming about the representation of the judicial process itself.) The range of views expressed was consistent, irrespective of whether the women concerned had or had not experienced violence. The following testimony from a rape victim offers a poignant insight into both the 'realism' of how the physical examination was portrayed, and also into its necessity if legal action is to be taken:

> When she'd just been raped and taken to the hospital – you have no choice but to let them photograph the bruises. You've got no choice but to be examined because they've got to prove you've been raped. So you can't sit there and say, 'No, you can't touch me.' I went through ten hours of it. I had a man doctor. She had women, I'd a man. Because it was different; mine was buggery. That was just, you know, rape. But – this man was specialised in it and I was on my own with a man in the room and that was it. I had nobody with me and then when I had my bruises and everything photographed, it was men again. And I was on my own. I mean, you've just got to – I wanted it to be proved that I'd been raped. I wanted my husband behind bars and I was willing to do it.
> [English white woman, with experience of violence]

This is very much a view from inside the particular experience that underlines the extreme need for sensitivity in handling victims of such attacks. The following observations, at one remove, since they came from women who had experienced domestic violence, express clearly the sentiments aroused by the perceived indifference of the medical staff and rape counsellor:

Speaker 1:   They didn't even sympathise with her in the beginning either. In the beginning, when she went to the hospital, they made her feel, like, 'Have you ever had a venereal disease?' They put ... questions as if to say, 'Are you a slag? Full stop.' They might as well have turned round and said, 'Are you a slag?'

Speaker 2:   But they should've explained that. Well, they should've done it after, like, when she went in and she hadn't even had a wash and they were doing all that. Sort of, put your legs open, and then that woman from Rape Crisis came and she was standing, and the woman was there with her, with her legs up. It was quite, you know, everybody was in and out, in and out, and it just didn't matter.

Speaker 1:   It was just raw. It looked like, you know ... say if you got raped you'd have all these people harassing you and badgering you. You know what I mean? Right at that time, she didn't need all of that.
[English Afro-Caribbean women, with experience of violence]

These are fiercely protective reactions, profoundly alive to the humiliation inflicted after the original violation. But women who had not experienced violence felt just as strongly as those who had about the workings of the system that were depicted in this scene:

I felt that at the beginning of the film, when she was taken to the hospital, immediately after it, she was treated as the criminal, not as a victim. And it was all so matter-of-fact, there was no care or concern for her, it was just – 'Do you have diseases? When did you last have sex?' I mean her body had been violated, not just by one person, but by three ... and that was awful.

She was just like a piece of meat. All they were concerned with was getting her photographs, and that was awful. And the cross-questioning was dreadful.
[English white working-class women, with no experience of violence]

However, not surprisingly, it was the long rape scene itself that evoked the most profound feelings of anger, outrage and distress. Those – the majority – who felt that the rape scene should have been included, tended to justify this on the basis of its impact, the horror of which could be argued to have a beneficial effect on audiences. Nevertheless, there are nuances and qualifications to such a line that do not emerge directly from the quantitative data.

Explicitness
For some, watching the rape scene could, quite simply, be a numbingly disorienting experience:

> My heart sunk like lead over it. I could feel myself moving about in the chair. It really quite disturbed me. If I'd seen that at the beginning – I wouldn't have been – for a good ten or fifteen minutes after it – I don't think I'd really have been aware of what was going on.
> [Scottish white middle-class woman, with no experience of violence]

Apart from offering an insight into the depth of the feelings that the rape scene could touch, this comment also reflects upon how the narrative in *The Accused* has been cleverly constructed to hold the audience by pulling some of its punches until they can be delivered with greatest impact. This was even more clearly expressed in the following observations:

> Because the whole point of the film was about her being raped and it would have lost all the impact if you just saw somebody sitting in the witness box, relating what happened. She had already done that herself.
> [Scottish white middle-class woman, with no experience of violence]

> The rape, in my opinion, it was put in the movie at the very end to sort of build you up, really, to this excitement of the rape scene. ... When the girl was telling the other lady about when she was raped, why wasn't it sort of flashed back as her story, rather than waiting to the trial and let another witness [tell it]? I suppose it was building it up as well, you know, in the movie. Get you probably excited and you think, 'Oh, this is a good part.'
> [English Afro-Caribbean woman, with no experience of violence]

Behind this recognition that the impact of the rape scene is the product of cinematic artifice lay a concern – articulated by a number of women – that *The Accused* might be exploiting sexual violence. The quantitative data has shown that substantial minorities of women had reservations about this scene. The kinds of division that it could provoke emerge very clearly from the following exchange between women who had no experience of violence:

> *Speaker 1:*   I think ... that they could've explained it. They could easily leave that rape scene.

Speaker 2:	But it's like that other film we watched. You don't realise the full impact, like, the one we were watching, the first one [*Crimewatch*], until you've got the reconstruction.
Speaker 3:	Yeah, but I think with that sort of film, it would cause more damage than it would any good. I mean, if someone had been raped, would you like to have [to] sit through that again?
	[English Afro-Caribbean women, with no experience of violence]

Here, the argument hinges upon whether or not *The Accused* could have achieved its impact without employing such explicit and graphic means. The counter-argument interestingly cites how *Crimewatch* could manage to discuss a rape case without showing anything graphic at all – a point that demonstrates, incidentally, how cross-references to other programmes may be used in debates about what it is acceptable to show on television. The exchange then continued:

Speaker 1:	But you wouldn't miss anything, would you? What would you? All right, if you didn't watch that particular part, would you miss anything? You could still grasp it, couldn't you?
Speaker 2:	You could still grasp it but the enormous effect that it's had on us at the moment, it wouldn't be as drastic ... without those.
Speaker 1:	Yeah, but I'm thinking how would men see it? How would men see it?
Speaker 3:	That's what I'm saying, how would they view that scene?
Speaker 4:	They couldn't believe it either, I mean, they didn't – they didn't think they were doing any wrong.
Speaker 1:	Men would probably sit down and think, 'Well, she asked for it. She was enjoying it and look, the men around enjoyed it.'
	[English Afro-Caribbean women, with no experience of violence]

Here, the argument about the need for explicitness in order to ensure impact is both denied and repeated. The debate then shifts onto new territory, namely a concern about how 'men' as a general category of viewer would respond, with sharp doubts expressed about whether their interpretation would be anything other than from a potential rapist's point of view. This latter point was developed further by several women, who expressly suggested that if the present study had been conducted on men, then the outcome would have been radically different:

152

If you'd got six men sat in – or five men sat in the room next door, they'd probably ... I bet you one of the first things that would come out was that she'd asked for that. They'd think that she asked for that, the way she was dressed, the way she was wiggling her backside and she aroused him and she asked for it. I think that's what you'd get from them.
[English white working-class woman, with no experience of violence]

This proved to be far from an isolated comment. Supporting evidence was produced by other women who reflected upon their experiences of seeing *The Accused* in mixed company:

When I watched it there were men present, and they were quite disturbed about it – but they didn't have so much to say about it than, 'Oh well, no comment. She did really ask for it. It was her own fault.' And I said, 'How could you say that?' And they still couldn't see what we were pointing out, they were saying, 'But look, if you play it back you could see that she did ask for it.'

And several of the girls as well were saying, 'Yes, she asked for it' and everything like that. But I don't think anybody asks to be raped.
[English Afro-Caribbean women, with no experience of violence]

A similar point was made by a woman whose husband had rented *The Accused* from a video shop, who said:

We had an argument about it because he reckoned that she was dressed provocatively and that she deserved it, and I reckoned she didn't. I got quite angry about it.
[English white woman, with experience of violence]

These observations point to a profound diversity of interpretation between men and women who had watched the film and to their failure to bridge the gap in debate. Moreover, the comments made also underline the fact that the 'male' perspective may also be shared by some women. Underlying this 'male' perspective is a broader set of widely diffused cultural assumptions. The evidence suggests that in some cases these assumptions are rejected due to some women's direct experience of violence, and in others by their refusal to accept as legitimate such categorisations of female behaviour. The testimony of yet another woman shed further light upon the experience described above:

Shall I tell you something? When I went to see that film first, there was about ten of us, five of them were male. After we walked out of that film the women were devastated, one out of the five men was, the other four were cracking jokes. That upset me more after that

than the film did. Their responses afterwards.
[English Asian woman, with no experience of violence]

Although it would be wildly exaggerated to imply that this was a generally held view, it was, nevertheless, one that was expressed sufficiently often to open up a further set of questions about the more general conceptions of the differences between men and women that informed much of the interpretation of the film. Even where it might be conceded that watching the film could change views, this was nevertheless grounded in the belief that habitually men simply do not think about such questions:

> I think it's opened a lot of people's eyes, I know a few males that have gone to see it and they said before ... [of] rape, 'So what, what's the big thing about it?' And they watched that film and they say that they never realised how much effect on the female, and how disturbing it is, and how horrific and everything ... I think it was more they never thought about it before. But I think it really opened ... their eyes. Because I really don't think males really think about it, do they? It's not happening to them.
> [Scottish white middle-class woman, with no experience of violence]

Contexts of viewing

Finally, some points should be made about the profound anxieties aroused by how such a film as *The Accused* might be viewed. We have already alluded to the differences between masculine and feminine perspectives on the rape scene suggested by a number of women in our sample. We have argued that this is related to some quite profound differences in male and female culture and the kinds of identities that these sustain for men and women.

Most concern was expressed about pleasure and sexual gratification being derived from viewing *The Accused*, together with the possible result of 'copycat' behaviour resulting in rape. General worries about the imitation of violent action resulting from media consumption are well established and have accompanied the rise of the mass media themselves. A very clear statement of this line of argument was expressed thus:

> Some males would perhaps enjoy it. If males were watching it and say, 'Oh, that's disgusting', and go away and not do anything [that would be all right]. But the thing is, that scene could provoke someone and it could lead on to an actual rape.
> [Scottish white middle-class woman, with no experience of violence]

Or again, in these very similar terms:

> I don't think they should have made the film with the rape scene in

it. I think they could have done it without it because there's a lot of people who would actually watch the film and would not see it the way we're seeing it at the moment and would think, 'Oh, a bit of fun', or take it the wrong way, and it could lead to rape. So, in that case I don't think the film should have been made with the rape scene in it.

[Scottish white middle-class woman, with no experience of violence]

Such worries about how *The Accused*, in the view of numerous women, might be open to misinterpretation, led naturally enough into the making of suggestions as to how it ought to be viewed. The exchange quoted below shows how this kind of discussion occurred in one Scottish group with experience of violence, encompassing the idea that there should be group discussions, or that extracts could be shown in schools, and that such segments might be used in counselling:

Speaker 1: It would be good in groups, in a controlled situation, you know, and talking about rape ... using it that way. But to actually just have it to watch for kicks.

Speaker 2: I think perhaps up until the rape scene, if it could be cut up into bits, even in, like, schools – four, five, sixth formers [High School], that sort of thing .

Speaker 3: Uhuh, but delete the actual rape scene.

Speaker 2: But for to keep it as a whole thing like that, I don't think so.

Speaker 1: They could use different parts of it for different things like counselling, for actually understanding how the person feels or if you broke it up. But that actual rape scene, I found that really upsetting.

[Scottish white women, with experience of violence]

This latter point was developed further by a rape counsellor who placed *The Accused* very much in a potential training framework, underlining her strong doubts about the desirability of its general availability:

I'm looking at it from two points of view. I'm looking at it [as] a good training film for my recruits, to get them used to certain things that they're going to come across. But to put [it] on general release and to have people sitting in their homes or in cinemas watching it and getting some form of enjoyment, I think is wrong.

[Scottish white woman, rape counsellor, in group with experience of violence]

In a different group of women with experience of violence, a very similar line of argument developed, in almost identical terminology, where, once again, the emphasis was placed upon the need for putting the representation of rape into the right context, which would permit the responsible exercise of control over the audience's reactions:

> I think within a context like this, when we're sitting watching it and discussing it, it has some value. But when it's just people going in to watch it as an evening's entertainment, and then going home and there's nothing, no kind of educational follow-up, or no kind of discussion round it, no awareness, or consciousness around those issues, I feel really uncomfortable about that. I mean it is basically a money-spinner. It's an American film, it's made lots of money.
> [English white woman, with experience of violence]

These comments further reveal the depth of the underlying fears and anxieties that were elicited in the questionnaires.

Gender and male culture

The Accused, much more so than any of the other programmes screened, provoked reactions that mobilised broader sentiments and beliefs about the nature of gender. Such views emerged with particular clarity among members of the ethnic-minority groups. The classic attributes of masculinity and femininity were summed up in a list of stereotypes during one discussion:

> *Speaker 1*: Well, the men are brought up conditioned in a way to see women – well, men are brought up to be the fighters, the protectors, everything.
> *Speaker 2*: The breadwinners.
> *Speaker 1*: Women are the homemakers, the carers, the …
> *Speaker 2*: Babymakers [laugh].
> [Scottish Asian women, with experience of violence]

These rather ironic categorisations offer a strong sense of how the women concerned thought that they were perceived by men, and are grounded in an acute sense of how far-reaching gender divisions can be. For some, this shaded into how male fantasy made use of pornography and used this as a yardstick for judging women's sexual allure and performance:

> Men – a lot of them play out what they see and there are a lot of women who are abused by husbands because men see things in pornographic magazines. I'm talking about in general. And they see a woman on page three, and they expect that their woman is going to be like that, and if she's not like that, then it's her fault and she's going to be made to feel she should be like that. And then they expect a lot of women to behave like the way they see it in a film. And I think women suffer as a result of that because we're supposed to be what we're not, you know? You haven't got size forty boobs anyway. But that's how they visualise you and it's like you have to live

up to the expectations.
[English Afro-Caribbean woman, with no experience of violence]

One pointed remark went even further, where the rape victim was seen as being dehumanised:

It was like a machine that was holding a jackpot or something.
[Scottish Asian woman, with no experience of violence]

It is hardly surprising, then, that where doubts were raised about the moral capacities of 'men', as viewers, to be sensitive to a woman's point of view, such dubiety articulated with a much broader set of concerns about the relationship between rape and male culture. Inevitably, given the scenario in the film, much discussion of maleness focused upon men drinking in groups as an archetypal pastime, both as a leisure pursuit and more profoundly as an assertion of a particular form of bonding. Male friendship was pithily summed up by one woman with experience of violence:

Men have got a sort of thing about friends and if your friend said to do it, you're going to do it. If your friend said jump off a bridge, you do it.
[English white woman, with experience of violence]

And the role of drink in cementing such relationships was also the object of disenchanted observations:

They have a drinking competition in the pub. One swills down a pint, the rest of them have got to do it, even if it makes them sick. And if it makes them sick they cheer even more.

They've got to get into the same round as everybody else. I mean, I've seen my husband do it and he's no great drinker, and they'll all get a round in, you know. Everybody's got the round in. But this is probably four pints later or five pints later, I mean, 'You don't really want that.' 'I know, but I bought it.' 'Well, leave it.' 'Oh no, I've got to drink it.' And I'm sitting there thinking, 'Oh, for goodness' sake.' In the end I sort of just tip it into everybody else's glasses when he's gone to the loo [laugh]. You know, he just sort of goes with the flow.
[English white women, with no experience of violence]

These comments are particularly interesting for the way in which they suggest the role of peer pressure in producing conformity. However, it is a long step from feeling obliged to drink as a sign of comradeship and manhood to that of being obliged to join in a gang rape for the same right to belong. Yet there can be no doubt that such interpretative connections were made by some members of the groups in this study.

157

For example, the links between the male culture of group solidarity, the social milieu in which drinking takes place, and the threat to women of – at the very least – sexual harassment, are all made in this sketch of the bar scenario in *The Accused*:

> You had the guy at the bar who sent over the drinks and was eyeing them up. You had two behind them at a table who were also doing the same. So there you had three men watching this one particular girl. So if one didn't get her, you know – not necessarily to rape her – I'm not saying the three of them were sitting there saying, 'We're going to rape her.' But there was three guys sitting looking at her so there was bound to be one of those three who would approach her eventually, whether to sexually harass her or just to have a night out with her. But through events it turned into a gang rape.
> [Scottish white woman, rape counsellor, member of group with experience of violence]

This predatory and inherently unstable masculine environment, evoked here by a rape counsellor, loudly echoes the fears expressed about women's safety in the world at large in the responses made to *Crimewatch UK*.

However, it was precisely the insight that many of the women possessed into the pressures exerted by certain forms of male bonding that allowed some to make highly nuanced distinctions of responsibility between the rapists and their supporting crowd. Here we can discern a number of arguments about how and why the rape happened and the roles played in it by different men. One way into this issue was to see the entire rape as produced by the characteristic peer pressures of a male group, as in this quotation:

> She'd said to him, she said, 'I've had too much to drink, you know, I've got to go to work in the morning', and I think he was aroused too much then to let it go. And when the goading started, he carried on. And then the others, they just followed like sheep. They were just goaded and goaded and goaded. And it's like anything, to turn and to say 'no', you know, it's so hard in a crowd. I can't even imagine what it's like with something like that because I don't know how men feel about things like that. It's enough to make anybody vomit, you know, forcing sex on somebody who doesn't want it. ... But let alone one, two, three. ... And they just followed on. And I think, like that young lad, he was shocked when they said, 'Come on, college boy, it's your turn', and he just got carried along with the momentum, you know.
> [English white working-class woman, with no experience of violence]

Here, Danny, the first rapist, and Bob, the second, are almost excused for being aroused, and therefore out of control and susceptible to the mob support of their buddies. Beneath this lies an implicit conception of male sexuality as beyond rationality and self-regulation. It is not condoned, but rather seen as virtually a force of nature.

A further way of handling the question was to render it mundane; the rapist is part and parcel of society, by this account:

> I think they're perfectly everyday men, that's what you've got to remember. They're not monsters, you know, and I think ... your initial response is 'Monsters, hang them, cut them and draw them. ...' But they are everyday men. They are ... the college kids, you know; the man with the scorpion, he's got a wife; he's got responsibilities, and yet he still went and behaved the way he did.
> [English Asian woman, with no experience of violence]

In many respects, such domestication of the problem makes it even more troubling as there are no signs of Cain that can help the would-be victim avoid her fate. The logical consequence of such a view is that all men harbour the potential to commit rape. However, the general terms of discussion implied that if such a potentiality did exist, it required particular circumstances to activate it. So far as *The Accused* was concerned, a number of our sample made clear distinctions between the different rapists and their degree of moral responsibility. Such distinctions should be seen in the broader context of a general detestation and fear of rape, in which epithets such as 'animals', 'perverts', 'monsters' and 'rubbish' were used as ways of describing the rapists. There was also generalised contempt for the role of the male group in supporting the rape.

Some of the women were quite conscious of the extent that excuses were at times actually being offered, and went on to deny this:

> He was disgusting really, doing something like that, but I mean they were – they were pushed into it as well. I'm not making excuses for them, but they were more pushed into it.
> [English white woman, with experience of violence]

There was no uniformity of view about precisely where the line was to be drawn. In the following exchange, for instance, greater onus of responsibility is placed upon the first of the rapists:

Speaker 1: Because that student would never ever have committed rape. That was the crowd that made him do that. It's amazing what you do in a crowd that you wouldn't do on your own.

Speaker 2: I think the first guy would have done. I think he had every intention of committing rape, but the other two wouldn't.

Researcher:	You said the college boy wouldn't have committed it without the crowd?
Speaker 3:	No, he wouldn't have, no way. I mean he wasn't even going to do it – but the crowd egged him on so much. He didn't have to. Obviously he didn't have to do it, but ... they just egged him on so much that he just thought 'do it', you know ...
Researcher:	So was it the crowd's responsibility?
Speaker 3:	Yes. Not totally, I mean obviously he should still have turned round and said 'No way!', and walked away, but he wouldn't have done it if the crowd hadn't egged him on so much.
	[Scottish white middle-class women, with no experience of violence]

What is noticeable, once again, however, is the remarkable consistency with which crowd pressure is invoked as an explanation. A much more emphatic distinction came into play between relative responsibilities in the case of the third rapist, Kurt:

> There was one instance where the third rapist – you were almost in there willing him to say 'No'. There was a minute in there when you felt, when you felt ... this is a very naive man and he, I felt, certainly wouldn't have done it if it hadn't been that there were so many people round about him. And, even when he was doing it – he seemed such a naive kind of person, you could almost feel his naivety. Well, to a certain extent you could identify with him. Yes, you know, that you were being coerced into a situation ... You could feel his feelings to a certain extent. This was maybe a man who maybe didn't have opportunities with women or whatever. And yet, he hung back and at that moment when he hung back you were there with him. Even if there had just been two people and one of them said, 'Right, I've done it. You do it', he would have said 'No.'
> [Scottish white middle-class woman, with no experience of violence]

The above view was offered by a woman with no experience of violence, as were those immediately preceding it. However, one could find precisely the same line taken by those who had such experience, a point that emerged consensually from the following exchange:

Speaker 1:	I don't think it would've went near that far if it wasn't for the guys egging him on. I think that played a vital part in the film that made your heart bleed. Because it seemed a secondary thing to me that they weren't equally as guilty as the rapists, but they were a helluva lot guiltier than just bystanders. Yeah, there wasn't just the three who actually raped or penetrated her. I

	think they all raped her in some way or another.
Speaker 2:	I think they were equally guilty. Aye, the ones that were egging on. Because I took it that the third one that raped her, I don't think that if the guys hadn't been egging and egging and egging at him, he wouldn't have done it really. You could see he was sort of ...
Speaker 3:	They were sort of saying, 'Oh, you cannot do it. You cannot do it.' They were plaguing him, saying he was not a man as such, in so many words.
Speaker 1:	They were talking about the size of his penis and things like that, ridiculing.
Speaker 3:	So, of course, he just done it to actually prove himself.
Researcher:	So he – was less willing to ...
Speaker 3:	I wouldn't say he was less wanting to do it, but he just knew himself, in himself, that it was wrong to do it. But because of the egging on.
	[Scottish white women, with experience of violence]

Thus, at the same time as the guilt is spread around, it is also possible to find a mitigating explanation for one man, if certainly not an exculpation. At the heart of this is a widespread recognition that proving one's manliness by whatever means necessary is an unpredictable force to be reckoned with. Thus other women talked in relevant terms of it being necessary for a man to prove that he was not a 'wimp' or impotent.

Other characters

Most of the discussion of character focused on Sarah Tobias, who engaged the most complex reactions. As demonstrated above, discussion of the rapists largely took place in the context of conceptions of masculinity and femininity. This framework also held the key to the reactions expressed about other characters in *The Accused*. In fact, despite our working assumption that the discussion of characterisation might be quite extensive, we found that it was not. Nevertheless, sufficient indicative comments emerged in the various groups to offer some insights. In particular, judgments were focused upon the lawyer, Katheryn, and the friend, Sally, with more being said about the former.

Broadly speaking, among those who commented on her characterisation, Katheryn was depicted as a woman having to make her way in a man's professional world. Hardened by this, she shares the scepticism and indifference of her male colleagues to Sarah's fate, despite being a woman:

I think to begin with she was portrayed, and probably quite realistically so, as a woman in a man's world, who'd taken on their values, and their valuations of the situation. But I think the turning point did come for her – or it seemed to – when Sarah went to her home, where

161

she wasn't in her professional territory and it's intruding in her personal life, and the point where the lawyer went to the bar and saw the pin-ball machine and the images. And, for me, the feeling that I got at that point was that the lawyer's thinking it could've been anybody. There was these images around, it could've been any of us. That's the way I felt about it, from then on it was very much a personal thing.

[English white woman, with experience of violence]

The transformation of Katheryn's thinking comes about, on the above account, as a result of realising her own vulnerability. It is akin to a conversion. For others, the moment of change occurred when she encountered the chief egger-on of the rapists, the man with the scorpion tattoo, in the hospital, and then realised that Sarah was telling the truth. This, some argued, fuelled her feelings of guilt and made her all the more determined to prosecute the case. For them, the fact that she was a woman ensured that she was determined to see things through to the end:

She felt it more. I think women would feel it more than a man dealing with the case because it could happen to her. She sort of started to feel what the girl actually felt. Played on her emotions a bit.

[Scottish white middle-class woman, with no experience of violence]

The opposition between male and female also offers the key to the passing comments made about Sally, these in essence being that she had been disloyal and that by not seeking help she had betrayed the solidarity that one woman owes to another in such situations of risk:

Her best friend, although she did give a statement at the end of the day, but she wasn't very willing. ... See, no matter what happens at the end of the day, even your best friends will turn their back on you when it comes to involvement with the police and court and things like that. ... I don't blame them, but then I can understand why they don't want to be involved because it's, like, then they're seen in a different way as well. When they're accused of, you know, 'Why did you give evidence against a man?' and then it's their reputation. That was something else that it showed, and you know it's very important to see that because ... if your best friend ... ran, then you've got nobody else really.

[Scottish Asian woman, with experience of violence]

As a counterpoint, the man who does enlist aid, Ken, is correspondingly feminised, since he offers such a strong contrast with the macho norm of maleness represented in the film:

162

He was portrayed as a real effeminate bloke, wasn't he? Compared with everybody else in that bar. They were bawdy and loud and you looked at him in his neat little jacket and his sweet little face, standing there with absolute shock and horror. The only thing that I found a bit strange was that he never moved before he did. That he stood and watched the whole thing.
[English white working-class woman, with no experience of violence]

These are but pointers to the possible working out of some underlying assumptions. But they are completely consistent with the view that femininity and masculinity functioned as strong interpretive categories in how the women in the study reacted to *The Accused*.

Conclusion

As will be apparent, of all the programmes screened, *The Accused* had the most profound impact upon our viewing groups. The responses evoked touched the emotional core of virtually all the women present. What was particularly striking – and this emerged in the course of group discussions much more clearly than from the quantitative data – was the *universal* identification with the situation of the rape victim, although many reservations and qualifications were forthcoming about her character. This stands in strong contrast to the reactions to portrayals of domestic violence, where the identification with the victim was much less evenly distributed, being most apparent among women with experience of violence.

There was considerable concern about the appropriateness of a Hollywood film – one essentially premised upon entertainment values – as the most suitable vehicle for dealing with this troubling subject. A consequence of this was the frequently articulated desire for there to be a responsible, controlled context for viewing. This, however, did not express itself as a demand for outright censorship, for the most part. Rather, it produced suggestions about how such a controlled context might ideally be created while recognising that it was not really likely to be realised. The worries were centred upon what 'men' were likely to make of this film. *The Accused* evoked extremely powerful feelings and sharp observations about the culture of male solidarity and its negative impact upon women. Anxieties about men as viewers were completely consistent with these wider assumptions.

WOMEN VIEWING VIOLENCE

Viewing televised violence may, for some women, involve the re-creation of a painful and dangerous personal experience; for others, it approximates a feared event; and, for others still, it is merely the depiction of a relatively abstract and distant act. Differentiated by life experience, social class and ethnicity, viewers interpret sexual and domestic violence, given scenes and characters, as well as entire programmes, in a variety of ways. Some issues are more salient for particular categories of viewers than for others. Thus the viewing group or audience cannot be treated as a single entity but, rather, manifests a patterned diversity. Accordingly, the viewing audience becomes several viewing audiences.

Diversity among viewers

Ethnicity proved to be a strong differentiating factor between different groups of women viewers. This manifested itself in two ways: first, some were critical of the depictions of their own ethnic group, seeing these as uninformed, biased or bigoted, and second, others were alienated because of the perceived irrelevance to them of some of what they saw due to their own distance from the dominant, white culture. Ethnicity, therefore, played a crucial role in two quite distinctive ways: it was an indicator of alienation among Afro-Caribbean women and a way of affirming difference among Asian women.

The point about alienation emerged particularly clearly in the case of *EastEnders* for Afro-Caribbean women, who believed this programme to be making an essentially racist comment about mixed marriages and by extension about the general competence and character of black women. *Crimewatch* was also seen to be singling out black criminals. In the case of *The Accused,* ethnic identity also functioned to limit the measure of identification that the Afro-Caribbean women could find for the rape victim.

In the case of Asian women, *The Accused* offered information about practices and values at a considerable distance from their lived experience. They seemed to view the film almost anthropologically as a report upon the wider society. At the same time, their reading of the film validated their differences, showing them how their culture could operate to protect them from danger. Asian women were particularly remote from the depiction of white women, seeing them as beyond the cultural controls and restrictions which, in this case, were defined as protecting women from male violence. Their alienation, on the same basis as the Afro-Caribbean women's, was evident in observations made about *EastEnders*.

Social class appeared to create fewer obvious differences between viewers than ethnicity, and those differences were not as strong. In part, this may be attributed to the design of this research, given the problem of recruiting middle-class women who would admit to experiencing violence. However, where direct comparison was possible, by controlling for violence and social class, some differences were in evidence. For example, in the case of *Closing Ranks*, distance from Shirley on the part of the middle-class women was clearly related to her perceived class position. In similar vein, the refusal to think badly about the police and the ways they might at times behave appeared to be rooted in a commitment to a given view of the social order and an uncontested respect for authority. Much of the discussion of the differences between Carmel and Matthew in *EastEnders* focused on the woman's seniority of status in the employment hierarchy – compounded, of course, by the fact that she was a woman (and tacitly, we suspect, for some white respondents, by the additional fact that she was black).

The most obvious differentiating factor between viewers was the experience, or alternatively the lack of experience, of violence. Viewers with such life-experience were more sensitive to televised violence, more subtle and complex in their readings, more concerned about possible effects and more demanding in their expectations of the producers of such content. Having experience of violence allows given portrayals and moments leading to the violent event to be interpreted with considerable finesse: the finer points of discrimination were entirely linked to what women had undergone in their own lives. There was also a knowledge of all the excuses offered for male violence towards women and a consequential refusal to play the game of exculpation which contrasted with the greater willingness to do so among some of the women with no experience of violence.

This could be seen in the proportion of women able to relate either to the character and/or the situations across all four of the programmes screened. With only one exception, anywhere from one-half to nearly all of the women with experience of violence were able to relate to the characters portrayed and the situations in which they were placed. Exceptionally, only one-third could relate to the character in *The Accused*. On the other hand, only around one-third or less of women with no experience of violence related to either the characters or scenes in any of the four programmes. They came closest to convergence in their inability to relate to the character in *The Accused* and the middling ability to relate to the rape/murder victim in *Crimewatch*. Greatest variance occurred in relation to *EastEnders*, where most of those with experience of violence were able to relate both to the characters and to the scenes, while few of those without experience did so. These differences are, no doubt, also affected by class, with middle-class women being less able to relate to the working-class characters portrayed, and, similarly, by ethnicity. Although further study might help tease out the amount of differentiation attributable to each of these factors, there can be little doubt that the experience of violence is a strong differentiator in women's ability to relate to depictions of violence against women on television.

Similarities among viewers

Despite the differences in response created by social status and life experience, there were also similarities across the viewing audiences. To a large extent, such similarities would appear to be associated with gender and the general commonalities of women's experiences rather than with class or ethnicity: as women in their own right; on the basis of relationships between women and men; and in virtue of women's relations with others, particularly children.

The most striking example of similarity across the group was the fear of male violence, particularly of rape. This was generally found across all of the viewers, despite class or ethnicity, as was a concern about the possible impact upon children of viewing violence against women on television. With rape, the distinctions based on women's experience of violence broke down. In effect, every woman could identify with the fear of rape: it would seem to be more universal. It is not necessary to have experienced rape in order to fear it, to condemn it out of hand or to imagine its consequences. In relation to the rape/murder in *Crimewatch* and the gang rape in *The Accused*, group discussions elicited by the screenings reveal a profound anxiety about personal safety. This is further supported by the high proportion of women who defined *The Accused* as 'disturbing' and the fact that, while *Crimewatch* was not generally viewed as 'disturbing' overall, the rape/murder segment was. In general, this tells us a great deal about everyday tacit fears that women have about men.

Here, we face two conundrums which warrant brief discussion and a possible explanation. First, women are more afraid of violent attacks yet, in reality, it is men who are more likely to experience them. Second, more women are afraid of rape by a stranger than of sexual or physical violence by an intimate, yet the obverse is more likely. These gender-based issues bear on how the audiences in this research are both similar, as women with a common concern (about rape), and yet also different from one another (based on the varying experience of domestic violence). A further axis of difference is that which distinguishes women from men. The questions raised by such gender-based issues are made even more complex because the perceptions commonly held about the chances of experiencing various types of violence do not correspond with the actual incidence of such offences. Crime statistics and studies of violence show that violence between males is the most common form of violence, followed by domestic violence, domestic rape and, finally, rape by a stranger.[1] Yet, despite these well-attested findings, far more women are afraid of rape by a stranger whereas few, except for those who are its victims, fear domestic violence or rape from an acquaintance. Popular cultural beliefs help explain what might otherwise seem contradictory or puzzling.

For the most part, all women learn from a very early age to be aware of, and guard against, the possibility of male sexual violence. From the childhood lessons of 'don't take sweets from a stranger' to later warnings about walking alone in dark places and the dangers of specific places and people, the potential of male violence, particularly sexual violence, is continually underlined throughout society. Since women are by far the most usual victims of such violence, the lessons are, accordingly, more specifically directed at them. The fact that males are more likely to be physically violent to other males and that they are more likely to be physically or sexually violent to wives, lovers or girlfriends than to total strangers is either ignored or relatively unstressed in the popular culture. Thus it is not surprising that most women learn to be aware of, and more or less to guard against, the probability of being sexually attacked by a male stranger, such as those presented in *Crimewatch* and *The Accused*. Only those with the relevant lived experience are similarly sensitised to and fearful of physical and sexual attack within the domestic setting, such as portrayed in *EastEnders* and *Closing Ranks*.

Thus, while both marital violence and rape are gender-based offences, rape by a stranger is more likely to be a matter of *universal* concern to women despite their class or ethnic background, while domestic violence is less likely to engender fear *except for those who have actually had such experience*. The one is a more universal fear among women, although less likely to be experienced, whereas the other differentiates women based on what is, in fact, a far more common experience. This more universal concern among women is not similarly matched among men whose lived experience and social training reflect a different reality, in which the asymmetrical nature of sexual violence leaves them relatively unconcerned about the possibility of being attacked and harmed by a female stranger. Such gender divisions emerged most clearly in relation to *The Accused*. Here, beliefs about the nature of male culture, and its connections with violent sexual assaults on women, crystallised in conceptions of the differences between how women interpret the rape scene and how they imagine men's interpretations (for the most part) to be. This offers eloquent testament to the role of gender in cultural interpretation.

Thus gender operates in three ways to shape reactions to viewing various forms of violence against women: it differentiates women from men; it differentiates women with experience of violence from those with none; and, finally, it operates as a factor that cuts across class, ethnicity and experience of violence, expressed in terms of women's generalised concerns about sexual violence from strangers. Thus the specific case studied here links to a more general point. Readings of televised violence among women can at times be treated as tending towards a universal framework of interpretation, and thus as more generalisable to the population of women as a whole, while at other times reactions must be differentiated, being generalisable only to specific subgroups or categories of viewers.

The findings of this research indicate that life experience, ethnic and class background, and gender are important factors around which both universality and particularity are organised and that cultural beliefs may play a mediating role. These factors often represent a complex cross-cutting in which the primacy of one is not always clear or possible to distinguish. However, the findings also seem to indicate that, in general, the salience in any particular programme of ethnicity, class, gender or a lived experience such as violence is greatest for those *most directly involved* and diminishes in importance with social distance. Having a particular experience or a particular background does significantly affect the interpretation of a given text. The four programmes screened are obviously open to various readings. However, on the evidence, *how* they are read is fundamentally affected by various socio-cultural factors and by lived experience.

This begins to open the broader question of the social identities available to women and how these shape their interpretations of culture. It is an obvious next step for research such as this to investigate this matter further and to make a systematic comparison with the social identities of men. We have addressed the apparent contradiction between audience reactions, fears of violence, and the 'reality' of their occurrence. This highlights the highly complex relationship between audience perceptions, popular culture, and material circumstances, in this case the known rates of crime. While the understanding of audience response has been enhanced through this approach, this would hardly have occurred had the research remained strictly within the distinct domains of either audience perceptions or criminal statistics.

The 'active audience'

Rather than being passive recipients of scenes and messages of audio-visual culture, viewers are active interpreters and evaluators of that which is viewed. This activity, however, takes place within definite limits, mobilising frameworks of interpretation that are rooted in diverse socio-cultural backgrounds and experience. In the present study, as in others, many have applied the test of realism to their viewing experience. In particular, women who have experienced violence expect the depiction of violence against women to be realistic, in order that it might best serve an educational purpose for the general public and for violent men who thereby might better understand the experiences of women who are abused. Accordingly, we have found a belief that depicting or discussing violence on television, provided it is done well and sensitively, may have a positive effect upon the lives of individual viewers and social life in general. Conversely, some viewers worry that violence casually or insensitively portrayed may actually contribute to more violence and/or frighten children, the elderly, and women on their own. We have uncovered a definite view that producing scenes of violence against women for public viewing brings with it a related responsibility for its possible consequences for viewers. It is not surprising, therefore, that, for the most part, the violence on television portrayed in this study was not defined as 'exciting' or 'entertaining', but rather as 'educational' or 'relevant', while at the same time as 'disturbing' and sometimes 'offensive'. Thus the importance attributed to what was viewed was not in terms of pleasure, escape or fantasy but in terms of relevance and social importance.

Reactions to viewing violence and fear of crime

While there have been several decades of research attempting to examine the effect of viewing violence upon subsequent perpetration of violence, on 'copycat' violence and the effects of pornography, the findings are not clear. We remain uncertain about whether the depiction of violence for popular consumption actually increases the occurrence of violence in daily life. Since the focus of this research was not upon the responses of the potential perpetrators of violence against women to depictions of such violence, the present findings cannot directly add to this very large body of literature nor, indeed, are they intended to do so. It is worth noting, however, that the female respondents spontaneously expressed some concern about the possible negative effects of depicting violence against women on television and generally felt that there should be some limits upon that which might be detrimental to the safety of women and the sensibilities of children.

Studies of the fear of crime generally show that those who are most afraid, such as elderly women, are among the least likely to become the victims of crime. Conversely, those most likely to become the victims of physical violence, young males victimised by other males, are among the least afraid of crime. Since women are in general more afraid of crime than men, although less likely to become its victims, there has been some speculation about the source of such anxieties and some initial comment about the 'irrationality' of women's fears. More complex analysis has reconsidered women's fear of crime in terms of their personal histories of violence, the higher probability of its occurrence than is reflected in criminal statistics and the increased level of severity of the violence, and arrived at more subtle explanations.[2] If, in the case of young men, there is a high probability of a scuffle with a mate outside a pub, but the likely *severity* of the violence is fairly low, then young men are not likely to experience a high level of fear of such crime. If, in the case of young women, the probability is low of being attacked and raped by a stranger while on the way home at night, but the *severity* of the attack is high, then the level of fear is likely to be much greater, even though the chances of occurrence are less. Accordingly, the levels of fear and anxiety about possible violence against women among the respondents in this research are to be expected, and accord with other findings.

There has been some controversy about the contribution of the media to fear of crime among viewers, but, as noted in the introduction, the evidence is not clear-cut. Of late, such programmes as *Crimewatch UK* have been the focus of specific official and critical attention concerning their effects upon fear of crime, although findings by the broadcasting organisations tend to be somewhat dismissive of this. *Crimewatch* was certainly the only programme spontaneously named by respondents when asked to identify programmes which increased their fear of crime (because of the types of crime depicted); but, ironically, it was also named, albeit by fewer respondents, as a programme reducing their fear of crime (because of its representation of police successes in solving crime).

To our knowledge, there is no other research of this kind on how the victims of violence react to and interpret the depiction of such acts on television.[3] Here, *the issue is not whether depictions of violence increase the likelihood of similar violence among potential perpetrators, but the feelings and reactions that it creates among those who are the actual or potential victims of violence.* Are women likely to feel more vulnerable, less safe or less valued members of our society if, as a category, they are with some frequency depicted as those who are subjected to abuse? If so, the portrayal of violence against women may be seen as negative, even if women viewers have never experienced such violence and/or its likelihood is not increased. Some indications of this can be found in three findings: women's concern that televised violence against women be portrayed realistically and sensitively and used to effect some positive outcome, such as public education or crime prevention; women's fear that such portrayals might have negative effects upon women and children; and indications by women that there are some outer limits beyond which the portrayal of violence against women should not go. This was expressed most strongly among women who had themselves been the victims of violence, perhaps looking for an enlightened reaffirmation of their lives and experiences within such portrayals, while at the same time fearing indifference or, worse still, confirmation of the perpetrators' rationales.

The method

This examination of women viewing violence has used both qualitative and quantitative methods in an attempt to obtain the advantages of each; notably the depth and detail obtainable from lengthy group discussions, and the structure, comparability across cases, and ability to generalise from quantitative data. Overall, the approach is systematic and reproducible. Diversity, rather than singularity, characterises the nature of the sample, the types of programmes viewed and the techniques of data collection and analysis. The sample was selected in order to ensure diversity among viewers and the design was also characterised by variation in factors such as experience, ethnicity and class, which we thought to be theoretically relevant to the topic under study. Selecting

170

diverse genres of programmes aimed to show the depiction of violence in a variety of audiovisual forms, each with quite distinct contents but still thematically connected. The aim was also to present a comparison of violence against women with other forms of crime, to provide elements of ethnic and class diversity in the programmes themselves, and to offer an overall 'package' of viewing in which the type and amount of violence increased in severity. Thus the viewers might be 'eased' into increasingly difficult topics, and comparisons of response might consequently be made across both diverse programmes and viewing groups. This proved fruitful, increasing the strength of generalisations that might be made about women's reactions to violence against women on television.

In selecting programmes, we opted for those that might be seen as realistic and relatively sympathetic, leaving aside the explicitly exploitative and pornographic as well as those employing fantasy. Although this obviously limited the range of representations offered, it did not predetermine the specific kinds of reading that viewing groups might bring to bear on what they saw. Programme choices were based on a mixture both of ethical and practical considerations about how far researchers might go, with particular sensitivity to just how far victims of violence might be exposed to disturbing scenes. This study has extended the genres usually looked at in feminist media studies and is also cross-generic, examining both factual and fictional representations of violence. Still further extension of genres to be viewed is both possible and desirable. We have sought quite explicitly to bring a sociological study of violence against women into media studies and media reception analysis into the present literature on violence against women. Both fields of research have thus far developed largely in relative ignorance of each other.

Where now?

Do we need a similar study of men in order to reflect upon the validity of these findings about women? A similar study of men would tell us about how men, the usual perpetrators of violence against women, view the depiction of violence against women on television. It would be an equally fascinating study, but in many ways quite distinct. That is because there is a crucial difference in terms of whether the viewer is prospective victim or perpetrator.

The representation of violence against women by men in our culture raises some broad questions about the acceptability of what is screened and printed. When women appear in books, newspapers, magazines, television programmes and films as the objects of male violence – whether domestic or sexual – questions may legitimately be posed about how appropriately gender is handled by different media. This brings us inevitably into debates about censorship, which have been particularly lively where they concern questions of pornography, although, interestingly enough, not at all where domestic violence has been concerned.[4] Domestic violence is plainly on an altogether different conceptual map. We trust that this analysis will at least begin to open a discussion about this neglected issue.

This study is relevant for debates about the regulation of television's (and the cinema's) content. Some strong sentiments have been expressed by women who participated in this research about the extent to which it is acceptable to show representations of violence between men and women in public without adding special safeguards. To the extent that such ideas are taken seriously, and enter the public domain to become part of regulatory thinking, they could affect what is produced and also therefore have an impact upon what is consumed. In short, considerations raised above have implications for the relations and processes that constitute the field of broadcasting censorship.[5]

The general issue of how women view television has also been related to other areas of concern. For instance, one much-discussed theme has been that of women's employment opportunities in the media industries. Here the central question is 'How well are they represented in positions of power and influence?' This in turn connects with arguments about how the presence of women in key decision-making positions (such as senior media executive posts concerned with management strategy and finance, editing and production) might have an impact on how gender and sexuality are represented in various media. There are two connected senses of representation here. One line of argument is that, if women are represented where it counts (in boardrooms and editors' chairs), this can change how they are represented symbolically (in sound, image and print) to the public via the output of the media. The debate about this question remains far from resolved. Of late, increasing scepticism has begun to be voiced and it is becoming more common to argue that there is no necessary connection between women occupying positions of power in the media and the content of what is produced.[6] As in other fields of work, it may still be premature to comment on the effect of women in important decision-making positions until there are enough women to form a sufficient 'critical mass' to make any difference.[7] Evaluations of any effect while the representation of women remains incomplete cannot be considered reliable.

Although specific to recent feminist criticism, these lines of argument about the nature of representation in the media are also part of a much wider debate about the relations between professional communicators and audiences. An issue of persistent interest is how communicators can be made more accountable for the power that they possess to define the imaginary shape of our society and culture. The particular question of how media represent violence has long been a focus of public concern about such accountability. In the present study, we believe that the women who have participated have raised issues that may give the broadcasters food for thought. One of our purposes is to offer this analysis as a specific focus for debate between those who work in television, those who regulate it, and last, but certainly not least, those who consume it, men as well as women.

This study has begun to open up a further important set of questions. These concern how the different meanings that women accord television's representations of gender relations might affect how they live their lives. It is this, after all, that has fuelled much of the research on what women make of television. By recognising that making sense of television is to a significant – but also highly structured – extent in the hands of the viewers, it is still as well to be cautious about just how much people's lives can be transformed by changes in routine programming. Certainly, to effect a change in the kinds of discourse that women may use when talking or thinking about television, or simply to give them the space and legitimacy for talking and thinking in ways that are relatively unconstrained, are far from unimportant matters. Previous studies have done precisely this. We accept that such changed contexts may offer and legitimise some subjective pleasures for women viewers. To concede this, however, still leaves us with an open question. Just what kind of impact – for most – can changing how you think about television (or how you consume culture more generally) have on the social, economic and political constraints of your life?[8] The question does need posing, for there is something of a temptation abroad almost to substitute television criticism for political action. We certainly would not accept that the two are identical by any means. Quite simply, there is in such a tendency a temptation altogether to overrate the importance of television.

Notes

Chapter 1

1. See Annette Kuhn, *Cinema, Censorship and Sexuality, 1909–1925* (London and New York: Routledge, 1988), for an account of the early regulation of the cinema.

2. This issue is analysed by Geoffrey Pearson, *Hooligan: A History of Respectable Fears* (Basingstoke and London: Macmillan, 1983).

3. For a consideration of these arguments and their connection to the issue of censorship in broadcasting, see Philip Schlesinger, *Media, State and Nation: Political Violence and Collective Identities* (London, New York and Delhi: Sage Publications, 1991), Part I.

4. For a comprehensive review of the evidence, see Guy Cumberbatch and Dennis Howitt, *A Measure of Uncertainty: The Effects of the Mass Media* (London and Paris: John Libbey, 1989).

5. On effects, see Denis McQuail, *Mass Communication Theory: An Introduction* (London: Sage, 1987, second edition), Chapter 9; and for a relevant review of crime studies, see Richard V. Ericson, 'Mass media, crime, law and justice: an institutional approach', *The British Journal of Criminology* vol. 31 no. 3, Summer 1991, pp. 219–49.

6. For an empirical development of this line of argument, see Barrie Gunter, *Dimensions of Television Violence* (Aldershot: Gower, 1985).

7. For a relevant analysis see Philip Schlesinger, Howard Tumber and Graham Murdock, 'The media politics of crime and criminal justice', *The British Journal of Sociology* vol. 42 no. 3, September 1991, pp. 397–420.

8. Susan J. Smith, 'News and the dissemination of fear' in J. Burgess and J. Gold (eds), *Geography, the Media and Popular Culture* (Kent: Croom Helm, 1985), pp. 229–58.

9. See Barrie Gunter, *Television and the Fear of Crime* (London: John Libbey, 1987), Chapter 7, for a discussion of these arguments.

10. For a comparative perspective on this question, see Ien Ang, *Desperately Seeking the Audience* (London: Routledge, 1991); also see Eileen R. Meehan, 'Why we don't count' in Patricia Mellencamp (ed.), *Logics of Television: Essays in Cultural Criticism* (Bloomington and Indianapolis: Indiana University Press; London: BFI Publishing, 1990), pp. 117–37.

11. Klaus Bruhn Jensen and Karl Erik Rosengren, 'Five traditions in search of the audience', *European Journal of Communication* vol. 5 nos. 2–3, June 1990, pp. 207–38.

12. Shaun Moores, 'Texts, readers and contexts of reading: developments in the study of media audiences', *Media, Culture and Society* vol. 12 no. 1, January 1990, pp. 1–29; Robert C. Allen, 'Reader-oriented criticism and television' in Robert C. Allen (ed.), *Channels of Discourse: Television and Contemporary Criticism* (London: Methuen, 1987), pp. 74–110.

13. James Curran, 'The new revisionism in mass communication research: a reappraisal', *European Journal of Communication* vol. 5 nos. 2–3, June 1990, pp. 135–64, argues for this latter point.

14. John Fiske, 'Moments of television: neither the text nor the audience' in Ellen Seiter, Hans Borchers, Gabriele Kreutzner and Eva-Maria Warth (eds), *Remote*

Control: Television, Audiences and Cultural Power (London and New York: Routledge, 1989), pp. 56–78; John Fiske, *Television Culture* (London and New York: Methuen 1987), pp. 62–83.

15. Klaus Bruhn Jensen, 'The politics of polysemy: television news, everyday consciousness and political action', *Media, Culture and Society* vol. 12 no. 1, January 1990, pp. 57–77.

16. See Fiske, *Television Culture*; Jensen, 'The politics of polysemy'; Peter Dahlgren, 'What's the meaning of all this? Viewers' plural sense-making of the news', *Media, Culture and Society* vol. 10 no. 3, July 1988, pp. 285–301; Kay Richardson and John Corner, 'Reading reception: mediation and transparency in viewers' accounts of a TV programme', *Media, Culture and Society* vol. 8 no. 4, July 1988, pp. 285–301.

17. For a key text that has influenced much subsequent work, see Hermann Bausinger, 'Media, technology and daily life', *Media, Culture and Society* vol. 6 no. 4, October 1984, pp. 343–51. For related approaches see David Morley, *Family Television: Cultural Power and Domestic Leisure* (London: Comedia, 1986); Roger Silverstone, 'Television and everyday life: towards an anthropology of the television audience', in Marjorie Ferguson (ed.), *Public Communication: The New Imperatives* (London, Newbury Park, New Delhi: Sage Publications, 1990), pp. 173–89; and James Lull, *Inside Family Viewing: Ethnographic Research on Television's Audiences* (London: Routledge/Comedia, 1990).

18. For related examples of variation in the constitution of groups, see Andrea L. Press, 'Class, gender and the female viewer: women's responses to *Dynasty*', in Mary Ellen Brown (ed.), *Television and Women's Culture: The Politics of the Popular* (London, Newbury Park, New Delhi: Sage Publications, 1990); Dorothy Hobson, 'Soap operas at work' in Seiter et al. (eds), *Remote Control*, pp. 150–67; John Corner, Kay Richardson and Natalie Fenton, *Nuclear Reactions: Form and Response in Public Issue Television* (London, Paris: John Libbey, 1990); Elihu Katz and Tamar Liebes, 'Mutual aid in the decoding of *Dallas*: preliminary notes from a cross-cultural study' in Phillip Drummond and Richard Paterson (eds), *Television in Transition* (London: BFI Publishing, 1986) pp. 187-98.

19. Janice Radway, *Reading the Romance: Women, Patriarchy, and Popular Literature* (Chapel Hill: University of North Carolina Press, 1984); Ien Ang, *Watching Dallas* (London: Methuen, 1985); Marjorie Ferguson, *Forever Feminine: Women's Magazines and the Cult of Femininity* (London: Gower, 1985); Elizabeth Frazer, 'Teenage girls reading *Jackie*', *Media, Culture and Society* vol. 9 no. 4, October 1987, pp. 407–25; Dorothy Hobson, *Crossroads: The Drama of a Soap Opera* (London: Methuen, 1982); Susan Kippax, 'Women as audience: the experience of unwaged women of the performing arts', *Media, Culture and Society* vol. 10 no. 1, January 1988, pp. 5–21; Annette Kuhn, 'Women's genres', *Screen* vol. 25 no. 1, January-February 1984, pp. 18–28; Michèle Mattelart, 'Women and the cultural industries', *Media, Culture and Society* vol. 4 no. 2, April 1982, pp. 133–51; Laura Mulvey, 'Visual pleasure and narrative cinema', *Screen* vol. 16 no. 3, Autumn 1975, pp. 6–18; Andrea L. Press, 'Class and gender in the hegemonic process: Class differences in women's perceptions of television realism and identification with television characters', *Media, Culture and Society* vol. 11 no. 2, April 1989, pp. 229–51; Dorothy Hobson, 'Soap Operas at Work'; Valerie Walkerdine, 'Video replay: Families, films and fantasy' in Victor Burgin, James Donald and Cora Caplan (eds), *Formations of Fantasy* (London and New York: Methuen, 1986).

20. Liesbet van Zoonen, 'Feminist perspectives on the media', in James Curran and Michael Gurevitch (eds), *Mass Media and Society* (London: Edward Arnold, 1991), pp. 33–54 ; Marjorie Ferguson, 'Images of power and the feminist fallacy', *Critical Studies in Mass Communication* vol. 7, September 1990, pp. 215–30.

21. See Klaus Bruhn Jensen, *Making Sense of the News: Towards a Theory of an*

Empirical Model of Reception for the Study of Mass Communication (Aarhus: Aarhus University Press, 1986), Chapter 5, and James Lull, *Inside Family Viewing*, Chapter 1, for well-argued cases.

22. For discussions of this point see Brown (ed.), *Television and Women's Culture*; Walkerdine, 'Video replay: Families, films and fantasy'; and van Zoonen, 'Feminist Perspectives on the Media'.

23. As for instance in Jan-Uwe Rogge, 'The media in everyday family life: some bibliographical and typological aspects', in Seiter et al. (eds), *Remote Control*, p. 174.

24. Recent examples include Birgitta Höijer, 'Studying viewers' reception of television programmes: theoretical and methodological considerations', *European Journal of Communication* vol. 5 no. 1, March 1990, pp. 29–56, and Sonia Livingstone, 'Interpreting a television narrative: how different viewers see a story', *Journal of Communication* vol. 40 no. 1, Winter 1990, pp. 72–85.

25. See Janice Radway's argument on the need for more differentiation and systematic comparison, and more genre-differentiated study in *Reading the Romance*, pp. 9–10.

26. For example, middle-class and working-class women might be found to have different notions of whether or not situations in a television narrative are 'realistic' and to identify in quite distinctive ways with different characters and situations. Arguably, such patterns of perception and of use have their basis in different forms of class experience and particular cultural patterns (on this, see Andrea Press, 'Class, gender and the female viewer', pp. 158–80, and 'Class and gender in the hegemonic process', pp. 229–51). Much the same could be argued in respect of specific readings of the mainstream cinema's representation of blacks by black women – which may differ significantly not only from those of whites but also from those of black men (see Jacqueline Bobo, '*The Color Purple*: black women as cultural readers', in E. Deidre Pribram (ed.), *Female Spectators: Looking at Film and Television* (London and New York: Verso 1988), pp. 90–109.

27. Philip Schlesinger, Graham Murdock and Philip Elliott, *Televising 'Terrorism': Political Violence in Popular Culture* (London: Comedia, 1983).

28. John Corner et al., *Nuclear Reactions*.

29. For pertinent discussions, see Charlotte Brunsdon, 'Television: aesthetics and audiences' in Patricia Mellencamp (ed.), *Logics of Television: Essays in Cultural Criticism* (Bloomington and Indianapolis: Indiana University Press; London: BFI Publishing, 1990), pp. 59–72, and Corner et al., *Nuclear Reactions*, pp. 47–8.

30. R. Emerson Dobash and Russell P. Dobash, *Violence Against Wives* (New York: Free Press; Basingstoke: Macmillan Distributing, 1979), p. 247; Ruth E. Hall, *Ask Any Woman: A London Inquiry into Rape and Sexual Assault* (Bristol: Falling Wall Press, 1985), pp. 21, 33, 38, 78; Diana E. H. Russell, *Rape in Marriage* (New York: Macmillan, 1982), cited in Elizabeth A. Stanko, *Intimate Intrusions: Women's Experience of Male Violence* (London: Routledge, 1985), pp. 37–8, 50.

31. Del Martin, *Battered Wives* (San Francisco: Glide Publications, 1976), pp. 1–5.

32. McNeill, 'Flashing: its effect on women', in Jalna Hanmer and Mary Maynard (eds), *Women, Violence and Social Control* (London: Macmillan, 1987), p. 99.

33. McNeill, 'Flashing', pp. 102–8.

34. McNeill, 'Flashing', p. 101.

35. Liz Kelly, *Surviving Sexual Violence* (Cambridge: Polity Press, 1988), p. 167.

36. McNeill, 'Flashing', pp. 101–2.

37. Christopher Bagley and Kathleen King, *Child Sexual Abuse: The Search for Healing* (London and New York: Tavistock/Routledge, 1990), p. 17.

38. Diana E. H. Russell, *The Secret Trauma: Incest in the Lives of Girls and Women* (New York: Basic Books, 1986), p. 175.

39. See Dobash and Dobash, *Violence Against Wives*, p. 107.

40. Pat Kincaid, *The Omitted Reality* (Ontario, Canada: Learnxs Press, 1982), p. 23.
41. R. Emerson Dobash and Russell P. Dobash, *Women, Violence and Social Change* (London: Routledge, 1992), p. 2.
42. See Lee Ann Hoff, *Battered Women as Survivors* (London: Routledge, 1990), and Liz Kelly, *Surviving Sexual Violence*.
43. Hoff, *Battered Women as Survivors*, pp. 36–7.
44. Susan Brownmiller, *Against Our Will: Men, Women and Rape* (London: Secker & Warburg, 1975), p. 347.
45. Brownmiller, *Against Our Will*, p. 359.
46. Kelly, *Surviving Sexual Violence*, p. 123.
47. Kelly, *Surviving Sexual Violence*, p. 175.
48. Sylva Fraser, *My Father's House: A Memoir of Incest and Healing* (Toronto: Doubleday, 1987), p. 220, cited in Bagley and King, *Child Sexual Abuse*, p. 19.
49. Kelly, *Surviving Sexual Violence*, p. 124.
50. Kelly, *Surviving Sexual Violence*, p. 198.
51. Kelly, *Surviving Sexual Violence*, p. 199.
52. Brownmiller, *Against Our Will*, pp. 362–3.
53. Kelly, *Surviving Sexual Violence*, p. 200.
54. Kelly, *Surviving Sexual Violence*, p. 193.
55. Kelly, *Surviving Sexual Violence*, p. 200.

Chapter 2

1. Ien Ang, 'Wanted audiences: on the politics of empirical audience studies' in Ellen Seiter et al. (eds), *Remote Control: Television, Audiences and Cultural Power* (London and New York: Routledge, 1989), pp. 96–115.
2. See Höijer's critique of group interviews in reception studies in Birgitta Höijer, 'Studying viewers' reception of television programmes', *European Journal of Communication* vol. 5 no. 1, March 1990, pp. 29–56. While we agree with many of Höijer's criticisms and reservations, we do not accept her conclusion that ethnographic and psychotherapeutic approaches relying on individual interviews are necessarily the best way forward.
3. E. Mishler, 'Meaning in context: Is there any other kind?', *Harvard Educational Review* vol. 49, no. 1, pp. 1–19; Russell P. Dobash and R. Emerson Dobash, 'The context specific approach [to studying violence]', in D. Finkelhor et al. (eds), *The Dark Side of Families* (Newbury Park, CA: Sage, 1983); P. Rabinow and W. M. Sullivan (eds), *Interpretive Social Science* (Berkeley: University of California Press, 1979); D. Callahan and B. Jennings, *Ethics, the Social Sciences and Policy Analysis* (New York: Plenum, 1983).
4. See for example, N. K. Denzin, *The Research Act* (Chicago: Aldine, 1970); Nigel G. Fielding and Jane L. Fielding, *Linking Data* (Beverly Hills: Sage, 1986).
5. See H. L. Dreyfus and P. Rabinow, *Michel Foucault: Beyond Structuralism and Hermeneutics* (Chicago: University of Chicago Press, 1986) for a discussion of interpretative analytics as developed within the context of Foucault's structuralist agenda.
6. A pertinent example is Press, 'Class and gender in the hegemonic process', pp. 229–51. In Press' otherwise interesting article, she relegates her brief discussion of methods to a footnote. A similar point applies to Morley, *Family Television*.
7. See the discussion in Chapter 3 below.
8. See for example Muriel G. Cantor and Suzanne Pingree, *The Soap Opera* (Beverly Hills: Sage, 1983).
9. In forming groups 4 and 5 it was impossible to produce class-differentiated groups for reasons explained in Appendix V.
10. In the case of Groups 3, 6, 9, 10, 13 and 14, it was decided that ethnic background rather than social class should operate as the key criterion of selection.

11. R. Emerson Dobash and Russell P. Dobash, *Women, Violence and Social Change* (London: Routledge, 1992); Marjorie Homer, Anne Leonard, and Pat Taylor, *Private Violence: Public Shame, A Report on the Circumstances of Women Leaving Domestic Violence in Cleveland* (Middlesbrough, England: Cleveland Refuge and Aid for Women and Children, 1984); Amina Mama, *The Hidden Struggle: Statutory and Voluntary Sector Responses to Violence against Black Women in the Home* (London: London Race and Housing Research Unit, 1989); Scottish Women's Aid, *The Herstory of Women's Aid in Scotland* (Edinburgh: Scottish Women's Aid, 1988).

12. See Morley, *Family Television* and Hobson, *Crossroads*.

13. Robert K. Merton, Marjorie Fiske, and Patricia L. Kendall, *The Focused Interview: A Manual of Procedures* (New York: Free Press, 1990, second edition). Merton first developed the focused group interview with individuals in sociological communications research through his collaborative work with Paul Lazarsfeld.

14. Cumberbatch and Howitt, *A Measure of Uncertainty*.

15. Ian Dey, Hypersoft, available from Ian Dey, Department of Social Policy and Social Work, University of Edinburgh.

16. Daniel S. Feldman, Jr., Rick Hoffman, Jim Gagnon, and Joe Simpson, *StatView II SE + Graphics* (California: Abacus Concepts, 1988).

17. Höijer, 'Studying viewers' perceptions of television programmes'.

18. Only the results of the Programme Questionnaires administered before discussion are analysed here.

19. A Likert-type scale usually involves presenting respondents with a word or statement which they are asked to rate on a numerical scale, usually from one to five, although another range of numbers might be employed. Likert procedures usually involve summating an individual's answers on a range of questions about the same issue and giving them an overall scale score. In this way, individual respondents can be compared. Although we asked women to rate the various programmes on a series of issues using a range from one to five, we did not constitute these as an overall scale or sum their responses in order to give women individual scale scores (see Appendix II).

20. Andrew Hemming, 'Soap operas', in *BBC Broadcasting Research Annual Review 1989* (London and Paris: John Libbey, 1989), pp. 27–34; Karen Day and Eleanor Cowie, 'Trends in viewing and listening', in *BBC Broadcasting Research Annual Review 1990* (London and Paris: John Libbey, 1990), pp. 5–22.

21. For a summary of these findings, see Dobash and Dobash, *Women, Violence and Social Change*.

22. Martin Daly and Margo Wilson, *Homicide* (New York: Aldine de Gruyter, 1988).

23. See, for example, Dobash and Dobash, *Violence Against Wives*; Mildred Pagelow, *Woman-Battering* (Newbury Park, CA.: Sage, 1981); Russell, *Rape in Marriage*; Stanko, *Intimate Intrusions*: Hanmer and Maynard (eds), *Women, Violence and Social Control*; Kelly, *Surviving Sexual Violence*; Edwards, *Policing 'Domestic' Violence* (London: Sage, 1989); Dobash and Dobash, *Women, Violence and Social Change*.

24. It should not be assumed that the apparently less serious forms of abuse have no consequences for women. See McNeill, 'Flashing'; Kelly, *Surviving Sexual Violence*.

25. Kelly, *Surviving Sexual Violence*; Stanko, *Intimate Intrusions*.

26. L. Perloff, 'Perceptions of vulnerability to victimization', *Journal of Social Issues* vol. 39 no. 2, 1983, pp. 41–61; Elizabeth A. Stanko, 'Typical violence, normal precaution: men, women and interpersonal violence in England, Wales, Scotland and the USA', in Hanmer and Maynard (eds), *Women, Violence and Social Control*, pp. 122–34; Patrick McLaughlin, R. Emerson Dobash and Russell P. Dobash, *Women Thinking about Crime* (Stirling University: Report for Central Regional Council, 1991).

179

27. See also McLaughlin, Dobash and Dobash, *Women Thinking About Crime.*
28. Stanko, 'Typical violence, normal precaution'.
29. See Barrie Gunter, *Television and the Fear of Crime.*

Chapter 3

1. For a fuller account of the background to *Crimewatch UK,* see Philip Schlesinger and Howard Tumber, 'Fighting the war against crime: television, police and the audience', paper presented to the International Television Studies Conference, London: July 1991.
2. BBC Broadcasting Research, *Crimewatch UK* (London: BBC Special Projects Report, SP.88/45/88/16, October 1988), p. 7.
3. For a view from inside the programme see Nick Ross and Sue Cook, *Crimewatch UK* (London: Hodder & Stoughton, 1987). The present paragraphs draw upon Schlesinger, Tumber and Murdock, 'The media politics of crime and criminal justice', pp. 407–8.
4. Keith Soothill and Sylvia Walby, *Sex Crime in the News* (London and New York: Routledge, 1991), Chapter 2.
5. Soothill and Walby, *Sex Crime in the News,* p. 17.
6. Soothill and Walby, *Sex Crime in the News,* Chapter 3.
7. See BBC Broadcasting Research, *Crimewatch UK,* p. 31.
8. *Report of the Working Group on the Fear of Crime* (London: Home Office, 1989).
9. Ibid, pp. 32–4; Schlesinger and Tumber, 'Fighting the war against crime', p. 2.
10. BBC Broadcasting Research, *Crimewatch UK;* J.M. Wober and B. Gunter, *Crime Reconstruction Programmes: Viewing Experience in Three Regions, Linked with Perceptions of and Reactions to Crime* (London: IBA Research Department Research Paper, August 1990).
11. BBC Broadcasting Research, *Crimewatch UK,* p. 18.
12. Wober and Gunter, *Crime Reconstruction Programmes,* p. ii.
13. The percentages in Figures IV–X, Reactions to Programmes, are based on questions in the Programme Questionnaires (see Appendix II). The percentages were created by summing those who answered '4' or '5' to questions concerning reactions to programmes (e.g. 'realistic', 'upsetting'). For example, in Figure IV, the columns labelled 'realistic' were created by combining those who answered '4' or '5' to the following question:
   *How realistic do you think the reconstructions of crimes were in this programme?
   Not at all realistic 1 – 2 – 3 – 4 – 5 Very realistic
They were then defined as judging the programme to be 'realistic'. Thus 71% of women with experience of violence and 84% of women with no experience defined the programme as 'realistic' (see Figure IV).
14. Yule's Q is a statistical measure of the strength of association between two ordinal variables which assesses the degree of predictability of order on one variable from knowledge of order on a second. It is a special case of the widely used Gamma measure and varies from -1 to +1. Zero indicates no association and +1 indicates perfect predictability of order between the two variables. Values between 0 and +1, such as those obtained in this study, indicate the proportional reduction of error in guessing order in direction on one variable using knowledge of order on the second variable. See John H. Mueller, Karl F. Schuessler and Herbert L. Costner, *Statistical Reasoning in Sociology* (Boston: Houghton Mifflin, 1970).

Chapter 4

1. Julia Smith and Tony Holland, *EastEnders: The Inside Story* (London: BBC Books, 1987), p. 19.
2. David Buckingham, *Public Secrets: EastEnders and its Audience* (London: BFI Publishing, 1987), Chapter 3.

3. Buckingham, *Public Secrets*, p. 83.
4. Buckingham, *Public Secrets*, pp. 83–4.
5. Buckingham, *Public Secrets*, p. 62.
6. Buckingham, *Public Secrets*, p. 196, his emphasis.
7. Stephen Bourne, 'Coming Clean: Soap Operas', pp. 128–9 and Lucy O'Brien, 'We'll make a drama out of your crisis', pp. 156–9 in Therese Daniels and Jane Gerson (eds), *The Colour Black: Black Images in British Television* (London: BFI, 1989); Hilary Kingsley, *Soap Box: The Papermac Guide to Soap Opera* (London and Basingstoke: Papermac, 1988), pp. 270–1.
8. Kingsley, *Soap Box*, p. 269.
9. Jacqui Roach and Petal Felix, 'Black Looks', in L. Gamman and M. Marshment (eds), *The Female Gaze: Women as Viewers of Popular Culture* (London: Women's Press, 1988), p. 137: this is the authors' gloss on her views, not her own words.
10. Roach and Felix, 'Black Looks', p. 137.
11. Kingsley, *Soap Box*, p. 272.

Chapter 5

1. On this matter see Paddy Hillyard and Janie Percy-Smith, *The Coercive State: The Decline of Democracy in Britain* (London: Fontana, 1988); K.D. Ewing and C.A Gearty, *Freedom under Thatcher: Civil Liberties in Modern Britain* (Oxford: Clarendon Press, 1990).
2. Roger Graef, *Talking Blues : The Police in Their Own Words* (London: Collins Harvill, 1989), p. 11.
3. Graef, *Talking Blues*, p. 214.
4. Graef, *Talking Blues*, p. 241.
5. Graef, *Talking Blues*, p. 235.
6. Graef, *Talking Blues*, p. 241.
7. Graef, *Talking Blues*, p. 337.
8. Minette Marrin, 'Understated vision world supremacy', *The Daily Telegraph*, 11 January 1988.
9. Quoted in Peter Guttridge, 'Stress: a force to be reckoned with', *TV Times*, 9–15 January 1988. For further discussion by the director, see Roger Graef, 'Taking liberties', in Andrea Millwood Hargrave (ed.), *A Matter of Manners? The Limits of Broadcasting Language*, Broadcasting Standards Council Research Monograph Series: 3 (London, Paris, Rome: John Libbey, 1991), pp. 77–8.
10. Hugh Hebert, 'The baddies in blue', *The Guardian*, 11 January 1988.

Chapter 6

1. Pam Cook, '*The Accused*', *Monthly Film Bulletin*, vol. 56 no. 661, February 1989, pp. 35–6.
2. Derek Malcolm, 'The lust picture show', *The Guardian*, 16 February 1989.
3. Cook, '*The Accused*', pp. 35–6.
4. Adam Mars-Jones, 'Unmoving Violation', *The Independent*, 16 February 1989.
5. Anne Simpson, 'Actress who has grown up on the film set', *The Glasgow Herald*, 14 March 1989.
6. Simpson, 'Actress who has grown up on the film set'; Cook, '*The Accused*'.
7. Larry W. Riggs and Paula Willoquet, 'Up against the looking glass!: Heterosexual rape as homosexual epiphany in *The Accused*', *Film Literature Quarterly* vol. 17 no. 14, 1989, pp. 214–23.
8. Lynn A. Higgins and Brenda R. Silver (eds), *Rape and Representation* (New York: Columbia University Press, 1991).
9. Soothill and Walby, *Sex Crime in the News*, p.147. See also Lorraine Radford, 'Legalising woman abuse', in Hanmar and Maynard (eds), *Women, Violence and Social Control*, pp. 135–51, on how the discourses of the court and legal documents construct the culpability of women victims.

Chapter 7

1. Stanko, 'Typical violence, normal precaution'; M. Hinderlang, M. Gottfredson and J. Garofalo, *The Victims of Personal Crime* (Cambridge, Mass: Ballinger, 1978); W. Skogan and M. Maxfield, *Coping with Crime* (Beverly Hills, California: Sage, 1981; M. Hough and P. Mayhew, *The British Crime Survey* (London: HMSO, 1983); M. Maxfield, *Fear of Crime in England and Wales* (London: HMSO, 1984); G. Chambers and J. Tombs, *The British Crime Survey. Scotland* (Edinburgh: HMSO, 1984).

2. Stanko, 'Typical violence, normal precaution'.

3. Ann Shearer in a related study, *Survivors and the Media,* commissioned by the Broadcasting Standards Council, has a focus quite distinct from this book, as the main research interest lay in establishing survivors' reactions to the portrayal of disasters, rape or assault and the violent deaths of relatives. Those researched in most detail by the study had a *direct* involvement in these kinds of events. By comparison, although many of the women who participated in *Women Viewing Violence* brought relevant experience of violence to bear in their reactions, they did not discuss specific scenarios or view given events in which they themselves had been directly involved. Thus where the survivors' study has an obvious point of contact with the current work is in its concern with the more general role of *personal experience* and its relation to how media representations are read.

   Two specific findings were of particular relevance to the present study because they relate to programmes that we ourselves discuss. First, twenty of the thirty-eight survivors who responded to a questionnaire 'said they would want to see *Crimewatch UK* ... irrespective of their own experiences' and 'a further seven said that they would watch it *because* of these' (p. 30). In a second relevant observation, it is noted that 'Four of the six rape and sexual abuse survivors had in fact particularly chosen to watch *The Accused*, a film about rape which did not figure on the interviewers' list, one of them on the recommendation of her counsellor as preparation for her court case' (p. 31). This evident willingness to confront potentially difficult coverage does open up questions about relations between the experience of violence, distress and television viewing. The evidence of the present study does not suggest, on the whole, that negative experience results in calculated avoidance. See Ann Shearer, *Survivors and the Media,* Broadcasting Standards Council Research Monograph Series: 2 (London: John Libbey, 1991).

4. For a thoughtful overview of debates on pornography see Suzanne Kappeler, *The Pornography of Representation* (Cambridge: Polity Press, 1986). An illuminating discussion by broadcasters is to be found in 'The treatment of rape in a TV drama' in Brian Lapping (ed.), *The Bounds of Freedom* (London: Constable/Granada Television, 1980), pp. 95–128.

5. For a relevant discussion, see Annette Kuhn, *Cinema, Censorship and Sexuality,* in which a critique of what she terms the 'prohibitions/institutions model' of censorship is offered.

6. These questions are aired in van Zoonen, 'Feminist perspectives on the media', and Ferguson, 'Images of power and the feminist fallacy'.

7. See Dobash and Dobash, *Women, Violence and Social Change* for instances where the presence of women has made a difference in organisational policy and practice.

8. For a view which tends to overrate the 'empowerment' offered by 'feminine discourse' see Brown, 'Conclusion: consumption and resistance – the problem of pleasure' in *Television and Women's Culture.*

Selected References

Allen, Robert C. (ed.), *Channels of Discourse: Television and Contemporary Criticism* (London: Methuen, 1987).

Brown, Mary Ellen (ed.), *Television and Women's Culture: The Politics of the Popular* (London: Sage Publications, 1990).

Buckingham, David, *Public Secrets: EastEnders and its Audience* (London: BFI Publishing, 1987).

Corner, John, Richardson, Kay and Fenton, Natalie, *Nuclear Reactions: Form and Response in Public Issue Television* (London, Paris: John Libbey, 1990).

Cumberbatch, Guy and Howitt, Dennis, *A Measure of Uncertainty: The Effects of the Mass Media* (London and Paris: John Libbey, 1989).

Dobash, R. Emerson and Dobash, Russell P., *Violence Against Wives* (New York: Free Press and Macmillan Distributing, Brunel Road, Houndmills, Basingstoke, England ISBN 0-02-907810-5, 1979).

Dobash, Russell P. and Dobash, R. Emerson, 'The context-specific approach to studying violence', in D. Finkelhor et al. (eds), *The Dark Side of Families* (Newbury Park, CA: Sage, 1983).

Dobash, R. Emerson and Dobash, Russell P., *Women, Violence and Social Change* (London: Routledge, 1992).

Dobash, R. Emerson and Dobash, Russell P., 'The nature and antecedents of violent events', *The British Journal of Criminology* vol. 24 no. 3, July 1984.

Edwards, Susan S. M., *Policing 'Domestic' Violence* (London: Sage, 1989).

Graef, Roger, *Talking Blues: The Police in Their Own Words* (London: Collins Harvill, 1989).

Gunter, Barrie, *Dimensions of Television Violence* (Aldershot: Gower, 1985).

Gunter, Barrie, *Television and the Fear of Crime* (London: John Libbey, 1987).

Hanmer, Jalna and Maynard, Mary (eds), *Women, Violence and Social Control* (London: Macmillan, 1987).

Hoff, Lee Ann, *Battered Women as Survivors* (London: Routledge, 1990).

Hough, M. and Mayhew, P., *The British Crime Survey* (London: HMSO, 1983).

Jensen, Klaus Bruhn, *Making Sense of the News: Towards a Theory of an Empirical Model of Reception for the Study of Mass Communication* (Aarhus: Aarhus University Press, 1986).

Kelly, Liz, *Surviving Sexual Violence* (Cambridge: Polity Press, 1988).

Kuhn, Annette, *Cinema, Censorship and Sexuality, 1909-25* (London and New York: Routledge, 1988).

Martin, Del, *Battered Wives* (San Francisco: Glide Publications, 1976).

Rabinow, P. and Sullivan, W. M. (eds), *Interpretive Social Science* (Berkeley: University of California Press, 1979).

Ross, Nick and Cook, Sue, *Crimewatch UK* (London: Hodder & Stoughton, 1987).

Schlesinger, Philip, Murdock, Graham and Elliott, Philip, *Televising 'Terrorism': Political Violence in Popular Culture* (London: Comedia, 1983).

Schlesinger, Philip, Tumber, Howard and Murdock, Graham, 'The media politics of crime and criminal justice', *The British Journal of Sociology* vol. 42 no. 3, September 1991.

Schlesinger, Philip, *Media, State and Nation: Political Violence and Collective Identities* (London, New York and Delhi: Sage Publications, 1991).

Seiter, Ellen, Borchers, Hans, Kreutzner, Gabriele and Warth, Eva-Maria (eds), *Remote Control: Television, Audiences and Cultural Power* (London and New York: Routledge, 1989).

Smith, Julia and Holland, Tony, *EastEnders: The Inside Story* (London: BBC Books 1987).

Soothill, Keith and Walby, Sylvia, *Sex Crime in the News* (London and New York: Routledge, 1991).

Stanko, Elizabeth, *Intimate Intrusions: Women's Experience of Male Violence* (London: Routledge, 1985).

Appendices

I BACKGROUND QUESTIONNAIRE

Women's Interpretations of Violence Against Women on Television

Background Questionnaire
1990

Departments of Film and Media Studies
and Sociology & Social Policy

Please complete this questionnaire and bring it with you on Saturday.

All information given in this questionnaire will be treated in the strictest confidence. Your name will not be used in any reports which use the details collected here. In order to better understand your ideas and feelings about television, we would first like to ask some of your personal details.

1. Name _____

2. Age _____years

3. Ethnic Origin _____

4. In which city/town/village do you live? _____

5. In which part of that town/city do you live? _____

6. Marital Status:
   Single   [   ]
   Married [   ]
   Separated [   ]
   Divorced [   ]
   Widowed [   ]

7(a). At what age did you leave full-time education?_____years

  (b). What was the last educational qualification for which you studied?
   Please tick box.
   'O' levels/CSE's   [   ]
   'A' levels/Highers   [   ]
   Technical qualifications   [   ]
   University degree   [   ]
   Other, please specify_____

8. Occupational status. Please tick appropriate box.
   Employed full-time   [   ]
   Employed part-time   [   ]
   Self-employed   [   ]
   Government training scheme [   ]

Unemployed (seeking work) [ ]
Housewife [ ]
Full-time student [ ]
Part-time student [ ]
Other, please specify_____

9. If employed, what is your occupation?___

10. Do you have a partner, and is that person employed?
    No   [ ]
    Yes   [ ], Full-time [ ] or Part-time [ ]
    What is that person's occupation?_____

11. Do you have any children?
    No   [ ]
    Yes   [ ], please indicate their sex and ages below:
    Child 1 Male or female   Age _____yrs
    Child 2 Male or female   Age _____yrs
    Child 3 Male or female   Age _____yrs
    Child 4 Male or female   Age _____yrs
    Child 5 Male or female   Age _____yrs
    Child 6 Male or female   Age _____yrs
    Child 7 Male or female   Age _____yrs

12. With whom do you live? Please tick box.
    Husband [ ]   Boyfriend   [ ]
    Children [ ]   Friend/s female   [ ]
    Relatives [ ]   Female partner   [ ]
    Parents [ ]   Friend/s male   [ ]
                      Friends (male and female)   [ ]

13. What type of accommodation do you live in?
    Own private house   [ ]
    Rented council accommodation   [ ]
    Rented private accommodation   [ ]
    Hostel   [ ]
    Student residence on a campus   [ ]
    Other, please specify_____

14. Do you own your own car?

    Yes   [ ]
    No   [ ] Do you have easy access to the use of a car? Yes [ ] No [ ]

15. Do you use public transport?
    No   [ ]
    Yes   [ ] Is this your main form of transportation? Yes [ ] No [ ]

16. Do you have a telephone?
    Yes   [ ]
    No   [ ] Do you have access to a neighbour's phone? Yes [ ] No [ ]
    Do you mainly use a public telephone?
    Yes   [ ]   No   [ ]

17. In what sort of community/leisure activities outside of home are you involved?
    Please tick appropriate boxes.
    None   [ ]   Sports clubs   [ ]
    Politics   [ ]   Scouts   [ ]
    Environmental groups [ ]   Guides   [ ]
    Youth Schemes   [ ]   Church   [ ]

| Care of Elderly | [ ] | Women's groups | [ ] |
| Amateur dramatics | [ ] | Residential groups | [ ] |

Other, please specify_____

18. Do you live in a NEIGHBOURHOOD WATCH area?
No   [ ]
Yes   [ ] Are you an active member of NEIGHBOURHOOD WATCH?
               Yes   [ ]   No   [ ]

19. Do you have any involvement with victim support schemes?
No   [ ]
Yes   [ ] What is the nature of your involvement?_____

20(a). Do you have an interest in national politics?   Yes [ ] No [ ]

   (b). Which political party do you support?

Conservative	[ ]
Green Party	[ ]
Labour	[ ]
Liberal Democrats	[ ]
SNP	[ ]

Other, please specify_____

21. On average, how many hours of television do you think you watch?
(a) per weekday   _____hrs
(b) per Saturday   _____hrs
(c) per Sunday   _____hrs

22. Which TV channel do YOU MOST like watching? Please tick one box.
BBC 1	[ ]	BBC 2	[ ]
ITV	[ ]	Channel 4	[ ]
SKY	[ ]	BSB	[ ]

23. In your household, which TV channel is watched most often?
Please tick one box.
BBC 1	[ ]	BBC 2	[ ]
ITV	[ ]	Channel 4	[ ]
SKY	[ ]	BSB	[ ]

24. Which are the TV programmes you watch MOST OFTEN?
_____

25. What are your FAVOURITE TV programmes? Please name them.
_____

26. What are the TV programmes you MOST DISLIKE? Please name them.
_____

27. Which radio station do YOU MOST like listening to?
_____

28. In your household, which radio station is listened to MOST OFTEN?
_____

29. What are your FAVOURITE radio programmes? Please name them.
_____

30(a). Which newspapers do you read? Please name them.
Daily newspapers   _____
Local newspapers   _____
Sunday newspapers   _____

(b). How often do you read a newspaper?

Every day   [ ]
Every other day   [ ]
More than once a week [ ]
Once a week   [ ]
Less than once a week [ ]

31.   What magazines do you read? _____

32(a). Of all the media, which do you find most entertaining?

Newspapers   [ ]   Radio   [ ]
Magazines   [ ]   Television [ ]

(b). Which provides you with the most information on national and international affairs?

Newspapers   [ ]   Radio   [ ]
Magazines   [ ]   Television [ ]

33(a). Have you ever been a victim of any form of crime against your property? Please tick boxes.

Theft of, or from your car?

No   [ ]
Yes   [ ]   Did you report it to the police?
                No   [ ]
                Yes   [ ]
               After reporting it did you have any further contact with the police/courts about this offence?
                Yes   [ ]
                No   [ ]

(b). Against your home?

No   [ ]
Yes   [ ]   Did you report it to the police?
                No   [ ]
                Yes   [ ]
               After reporting it did you have any further contact with the police/courts about this offence?
                Yes   [ ]
                No   [ ]

Briefly give details of the crime/s committed against your property.

_____
_____
_____

34(a). Have you ever been the victim of a violent act (not sexual) committed in a public place?

No   [ ]
Yes   [ ] What did this act against you involve?

(b). If yes, please tick appropriate boxes.   Were you:

Grabbed [ ]   Pushed   [ ]
Slapped [ ]   Kicked   [ ]
Punched [ ]   Beaten up [ ]
Attacked with a weapon   [ ]
Other, please specify_____

(c). Altogether, how often have you been a victim of violent acts in a public place?____times.

(d). Did you report any of these incidents to the police?

No   [ ]
Yes   [ ] Did you have any further contact with the police/courts after
you reported the incidents? Yes   [ ]   No   [ ]

35(a). As an adult woman have you ever been a victim of a physical attack in your
        own home?
        No   [ ]
        Yes   [ ]

  (b). Who attacked you?
        Husband   [ ]   Boyfriend   [ ]
        Father   [ ]   Brother   [ ]
        Sister   [ ]   Mother   [ ]
        Other relative   [ ]   Neighbour   [ ]
        A stranger   [ ]

36(a). Have you ever been a victim of any of the following? Please tick
        appropriate boxes:
                Obscene phone calls   [ ]
                Sexual harassment at work   [ ]
                Groping/unwelcome contact   [ ]
                A male exposing himself to you   [ ]
                Incest   [ ]
                Rape   [ ]

  (b). How often have you been a victim of the following?
                Obscene phone calls   _____times
                Sexual harassment at work   _____times
                Groping/unwelcome contact   _____times
                A male exposing himself to you_____times
                Incest   _____times
                Rape   _____times

  (c). Were any of these incidents reported to the police?
        No   [ ]
        Yes   [ ]
        Did you have any further contact with the police/courts after you reported
        the incidents?
        Yes   [ ]
        No   [ ]

  (d). Who committed these acts?
        Husband   [ ]   Boyfriend   [ ]
        Father   [ ]   Brother   [ ]
        Sister   [ ]   Mother   [ ]
        Other relative   [ ]   Neighbour   [ ]
        A stranger   [ ]
        Other, please specify_____

37.   Do you worry about crime?
        A lot   [ ]
        Sometimes   [ ]
        Rarely   [ ]
        Never   [ ]

38.   Do you worry about being physically attacked:
        (a) In public places?   Yes   [ ]   No   [ ]
        (b) In your own home?   Yes   [ ]   No   [ ]

39.   Is there anything about the area in which you live that you feel is threatening?

189

No   [ ]
Yes   [ ] Please give details_____

40.   Are you apprehensive about going out at night in your local area?
      Yes   [ ]   No   [ ]

41.   How do you feel about the media's reporting of crimes committed against
      women?
      Do you feel it might:

      Make women more aware and safety-conscious?   Yes [ ]
                                                                 No   [ ]
                                                          Don't know [ ]
      Make women more afraid of being attacked?   Yes [ ]
                                                                 No   [ ]
                                                          Don't know [ ]
      Encourage men to commit violent acts against women?   Yes [ ]
                                                                 No   [ ]
                                                          Don't know [ ]
      Result in the issue being blown out of proportion?   Yes [ ]
                                                                 No   [ ]
                                                          Don't know [ ]
      Make men more aware of other men's acts against women?   Yes [ ]
                                                                 No   [ ]
                                                          Don't know [ ]

42.   Do you think that the courts should impose heavier sentences for crimes
      committed against women?   Yes [ ]
                                                                 No   [ ]
                                                          Don't know [ ]

43.   Do any types of media tend to <u>INCREASE</u> your fear of crime?
      No   [ ]
      Yes   [ ] Please tick one or more boxes.

      Television news:
      ITN   [ ]   BBC 1   [ ]
      Channel 4   [ ]   BBC 2 Newsnight   [ ]

      TV current affairs   [ ]   Radio news   [ ]
      TV drama   [ ]   Cinema   [ ]
      TV documentary   [ ]   Magazines   [ ]
      TV films   [ ]

      Newspapers:
      Local press   [ ]   Free papers   [ ]
      Tabloid newspapers   [ ]   Broadsheet newspapers   [ ]
      (e.g. Daily Record, Sun)   (e.g. Scotsman, Times, Guardian)
      Other, please specify_____

44.   Is there one particular type of newspaper coverage or TV programme which
      <u>INCREASES</u> your fear of crime?
      No   [ ]
      Yes   [ ] Which?_____

45.   Do any types of media tend to <u>REDUCE</u> your fear of crime?
      No   [ ]
      Yes   [ ] Please tick one or more boxes.

      Television news:

ITN	[ ]	BBC 1	[ ]
Channel 4	[ ]	BBC 2 Newsnight	[ ]
TV current affairs	[ ]	Radio news	[ ]
TV drama	[ ]	Cinema	[ ]
TV documentary	[ ]	Magazines	[ ]
TV films	[ ]		

Newspapers:

Local press	[ ]	Free papers	[ ]
Tabloid newspapers	[ ]	Broadsheet newspapers	[ ]
(e.g. Daily Record, Sun)		(e.g. Scotsman, Times, Guardian)	

Other, please specify_____

46. Is there one particular type of newspaper coverage or TV programme which REDUCES your fear of crime?

No [ ]

Yes [ ] Which?_____

47(a). Do you think there should be more control over the media's portrayal of women?

No [ ]

Yes [ ]

(b). If YES to 47(a) above, restrictions on, for example:

Newspaper pin-ups (e.g. page 3)?

Yes [ ]

No [ ]

Don't know [ ]

Adult magazines (e.g. Playboy)?

Yes [ ]

No [ ]

Don't know [ ]

Portrayals of violence against women on TV?

Yes [ ]

No [ ]

Don't know [ ]

Portrayals of violence against women in the cinema?

Yes [ ]

No [ ]

Don't know [ ]

Portrayals of violence against women on video?

Yes [ ]

No [ ]

Don't know [ ]

48. Are you concerned about women's issues?

Yes [ ]

No [ ]

Don't know [ ]

49. Are you concerned about women's rights?

Yes [ ]

No [ ]

Don't know [ ]

50. Do you think that men do enough to help women gain equal rights in society?

Yes [ ]

No [ ]
Don't know [ ]

51. Do you think that men and women are equals today?

Yes [ ]
No [ ]
Don't know [ ]

52. Do you think that men have more privileges in society than women? Yes [ ]
No [ ]
Don't know [ ]

53. Do you think that feminists have helped women gain a better position in society?

Yes [ ]
No [ ]
Don't know [ ]

54. Do you think that feminism has caused a breakdown in understanding between men and women?

Yes [ ]
No [ ]
Don't know [ ]

55. Do you think that you have ever lost out on an opportunity because you are a woman?

Yes [ ]
No [ ]
Don't know [ ]

56. Do you call yourself a feminist?

Yes [ ]
No [ ]

THANK YOU FOR FILLING IN THIS QUESTIONNAIRE

II PROGRAMME QUESTIONNAIRES

Crimewatch

1. Have you seen this particular *Crimewatch* programme before?
   Yes   [ ]
   No   [ ]
   Don't know   [ ]

2. How often do you watch *Crimewatch*?
   Regularly   [ ]
   Occasionally   [ ]
   Not very often [ ]
   Never   [ ]
   Do you then watch the *Crimewatch Update* presented on the same night?
   Yes always   [ ]
   Yes sometimes [ ]
   No   [ ]

3. What is your reaction to this *Crimewatch* programme? Please indicate your
   reaction by circling the appropriate number on a scale of 1 to 5. For example,
   if you think that it was very realistic, you would circle number 5.

   *How IMPORTANT do you think that *Crimewatch* is as a television
   programme?

   Not at all important   1 – 2 – 3 – 4 – 5   Very Important

   *How REALISTIC do you think the reconstructions of crimes were in this
   programme?

   Not at all realistic   1 – 2 – 3 – 4 – 5   Very realistic

   *How ENTERTAINING did you find this programme?

   Not at all entertaining 1 – 2 – 3 – 4 – 5   Very entertaining

   *How VIOLENT do you think that this programme was?

   Not at all violent   1 – 2 – 3 – 4 – 5   Very violent

   *Was this programme OFFENSIVE to you?

   Not at all offensive   1 – 2 – 3 – 4 – 5   Very offensive

   *How SERIOUSLY did you take this programme?

   Not at all seriously   1 – 2 – 3 – 4 – 5   Very seriously

   *How DISTURBING was this programme to you?

   Not at all disturbing   1 – 2 – 3 – 4 – 5   Very disturbing

*How <u>EXCITING</u> do you think this programme was?

Not at all exciting   1 – 2 – 3 – 4 – 5   Very exciting

*How <u>BELIEVABLE</u> do you think that the crimes presented in this programme were?

Not at all believable   1 – 2 – 3 – 4 – 5   Very believable

4. Do you think that *Crimewatch* should use reconstructions to show how the crimes are committed?

     Yes   [ ]
     No   [ ]
     Don't know   [ ]

5. Which three crimes presented in the *Crimewatch* programme you have just seen can you remember? Please write which three you can remember in the space below.

_____

6. Of all the crimes presented on this *Crimewatch*, which do you think was the most serious crime?

_____

Which was the least serious crime <u>to you</u>?

_____

7. Of all the crimes presented on this *Crimewatch* which do you think is the most serious in terms of its effects upon society?_____
     Which was the least serious in terms of its effects upon society?_____

8. Does *Crimewatch* increase, or reduce your fear of crime?

     Increases it   [ ]
     Reduces it   [ ]
     Does not affect me [ ]

9. Could you identify with any of the victims of crimes shown in the *Crimewatch* reconstructions you have just seen?

     No   [ ]
     Yes   [ ] Which ones? _____

10. If you knew someone who you thought might have committed one of the crimes shown on *Crimewatch*, would you report that person to the police?

     Yes   [ ]
     No   [ ]
     Don't know   [ ]

11. Do you think that *Crimewatch* encourages people to think about committing crime?

     Yes   [ ]
     No   [ ]
     Don't know   [ ]

12. How do you feel after watching *Crimewatch*? Please tick any of the following boxes.

     I would like to be able to help solve the crimes   [ ]
     I feel sorry for the victims of the crimes   [ ]
     I feel safe from crime   [ ]
     I feel more afraid of crime   [ ]
     It makes me feel upset   [ ]
     It makes me feel afraid   [ ]
     It gives me more confidence in the police   [ ]

I feel angry that these crimes happen   [ ]
I'm pleased that something is being done about crime   [ ]
It is important to know that crimes are happening   [ ]
It sensationalises crime   [ ]
Other, please specify_____

EastEnders

1(a). Have you seen this particular episode of *EastEnders* before?
        Yes   [ ]
        No   [ ]
        Don't know   [ ]

(b). How often do you watch *EastEnders*?
        Regularly   [ ]
        Occasionally   [ ]
        Not very often   [ ]
        Never   [ ]

2. What is your reaction to this episode of *EastEnders*? Please indicate your
   reaction by circling the appropriate number on a scale of 1 to 5. For example,
   if you think that it was very realistic you would circle number 5.

   *How <u>REALISTIC</u> do you think that this episode of *EastEnders* was?

   Not at all realistic   1 – 2 – 3 – 4 – 5   Very realistic

   *How <u>ENTERTAINING</u> did you find this programme?

   Not at all entertaining   1 – 2 – 3 – 4 – 5   Very entertaining

   *How <u>VIOLENT</u> do you think this episode was?

   Not at all violent   1 – 2 – 3 – 4 – 5   Very violent

   *How <u>OFFENSIVE</u> was this episode to you?

   Not at all offensive   1 – 2 – 3 – 4 – 5   Very offensive

   *How <u>SERIOUSLY</u> did you take this programme?

   Not at all seriously   1 – 2 – 3 – 4 – 5   Very seriously

   *How <u>DISTURBING</u> was this programme to you?

   Not at all disturbing   1 – 2 – 3 – 4 – 5   Very disturbing

   *How <u>EXCITING</u> do you think this programme was?

   Not at all exciting   1 – 2 – 3 – 4 – 5   Very exciting

   *How <u>BELIEVABLE</u> do you think this episode was?

   Not at all believable   1 – 2 – 3 – 4 – 5   Very believable

3. Could you <u>RELATE</u> to any of the <u>CHARACTERS</u> in this episode of *EastEnders*?
        Yes   [ ]   If so, to whom?   _____
        No   [ ]

4. Could you <u>RELATE</u> to any of the <u>SITUATIONS</u> in this episode of *EastEnders*?
        Yes   [ ]   If so, which?   _____
        No   [ ]

5. How RELEVANT is this episode's story to EVERYDAY LIFE?
    Very relevant   [   ]
    Moderately relevant [   ]
    Not relevant   [   ]

6. Do you think that this episode paints A FAIR PICTURE OF LIFE?
    Yes   [   ]
    No   [   ]
    Don't know   [   ]

7. Do you think that a SOAP OPERA is an appropriate programme in which to ADDRESS SOCIAL ISSUES.
    Yes   [   ]
    No   [   ]
    Don't know   [   ]

8. Do you think *EastEnders* HANDLES THE ISSUES IT ADDRESSES WELL?
    Yes   [   ]
    No   [   ]
    Don't know   [   ]

9. Do you watch any SOAP OPERAS OTHER THAN *EastEnders*?
    Yes   [   ]   If so, which?_____
    No   [   ]

10.Do you think that television soap operas like this SHOULD BE ALLOWED TO BE MADE?
    Yes   [   ]
    No   [   ]   If no, why not?_____

Closing Ranks

1. Have you previously seen this play?
    Yes   [   ]
    No   [   ]
    Don't know   [   ]

2. What is your reaction to this play? Please indicate your reaction by circling the appropriate number on a scale of 1 to 5. For example, if you think that it was very realistic you would circle number 5.

    *How REALISTIC do you think that *Closing Ranks* was?

Not at all realistic   1 – 2 – 3 – 4 – 5 Very realistic

    *How ENTERTAINING did you find this play?

Not at all entertaining   1 – 2 – 3 – 4 – 5 Very entertaining

    *How VIOLENT do you think this play was?

Not at all violent   1 – 2 – 3 – 4 – 5 Very violent

    *How OFFENSIVE do you think this play is?

Not at all offensive   1 – 2 – 3 – 4 – 5 Very offensive

    *How SERIOUSLY did you take this play?

Not at all seriously   1 – 2 – 3 – 4 – 5 Very seriously

*How <u>DISTURBING</u> was this play to you?

Not at all disturbing   1   –   2   –   3   –   4   –   5   Very disturbing

  *How <u>EXCITING</u> did you find *Closing Ranks*?

Not at all exciting   1   –   2   –   3   –   4   –   5   Very exciting

  *How <u>BELIEVABLE</u> do you think this play is?

Not at all believable   1   –   2   –   3   –   4   –   5   Very believable

3. Could you <u>RELATE</u> to any of the <u>CHARACTERS</u> in the play?
    Yes   [ ]   If so, to whom?   _____
    No   [ ]

4. Could you <u>RELATE</u> to any of the <u>SITUATIONS</u> in *Closing Ranks*?
    Yes   [ ]   If so, which?   _____
    No   [ ]

5. How <u>RELEVANT</u> is this play's story to <u>EVERYDAY LIFE?</u>
    Very relevant   [ ]
    Moderately relevant [ ]
    Not relevant   [ ]

6. What is the <u>MAIN ISSUE</u> with which *Closing Ranks* is concerned?
    Please tick <u>one</u> box.
    Police corruption   [ ]
    Domestic violence   [ ]
    Job stress in the police   [ ]
    CND   [ ]
    Family relationships   [ ]

7. Do you think that *Closing Ranks* paints a <u>FAIR PICTURE OF WOMEN</u>?
    Yes   [ ]
    No   [ ]
    Don't know   [ ]

8. Do you think that *Closing Ranks* <u>HANDLES THE ISSUES IT ADDRESSES WELL?</u>
    Yes   [ ]
    No   [ ]
    Don't know   [ ]

9. <u>WOULD YOU CHOOSE TO WATCH</u> *Closing Ranks* if you had seen it advertised in a newspaper or on television?
    Yes   [ ]
    No   [ ]   If no, why not?   _____
    Don't know   [ ]

10. Do you think that television dramas like this <u>SHOULD BE ALLOWED TO BE MADE?</u>
    Yes   [ ]
    No   [ ]   If no, why not?   _____
    Don't know   [ ]

The Accused

1. Have you previously seen this film?

Yes   [ ]
No   [ ]
Don't know   [ ]

2. What is your reaction to this film? Please indicate your reaction by circling the appropriate number on a scale of 1 to 5 . For example, if you think that it was very realistic, you would circle number 5.

*How REALISTIC do you think that *The Accused* was?

Not at all realistic   1 – 2 – 3 – 4 – 5   Very realistic

*How ENTERTAINING did you find the film?

Not at all entertaining   1 – 2 – 3 – 4 – 5   Very entertaining

*How VIOLENT do you think this film was?

Not at all violent   1 – 2 – 3 – 4 – 5   Very violent

*How OFFENSIVE do you think this film is?

Not at all offensive   1 – 2 – 3 – 4 – 5   Very offensive

*How SERIOUSLY did you take this film?

Not at all seriously   1 – 2 – 3 – 4 – 5   Very seriously

*How DISTURBING was this film to you?

Not at all disturbing   1 – 2 – 3 – 4 – 5   Very disturbing

*How EXCITING did you find this film?

Not at all exciting   1 – 2 – 3 – 4 – 5   Very exciting

*How BELIEVABLE do you think this film is?

Not at all believable   1 – 2 – 3 – 4 – 5   Very believable

3. Could you RELATE to any of the CHARACTERS in the film?
Yes   [ ]   If so, to whom?   _____
No   [ ]

4. Could you RELATE to any of the SITUATIONS in this film?
Yes   [ ]   If so, which?   _____
No   [ ]

5. How RELEVANT is this film's story to EVERYDAY LIFE?
Very relevant   [ ]
Moderately relevant [ ]
Not relevant   [ ]

6. Do you think that this film has any EDUCATIONAL VALUE?
Yes   [ ]
No   [ ]
Don't know   [ ]

7. Do you think that *The Accused* HANDLES THE ISSUES IT ADDRESSES WELL?
Yes   [ ]
No   [ ]
Don't know   [ ]

8. Do you think that the RAPE SCENE SHOULD HAVE BEEN SHOWN in this

film?

Yes	[ ]
No	[ ]
Don't know	[ ]

9. Do you think that this film SHOULD BE ALLOWED TO BE SHOWN ON TELEVISION?

Yes	[ ]
No	[ ]
Don't know	[ ]

10. Do you think that films like this SHOULD BE ALLOWED TO BE MADE?

Yes	[ ]	
No	[ ]	If no, why not? _____

III GUIDING QUESTIONS FOR DISCUSSION

Crimewatch

(i)   General discussion of programme:
- immediate reactions (gauge familiarity with programme)
- perceived purpose of programme
- gratifications from programme
- information and entertainment values

(ii)   Responses to the crimes presented: levels of seriousness of crimes

(iii)   Reactions to the final pay-off

(iv)   Reactions to the presenters:
–Nick Ross and Sue Cook
–Police presenters

(v)   Reactions to the perpetrators of crimes:
- Hitchin Bank fraudsters
- Mercedes car thieves
- Rapist and murderer of Rachael Partridge

(vi)   Reactions to the victims of crimes:
- Hitchin Bank fraud
- Mercedes car owners
- Rachael Partridge (rape/murder)

(vii)   Discussions of specific scenes presented in the reconstructions:
- car owners (victims) handing over keys to Mercedes
- Hitchin Bank, releasing of money
- rape and murder of Rachael Partridge
          - scene on sofa with boyfriend
          - sunbed scene
          - hitchhiking on the roadside

(viii) Reactions to the ten-minute *Crimewatch Update*.

(ix)   Value of *Crimewatch* to women – is there any specific value?

(x)   Fear of crime and *Crimewatch*.

(xi)   Any final points arising from the discussion.

EastEnders

(i)   General discussion of programme:
- immediate reactions (gauge familiarity with programme)
- perceived purpose of programme
- gratifications from programme
- entertainment values
- realism and storyline

(ii)   Reactions to characters:
- Matthew and Carmel
- Frank, Pat and their children
- Pauline and Arthur

(iii)   Reactions to specific scenes involving the violent relationship:
- Matthew and Carmel meeting in the street at lunchtime
- lunchtime scene involving the book on domestic violence
- Matthew's violence toward Carmel in the evening
- arrival of the ambulance at the close of the episode

(iv)   Reactions to scenes outside the violent relationship:
- Frank and Pat's party for Janine
- Pauline's decision to give up work
- Cindy's pregnancy

(v)   Specific reactions to the violence:
- at what point did the violence begin to become apparent?
- reactions to inclusion of this violence
- what is the value, if any, of including the violence?

Closing Ranks

(i)   General discussion of programme:
- immediate reactions (gauge familiarity with programme)
- perceived purpose of programme
- gratifications from programme
- entertainment values
- realism and storyline

(ii)   Reactions to characters:
- PC Sneaden and his wife, Shirley
- Billy, the couple's son
- Shirley's employer, the doctor
- policemen and the woman police constable
- CND women
- hippy character

(iii)   Reactions to scenes:
- first time Sneaden and Shirley seen together
- perception of the relationship when first moved house
- when Shirley visits the police station
- the family day out, CND women by the road
- breakfast scene involving Sneaden and Shirley
- Billy and Shirley at the ice-rink
- Sneaden's violence toward the hippy
- Sneaden's return home and rape of Shirley

                – final scene in which Sneaden stares into the mirror

(iv)   Reactions to the inclusion of the violence in this play

(v)   Perceived value of *Closing Ranks* as a television drama, overview.

The Accused

(i)   General discussion of programme:
           – immediate reactions (gauge familiarity with programme)
           – perceived purpose of programme
           – gratifications from programme
           – entertainment values
           – realism and storyline

(ii)   Reactions to characters:
           – Sarah Tobias
           – the three rapists
           – those who solicited the rape
           – the female lawyer
           – male lawyers
           – Sally, Sarah Tobias' friend
           – Kenneth Joyce

(iii)   Reactions to scenes:
           – initial scenes at The Mill when Sarah and Sally are together
           – when Sarah is dancing in the games room
           – as the men are watching Sarah's dancing
           – the rape
           – the female lawyer's transformation to supporting the case
           – Kenneth Joyce's decision to stand as a witness
           – winning the criminal solicitation case

(iv)   Reactions to inclusion of the rape scene.

(v)   Perceived value of *The Accused*, overview:
           – does the fact that the film is American have any effect on reactions?

TIMETABLE FOR VIEWING

9.50–10.00   Women arrive

9.50–10.30   Women welcomed, filling in of Questionnaires, name labels, voice checks, etc.

10.30–11.10   Viewing of first TV programme - *Crimewatch*

11.10–11.15   Fill in *Crimewatch* Questionnaires [before discussion]

11.15–11.50   Discuss *Crimewatch*

11.50–12.00   Viewing of *Crimewatch Update*

12.00–12.10   Discuss *Crimewatch Update*

12.10–12.15   Fill in *Crimewatch* Questionnaires [after discussion]

12.15–12.45   Viewing of *EastEnders*

12.45–12.50   Fill in *EastEnders* Questionnaires [before discussion]

12.50–13.35   Discussion of *EastEnders*

13.35–13.40   Fill in *EastEnders* Questionnaires [after discussion]

13.40–14.15   Lunch

14.15–16.00   Viewing of *The Accused*

16.00–16.05   Fill in *The Accused* Questionnaires [before discussion]

16.05–16.50   Discussion of *The Accused*

16.50–16.55   Fill in *The Accused* Questionnaires [after discussion]

16.55–17.05   Women give general reactions to the day. How they feel as women about such research.

17.05 Finish.

Note: When *Closing Ranks* was viewed by groups it replaced *The Accused* in the timetable.

IV QUALITATIVE DATA ANALYSIS

The qualitative analysis of the data was based upon a set of categories through which the transcript material from the group discussions was processed. The categorisations were designed to organise the main lines of response given by each group. The semi-formal approach to discussion used in the group interviews prevented a totally systematic categorisation of the data. Obviously, many comments made in the group discussions were either lacking in focus or were very brief in nature, depending on the individual's willingness to provide expansive replies as well as the area of discussion at any given time.

Construction of categories
The specific categories used in the processing of the transcript data were as follows:

Orientation to programme
Into this we have placed data on how the respondents generally reacted to each programme. For the three fictional programmes (*EastEnders, Closing Ranks* and *The Accused*), key issues identified were reactions to the violence depicted, their entertainment value and their perceived realism. For *Crimewatch*, as a factual programme concerned with crime, we categorised views on how the programme handled its subject matter and views about police involvement with the programme. Otherwise *Crimewatch* was categorised rather differently from the other three programmes, as is indicated below.

Victims and perpetrators of violence
Our main objective was to assess how groups reacted to violence in the programmes. Consequently we emphasised reactions to the victims and perpetrators of violent acts. In this connection, we placed any reactions by the groups not only to the characters themselves but also to how the programme portrayed these characters. Where possible the characterisation of explanations, causes, motives and justifications for violence was categorised.

Other characters
Responses to other characters beyond those specifically involved in the violence being investigated were categorised.

Scenes of violence
We categorised scenes between the victim and perpetrators of violence – including scenes of actual violence and those leading up to the violent act.

Other scenes
Of course, not all the scenes contained in the programmes used in this research were violent. Indeed, only a small minority of them were. It was therefore relevant to consider interpretations of non-violent scenes in order to appreciate how the programme was viewed in its entirety.

Plot
Here we categorised any responses concerning the narrative structure of the programmes, such as dramatic tension, realism of the narrative, and the use of narrative devices expressly identified by the groups.

Perceived programme goals
Here we categorised responses concerning the ascribed purposes and possible consequences of the televising of such programmes with violent content.

Issues
Where specific issues developed in the discussions, these have been placed in this category. These were specific to each programme, though common to all are gender relations. A major theme in the case of *EastEnders* was race relations; for *Closing Ranks*, questions concerning the police arose; and in *The Accused*, the social perception of rape assumed crucial importance.

Categories specific to *Crimewatch*
As stated above, *Crimewatch* required different categories from the other programmes. 'Orientation to Programme' was employed in common with the rest, but the following categories replaced the others used:

Relative importance of crime
This concerned the importance ascribed to the crimes contained in the programme. In particular, it allowed us to consider how the groups responded to crimes against property and to those against the person.

Experience relative to specific crime
This was assumed to be a significant determinant in the perception of crime, and to reveal potential identification with the victims of crimes in the programme.

Orientation to victims of specific crime
This was primarily concerned with the victims of the two reconstructions in the programme, the bank fraud, and the theft of the Mercedes

cars, though any other data concerning victims of crimes was also placed here. Data on the victim of the third reconstruction, the rape and murder of Rachael Partridge, was not placed under this category, as this was given its own separate category because of its importance.

Orientation to perpetrators of specific crimes
The same applies as to the above category, though obviously here the concern was with the perpetrators.

Rape and murder: orientations and issues
Four predominant issues were dealt with here: the question of hitchhiking; the question of youth and age (as the victim of the rape and murder was a teenager); living in the countryside and the difficulties of transport in such areas; and parenting, which considered the perceived role of the victim's parents in permitting that victim to hitchhike.

Orientation to victim of rape and murder
Data on the perception of Rachael Partridge and her position as a victim of violent crime.

Scenes from the reconstruction of the rape and murder
Perceptions of the scenes involved in the Rachael Partridge reconstruction, the programme's ascribed motives for including them and the feelings experienced were catalogued under this heading.

Crimewatch Update
All data specifically relating to *Crimewatch Update*, its purpose, value and assumed effect were placed under this broad heading.

Fear of crime
Here we were concerned with any data about how the programme might be assumed to increase or decrease viewers' fear of crime.

Applying the categories
Obviously data gained through the group discussions did not always fall easily into single categories. Hence one piece of data might well appear under anything up to four headings. This made for complications but allowed a particularly thorough analysis of group discussions. Group discussions could not be systematically controlled in quality or quantity. Nor could the same priorities in topics discussed be examined for all. This resulted in variations in the availability of data to be categorised under specific headings.

V RECRUITMENT

Recruitment of the women with experience of violence was necessarily begun up to two months prior to their sessions, due to the complexities discussed in the body of the book. One major difficulty in recruiting all of the women was the likelihood of recruitees' dropping out between the period of recruitment and their eventual attendance at the sessions.

Fusion Research were meticulous in their recruitment of women with no experience of violence, providing the researchers with back-up support right up to the day of attendance, and even on that day when necessary. However, even this amount of care and attention did not invariably secure six women per session.

Fusion's recruitment of Asian and Afro-Caribbean women was to prove particularly problematic for the agency. For the Scottish Asian group with no experience of violence, Fusion was forced to recruit women who were all related to one another, though some of them only distantly. This was the result of a certain wariness on the part of Asian women, and concern about taking part in activities outside of their families and the Asian community. The women finally recruited for this group were only willing to participate alongside other members of their families, considering themselves safe if they were with other women with whom they were familiar.

Despite a fortnight's lead time before a given group session, at times with two recruiters involved when problems were likely, it was still difficult to identify women and to commit them to attendance. The decision to recruit close to the date of group sessions was regarded as necessary, as otherwise volunteers could later find themselves unable to attend.

Fusion concentrated on recruiting the required six interviewees for each study, retaining back-up interviewees. On three occasions in England only five women finally attended. Two of these groups consisted of white women. Failure to attend at the very last minute was in one case due to a death in the family, and in another no explanation was offered. The third incomplete group was that of the English Asians. This group had been extremely difficult to recruit, as gaining the trust of Asian women in street interviews was particularly problematic for the recruiters. Eventually, members of this group were recruited through street interviews, while others were recruited on the advice of Birmingham City Council.

Within the groups of women with no experience of violence recruited by Fusion Research we encountered a few cases of women who had actually experienced violence but were not identified by the screening questions. In three instances, we discovered members of these groups to have had previous experience of sexual or domestic violence. At the time of recruitment, Fusion's recruiters requested interviewees to indicate whether they had experienced rape, battery, incest, or physical assault. In all these cases a negative response had been given. However, we subsequently discovered from individual questionnaires that the women concerned *had* experienced violence. On two occasions the women did not reveal their experiences of violence in public, while one group member did explain her experiences. We are aware that their individual responses would have reflected the experience of violence, and the impact that this might have had on group discussion requires further consideration.

Ensuring attendance at the viewing sessions was always difficult, given that women could find themselves with unforeseen commitments and obligations. Furthermore, there was always a possibility that at the last minute a woman might once again feel herself unable to face the fact that she had been a victim of violence. Many who attended group sessions stated that they were in a constant quandary about coming as they wished to avoid painful memories.

Due to recruitment difficulties with the group of women with experience of violence, we frequently over-recruited. At times this did lead to finally having the required six women in the group. On other occasions, however, we found ourselves with groups larger than essentially required, once with seven members, twice with eight, and once with nine. But this caused no particular difficulties in handling those groups.

Index